A Good Foundation

Holy Trinity Coleford

by

VALERIE BONHAM
JULIE DEXTER

CHURCH WINDOW BOOKS

Church Window Books
c/o the Revd Valerie Bonham
The Rectory
Church Street
Coleford BA3 5NG

FIRST EDITION
Text © Valerie Bonham and Julie Dexter 2009
Introduction © Phyllis Coles 2009
Memories © individual contributors 2009
Photographs © individual photographers 2009

All profits from the sale of this book will go to Holy Trinity, Coleford.

Cover photograph by Adrianne Fitzpatrick
Cover design by Adrianne Fitzpatrick and Ken Websdale
Typeset by AJF
Printed by CPI Antony Rowe

ISBN 978-1-84745-081-4

HOLY TRINITY COLEFORD

LIST OF INCUMBENTS

Annos

George Newnham	1831	Leonard Baker	1961
John West	1840	Sidney Wood	1969
Robert Whiteway	1846	E.W. Byles	1972
Thomas Yewens	1865	Alan Coleman	1975
W.A. Dwight	1896	M.E. Percival	1982
Joseph Wade	1900	J.D. Watson	1984
Henry Evans	1914	Peter M. Down	1992
H.F. Gane	1917	Valerie Bonham	2002
E.R. Oxby	1921		
H.F. Ralph-Bowman	1927		
Bernard Adams	1946		
John Sutters	1954		

GLORIA IN EXCELSIS DEO

List of Incumbents of Holy Trinity Coleford

CONTENTS

ACKNOWLEDGEMENTS

Research by Julie Dexter and Valerie Bonham.

Memories and contributions from Ron Brewer, Joyce Button, Dennis Chambers, Jean Chivers, Phyllis Coles, Clarissa Cridland, Esme Harrison, the late Jack Steeds, Bob Swallow, Robin Thompson, Colin Turner, Callum, Rhiannon and Fintan Pritchard, Mike Wells. **Note: The memory sometimes plays tricks, and some of the personal memories recorded here are not quite accurate chronologically. The authors have thoroughly researched the church records and are satisfied that the text of *A Good Foundation* is accurate. But we have left the personal memories of our contributors uncorrected because they reflect the contribution these people have made to the life of Holy Trinity.**

Photographs, illustrations and other material from Brian Allen, Karen Blacker, Valerie Bonham, Ron Brewer, Joyce Button, Jean Chivers, Phyllis Coles, Stuart Coles, Clarissa Cridland, Julie Dexter, Adrianne Fitzpatrick, Michael Hall, Sarah Ilott, Molly Kelly, Chris Lambert and Wendy Perry, Chris Osborne, Myra Perry, Hilary Plummer, Mary Plummer, Kate and Barry Pritchard, Eileen Smith, Jill Smith, Liz Smith, Colin Turner, Ann Woolley, and church records.

Mr R G Chambers via Liz Smith for information on Miss Ackroyd.

Fred Bonham for driving Revd Valerie to Taunton several times.

With thanks also to:

Lambeth Palace Library for information from the archives of the Incorporated Church Building Society.

The staff of the Somerset Record Office, the Somerset Local Studies Library and Frome Library.

Philip Nokes of Bath and Wells Diocesan Board of Finance for information about Coleford Church Hall.

The Society of St Margaret for permission to quote from St Margaret's Magazine as quoted in *The Planting of the Lord* by Sister Catherine Louise, SSM.

Michael McGarvie for clues about the windows from Mells.

Andy Foyle, editor of *Pevsner's Buildings of England: Somerset 1*; *The North with Bristol and Bath* for information about the building of Holy Trinity Church.

Jean Chivers, who first told Revd Valerie about the Haskins children, who died in the measles epidemic in 1916, and the child drowned at the Mill, and Sir Mervyn Medlycott, Bt., for information about the location of their graves.

The Revd Clarissa Cridland for her advice and encouragement.

LIST OF ILLUSTRATIONS

PREFACE

A CHURCH built as recently as 1831 may not be old when compared with the medieval churches of our neighbouring villages, but during that time Holy Trinity has imprinted itself into the life of Coleford. Today Holy Trinity stands at the centre of village life just as it has always done. Searching through the church records has made it very clear to me that many aspects of parish life do not change much. Concerns about finance, restoration projects, hopes that special events will be well supported, the joyful celebration of the church year, and sadness at times of loss. All these things are part and parcel of both village and church life. They are both part of our history and part of our ongoing life.

This book has helped me to focus my mind on the life and mission of Holy Trinity as we go forward together in the 21st century, drawing inspiration from the past. As the twentieth incumbent of this church and parish, it has been good to discover more about my predecessors. They are no longer simply a list of names on the church wall but individual priests who sought to serve the people of Coleford. And so, too, as I minister within the church, the names of those clergy and lay people who have gone before me now mean much more to me. Some, like Jack and Dorothy Coles, George Mounty, William Marchant Jones, Barbara Ackroyd, and the first four clergy, are commemorated in windows, furnishings, Communion vessels, and other memorials around the church. Others are in the corporate memory of present day church members, some of whom have worshipped here for many years.

While we would not wish to live in the past, or to rest on past laurels, it is right that we should honour the past and allow ourselves to be inspired by the love and dedication of those who have gone before us. For unless we are clear about where we have come from, we shall have no clear vision about where we are going. As Coleford continues to open out to new people coming to live here, so it is important for us all to understand about the heart and soul of this village. And despite the predictions of pessimists that Christianity is on the wane, I believe that Holy Trinity still has a very real part to play in the life of Coleford. For here in this village people still want to celebrate their joys and seek comfort in their sorrows at their parish church. And here, too, we celebrate the church year in Word and Sacrament, we support in prayer the sick, the needy, and the sorrowful, and we seek to proclaim the good news about Jesus.

A large number of people have helped in the production of this book, by contributing their personal memories, by lending photographs, by their expertise in research, writing and book production. I am grateful to all of them because this has been a real community effort, not just for the benefit of the church community but for the whole village. I am especially grateful to Julie Dexter, who readily accepted the challenge of initially co-ordinating this project, conducted a number of the interviews, did some of the research and in 2006 wrote some of the text.

VALERIE BONHAM, 2009

INTRODUCTION:
A LIFE AT HOLY TRINITY

For **Phyllis Coles**, like many before her, life has revolved around Holy Trinity. Born in 1920, Phyl started Sunday School at the age of four, and became a Sunday School teacher when she left school ten years later. A major focus of her life has been the choir, which she joined when she was nine and where she remains today; but there is much more to life at Holy Trinity, and Phyl shares her many memories on behalf of us all.

Phyllis Coles, aged 9 years, with her brothers, Fred and Maxwell

Mr E Steeds, Marilyn Burrows' granddad, was in charge of the Sunday School. We used to have Sunday School in the Church School. The Revd Ralph-Bowman was the Vicar then, and I remember his wife used to come over to the Sunday School and say some prayers and give us a chat. She was a very attractive woman and I used to watch out for her coming as she used to wear the most beautiful hats: wide brims and flowery crowns. The Sunday School had a free outing once a year when the coaches would be numbered—up to eight coaches; the parents paid their own fares. This was a great occasion as we didn't leave the village much in those days.

When I joined the choir, Mr W M Jones was the choirmaster and we were made to sing a verse of a hymn in front of all the choir, and Mr Jones decided whether your voice was good enough to join. We had choir practice every Thursday night, and if you didn't attend choir practice you were not allowed to sit in the choir on Sunday.

The organ was in the front of the church when I joined the choir—the men and boys were robed—but we sat in the front seats of the congregation. The ladies were not robed at the time. We didn't get robed until I was an adult. The organ had to be pumped by a young lad who sat behind a curtain. He sometimes fell asleep behind the curtain and when the organist started to play nothing came out, so someone had to dash behind the curtain to wake him up.

The choir was allocated some of the church collections for the Choir Fund, and we had a free outing to a seaside resort once a year. On the choir outing to Southsea one year, the coach broke down at Warminster. Luckily we broke down by a garage, but we were still there at one o'clock when we should have been at Southsea eating a lunch Mr W M Jones had booked for us. We arrived there about 3.30 pm or 4.00 pm—I can't quite remember which—but we were all hungry. This was one of the furthest trips we went on. It was usually Weston or Weymouth. The older choir members took it upon themselves to look after the younger ones whose parents were unable to look after them—so we all formed a large circle on the beach and picked out a landmark for the children to look out for, as they would wander about when they went for a paddle. We used to tuck our dresses in our knickers to go for a paddle with the rest. No bathing costumes for us, although I recall one child's mother knitted her a costume, which fitted her beautifully until she went in the sea. We all had a good laugh when she came out because her costume had stretched when it got wet and was nearly down to her ankles—she took it in good part and saw the funny side of it herself. We used to take sandwiches and cakes; Rose Plummer was well known for her sausage rolls and savoury tarts, which she shared with us all. We really enjoyed our picnics on the sand (eaten very often with sandy hands). Then we would buy cups of tea from the tea tents and ice creams.

I started going out with Eddie Coles after I sat with him on the coach at a choir outing (before I left school). He was my childhood sweetheart and we spent over sixty happy years together.

We had several organists over the years. The first I remember is Mr Soffy Hamblin, then Mrs Carpenter (Irene Heiron's mother); Mrs Baynton played the organ, and her daughter for a while. Roy Withers was a brilliant organist. He played for many years and played at our wedding. He was in the Air Force and applied for leave to play at our wedding, and at one o'clock we were beginning to panic, as he wasn't home then. However, all was well and he got there in time for the wedding. I remember my mum did the catering which was difficult with the rationing. I worked in the Messing Office when I was in the ATS, and the Messing Officers said, "Don't worry about your wedding cake,"—so I was lucky, as most people had to have cardboard over the cakes representing icing. Also, all leave was stopped the week of our wedding as the whole camp was moving from Barton Stacey to Aldershot. The Messing Officer saw my ATS Commanding Officer and said he was willing for me to go on leave, so I went on leave

from Barton Stacey and would have had to take all my kit home with me—but he said, "Bring it to the cookhouse and we will nail it into a tea chest and take it to the new cookhouse for you." Then he drew me a diagram of how to get back to camp in Aldershot.

Phyllis and Eddie Coles on their wedding day

After the war Norman Button, who was the organist at the Wesley Chapel, came back to find Mrs Willis had taken over—so as Roy Withers had retired, Norman became our church organist and a very good organist he was for many years. Unfortunately, he became ill and he collapsed and died at the organ—a terrible shock for us all, and especially for Joyce, his wife.

Norman and Joyce Button

I remember when there were fifteen boys in the choir. We have never been so few as we are today. I don't think I should forget to mention Beryl Rossiter in the choir. She had the most beautiful soprano voice, reaching the top notes without effort. She took the soprano solos when we had anthems, which was at every festival. Beryl and I used to sing duets as our voices blended so well. Wherever we went we were asked specially to sing *Silent Night*. When Jack Steeds' mum died, Jack asked us if we would sing *Silent Night* at her funeral, as she liked our singing of it. We were afraid we would get too emotional and break down; but Beryl said, "If you will, I will," so we did it and got through to the end. Jack's family were so pleased.

I remember Heather (Allen née Price) being in the choir, and that's when she started calling me Auntie Phyl. My brother Fred joined the choir, I believe a year before me, as they had boy choristers before girls. His wife Rose (Plummer) was also in the choir for well over forty years before they moved to Holcombe. She sang contralto with me, also Joan Mascord, now Mrs Sydney Jones, living in Frome, and another contralto was Gladys Mary Coleman, the Revd Alan Coleman's wife.

The choir joined the Royal School of Church Music and we were sent festival books—still in the vestry I believe. We had to learn the different settings for chants and *The Magnificat* and so on. There were also anthems, and then we attended Wells Cathedral each year for the diocesan music festival. We would go in the morning for rehearsals and then the public would attend in the afternoon when all the combined choirs would sing from that particular year's festival book. It was wonderful for me to have so many contraltos there and we all enjoyed our singing.

One practice night we had a visit from one of the directors of the Royal School of Church Music, and we chose to sing the anthem, *The strife is o'er*. We didn't realise he had written that anthem and when we finished he asked if we knew he had written it. We were rather taken aback to hear that, but he gave us a very good report and sent a letter of congratulation on our excellent performance and balance. Mr Jones was very strict on our diction and expression: loud, medium and soft, and said all the congregation should be able to hear every word clearly. We used anthems at every festival, and for harvest festival we had harvest Evensong on the Thursday evening, when the church was packed and chairs had to be placed in the aisles to seat everyone, and the same again on the Sunday.

Garden parties were held on the vicarage lawn each year. Stalls were manned—and in the evening there was dancing on the lawn. We also performed plays on the lawn in front of the vicarage.

We had a Girls' Friendly Society and Anglican Young Peoples' Association (AYPA). We travelled to Swindon one weekend and to Stourbridge another weekend. We stayed overnight with the local AYPA members and hosted AYPA members when they visited us. At one time we made breakfast in the kitchen at the vicarage once a month. The girls cooked breakfast and the boys did the washing up.

We put on a Nativity play and a Passion play each year in the church. The older members of the church used to meet in the "Bug Hut" on Tuesdays and did handicrafts to sell at the fete and jumble sales.

The church flowers were organised by Mrs Joyce Button, Joyce Donald (Marilyn Burrows' mum) and Nancy Seviour. They walked to the church every day to keep the flowers watered. We had a flower rota and each did the flowers for a fortnight a year and on all festivals. We very rarely had to buy flowers, as we all had our cottage gardens and had certain people we could call on for flowers for the church, such as Mr Percy Parfitt and Mr Robin Wheeler. I always got my chrysanthemums from him, and they were all pleased to give for the church. We had a flower fund for such times as Christmas and when it was difficult to find flowers in the garden. Jack Coles (Hilary Plummer's and Margaret Flower's dad) used to let us use his garden for coffee mornings to raise money for the flower fund. There was always plenty of greenery at the vicarage, and we were allowed to cut as much as we wanted.

About the church heating—there was a boiler house (now made into the Vicar's vestry). My brother Fred was responsible for lighting the boiler—which heated the water which ran through pipes all around the church. He used to go up at midnight on Saturday nights to stoke up the boiler to make sure the church was warm for eight o'clock Communion. On really frosty mornings we used to sit in the little side seats and put our feet on the pipes to warm them after getting them cold walking to church. I can't remember when electric heating was put in, but I know it was when the old boiler was wearing out, but it was never as good as the old boiler. If you sat under them, your head got too hot and your feet stayed cold as heat rises.

The Choir visited Coventry Cathedral and were very impressed. Graham Sutherland had designed the tapestry, and other artists had designed the windows for the Cathedral. As we had our south-east window in plain glass after the organ was moved, Mr W M Jones had arranged for a new window for our church by Keith New, who had designed some of the Coventry windows. It's much more modern than our other windows and we had mixed feelings about it at the time as it didn't match the others—however, I think we have got used to it by now. Mr Jones also purchased the Miners' Welfare Institute and presented it to the church.

Another thing I remember, we weren't allowed to speak in church, even before the service started. I much prefer the services now when we can speak and have a laugh and sing "happy birthday" in church and to see the children come along and be made welcome—even if they do run about sometimes. It's the way to encourage them. I may be going back to my second childhood—but I enjoy the children's services as much as they do.

I would love to see more join the choir, especially tenor and bass. I miss hearing Eddie's lovely bass voice behind me. He always took the bass solos, especially *Good King Wenceslas*. Malcolm Plummer, my nephew, took the part of the page. Rose, his mother, was so nervous for him that she asked me to join in if he broke down, but of course he didn't. I'm afraid we only average four in the choir most Sundays, sometimes five. How about it, sopranos, contraltos, tenor and bass? Eddie always carried the processional cross, leading the choir in until he joined the Army. Then my brother, Fred Plummer, took over, and after that his son, Malcolm, so we kept it in the family a long time.

PHYLLIS COLES

Part 1

THE HISTORY
OF
HOLY TRINITY

- 1 -

BEFORE HOLY TRINITY

COLEFORD as we know it today was once two settlements—Coleford and Highbury. Both lay in the parish of Kilmersdon and were served by Kilmersdon parish church. Holy Trinity now sits as a bridge between Coleford and Highbury, the focal point of a new ecclesiastical parish from the 1830s, which was recognised as a civil parish as recently as 1946. But it was not the first building that ministered to the spiritual needs of the people of the southern part of Kilmersdon parish.

The first place of worship that we know of was the Chapel of the Blessed Virgin, a daughter church of Kilmersdon. In 1982, long-serving Churchwarden Jack Coles noted that the Chapel was mentioned as early as 1488, when "it evidently had its own priest,

A modern picture of Holy Trinity taken from the Cinder Path

for Sir John of Colverd is one of ten priests named in a will of 1524. In a parliamentary return of 1551 the chapel of Coleford is again noted and it is spoken of as the Parish Church of Coleford in a will also as late as 1551. No trace of this building exists as far as we know, though according to Lord Hylton's *History of Kilmersdon*, published in 1912, local tradition says it was in a field called Norton Hill below the present Wesleyan chapel. They were troublesome times for the Church of England, and it must have fallen into decay and been swept away with scores of other free chapels at the time of the Reformation. It was apparently destroyed and its reverences [i.e. wealth] confiscated by … 1571, because no mention is made of it in the manorial survey of that year."

It was to be another 250 years before the village gained a new church, during which time the community was reliant on neighbouring parish churches and nonconformist chapels to meet their spiritual needs.

> **Jack Coles** noted in 1982:
> We can imagine that there must have been quite a number of people who wanted the ministration of the Established Church, which they couldn't get without walking to the neighbouring villages of Leigh, Holcombe, Mells and their parish church of Kilmersdon. We can imagine how they must have grumbled as they walked the dark country lanes to go to church, and it took a long time for the church authorities to wake up to the fact that a church was needed here in this village.

The Presbyterians began to worship in Coleford soon after 1662, under the Toleration Act. While the Act permitted nonconformist congregations to worship in their own buildings, it also required that such buildings should be at least five miles from the nearest market town, making Coleford an ideal location. Their chapel, which stood at the bottom of Springer's Hill, was later used by the Primitive Methodists before it was knocked down to make way for a new chapel in 1863 (*East Somerset Telegraph*, 30 May 1863).

The same Toleration Act that had allowed the foundation of the Presbyterian Chapel helped Methodism establish itself in the village in the mid 18th century. Its introduction was attributed to a peddler from Bristol, known as "the Singing Ragman". Looking back over the history of Methodism in the area, the *East Somerset Telegraph* reported on 17 May 1865 that "he was connected with a society of Wesleyans in Bristol, and his cheerful deportment, coupled with his hymn singing, frequently drew around him many of the inhabitants of Lipyeate, at the house occupied by Mr Flower. Subsequently, at the wishes of the people, Mr Wesley visited the place, and preached …"

On his first visit, on 1 January 1745, John Wesley noted that the colliers were "not as famous as those at Kingswood", and that he was forced to preach by the roadside, "for the house could not contain a tenth part of the congregation". The following year, Wesley returned to preach from the foundation stone of the first Methodist Chapel.

The Methodist Society flourished—its chapel needed enlarging within ten years—no doubt encouraged by Wesley's frequent visits (twenty-two in all), but perhaps also because of the lack of competition from the Established Church in meeting the spiritual needs of a growing community.

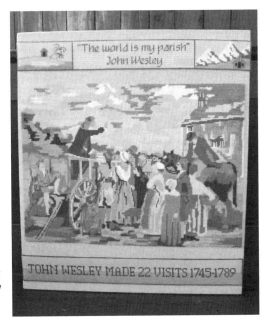

Millennium tapestry—John Wesley preaching in Coleford

2

A NEW CHURCH FOR COLEFORD

AT a meeting of the Kilmersdon Vestry on Friday, 24 April 1829, held at the Gauntlett Inn (now the Jolliffe Inn), Kilmersdon, it was "unanimously resolved that it is highly desirable to build a Church to contain not less than four hundred free sittings and a Residence for the officiating clergyman at Coleford in this parish, and subscriptions amounting to upwards of £1,000 having been already entered for this purpose that a Committee be appointed to carry the same into effect". (D/P/Coleford 8/3/1, p1) As the Vestry thanked Mr J M Paget "for his exertions in forwarding the above highly desirable business", news of the plans for a new church must have been warmly welcomed in the southern part of the parish.

The first formal meeting of the Committee charged with bringing the new church into being was held five days later, at the Greyhound Inn, Springer's Hill, Coleford. Fixing the location of the new church was impeded by difficulty in securing a site, presumably because those who owned land in the area hoped to make as much money as possible. Eventually, on 13 May, the Committee was informed that Mr Craddock, a yeoman farmer, had been able to trade two acres of his own land with two acres of land owned by Lord Hylton. This latter parcel of land Mr Craddock then sold to the Committee for £140.

On 23 June 1829 the Bishop of Bath and Wells wrote to the Incorporated Church Building Society regarding the intention to build a church at Coleford. The Bishop wrote: "A plan is in agitation for building a new Church at Colford [sic], in the Parish of Kilmersdon, capable of containing 4 or 500 persons. The Parishioners are making handsome subscriptions, and doing all they can towards completing this good work. They will, however, be obliged, I expect, to apply to your Society. With this view they will be obliged to you to send your Papers of enquiry to the Revd Mr Edwards, of Kilmersdon …" (ICBS 1109 fol 1/2, Lambeth Palace Library)

The papers of enquiry referred to were duly submitted by Thomas Candy and Joseph Britten, "Churchwardens in the Hamlet of Coleford in the Parish of Kilmersdon". The population was given as 1,991, quoting figures from 1821. The second question asked what is "the actual provision of Church room previous to the proposed building. Answer, 245. And of such present provision, the actual number of free and unappropriated sittings is none". Presumably the church room referred to is Kilmersdon Church, and the fact that none of the seats were free would be an indication that the poor of Coleford would not be accommodated at their parish church. Hence the need for a church in the

The Church Building Society. This body was formed in 1818 and incorporated by Act of Parliament in 1828. Its purpose was to "remedy the deficiencies of places set aside for Public Worship in our towns and cities". It also endeavoured to dispense with pew rents and often made this a condition of giving grants. In 1818 the **Church Building Act** had been passed by Parliament, whose members also voted a sum of £1,000,000 to build new churches in the rapidly expanding towns and cities. These are sometimes called "**Waterloo Churches**" because they were to be the nation's token of thanksgiving for the victory at Waterloo, although in recent years some historians have disputed this. The money was administered by the **Church Building Commission**, whose officials were called **Parliamentary Commissioners**, and the churches thus built were sometimes called "**Commissioners' Churches**" as well as Waterloo Churches. At the same time as this great growth in church building, the **Church Building Society**, later called the **Incorporated Church Building Society** (ICBS), also came into being, but was not the same body as the **Church Building Commission**. It was the **ICBS** which gave grant aid to Coleford Church, which was not a Commissioners' Church, the funding for it being mostly raised by subscription.

village, possibly a more pressing need than the distance between the two villages. From the document we learn that the new church would give "502 sittings, allowing 2 feet 4 inches by 18 inches to each sitting". The clergyman of the new church was to be maintained by "an allowance of twenty pounds [per year] from the Vicar [of Kilmersdon] and the certainty of an augmentation from the Commissioners of Queen Ann's [*sic*] Bounty". The provision for repairs to the building would come from the Church Rates. Of the 502 sittings, 408 would be free. The estimate for building the church was £1,169, and this was being raised by subscription of which £700 had been raised so far. The Churchwardens described the expectation of raising the rest by subscription as "very trifling". The work was expected to be completed by Midsummer Day 1830. The document was examined and approved by the Archdeacon of Wells on 31 July 1829. (ICBS 1109 fol 3/4, Lambeth Palace Library)

With the site secured by the purchase of Mr Craddock's land, advertisements were placed in the *Bath Herald*, *Bath Chronicle*, *Bath Journal*, *Felix Farley's* and the *Salisbury and Winchester Journal* inviting the submission of sealed tenders for the building of the church. On 28 October 1829

Queen Anne's Bounty A special fund formed by Queen Anne in 1704 whereby she bequeathed revenue coming to the Crown after the Reformation to augment the livings of Anglican clergy in poorer parishes. In 1948 Queen Anne's Bounty and the Ecclesiastical Commissioners were merged to form the present-day Church Commissioners.

the Revd William Batchelor, Stipendiary Curate of Chilcompton (and also of Babington), Secretary to the Coleford Church Building Committee, wrote to the ICBS to inform them that they had "received an estimate from a respectable builder who is willing to contract for erecting the proposed church at Coleford for the sum of eleven hundred and sixty nine pounds". (ICBS 1109 fol 5, Lambeth Palace Library) The contract was awarded on 3 February 1830 to Mr James Parfitt, but preliminary work had already got underway in September 1829 with the granting of permission to quarry "1000 common cart loads" at 2d per cart load.

On 5 December 1829 the Revd Batchelor again wrote to the ICBS "to return their thanks to the Board for the grant of the sum of two hundred and fifty pounds; and to request that the time for building the Church at Coleford may be extended from Ladyday 1830 [25 March] until Michaelmas 1830 [29 September], as the Committee find it necessary to make further exertions to obtain additional subscriptions". (ICBS 1109 fol 9, Lambeth Palace Library)

The contract (D/P/Coleford 8/3/2) gives details of the local landowners who had an interest in the project, as well as naming the contractors, James Parfitt, builder of Midsomer Norton, Henry Smith, blacksmith of Midsomer Norton, and Henry Smith, chandler of the same place (possibly the latter two are the same person in two roles). The list of landowners forms a directory of the local "great and good" consisting of John Twyford Jolliffe of Ammerdown, Esquire; Charles Neave of Bryely Hill in the County of Stafford, Clerk; William Edwards of Kilmersdon, Clerk; William Knatchbull of Babington, Esquire; John Moore Paget of Newbury House, Esquire; John Fussell of Mells, Esquire; Francis Craddock of Lipyeate, Gentleman; and Robert Green of Holcombe, Gentleman. Of the two Clerks (i.e. clergymen), William Edwards was the incumbent of Kilmersdon.

The original Minute book of the Church Building Committee (D/P/Coleford 8/3/1) lists the subscribers to the building. These included: J M Paget Esq. £300, Mrs Paget £200, Miss Paget £100, Colonel C Horner £50, W Knatchbull Esq. £100, and a second donation of £100, R Gough Esq. £325 (in 3 subscriptions), Mr F Craddock £20, J T Jolliffe Esq. £100.

On 8 September 1830 the Revd Batchelor wrote a further letter to the Board of the ICBS informing them that they had held a Committee meeting on Tuesday 31 August attended by the Surveyor/Clerk of Works (John Sperring—see chapter 10). "The Surveyor and Clerk of Works reported … that the Church had been built and roofed in, in a proper and workmanlike manner, and agreeably to the Contract and the Place approved by the Board, and might if absolutely necessary be compleated [sic] by the time specified. But at the same time he represented to the Committee that in consequence of the long protracted frost last winter a considerable delay had been occasioned in getting out the foundation, and of course the whole building had been delayed longer than was anticipated. He therefore recommended that the Church should not have the last coat of plaistering [sic] until March, nor be opened for service until Ladyday. The Committee personally inspected the Church, and agree in opinion with the surveyor, but before they acquiesce in the delay they are desirous of ascertaining whether it meets with the sanction of the Board."

It seemed that the Church Building Committee feared that the ICBS would not deliver the promised grant, so the Revd Batchelor continued, "The Committee request me to say that in addition to the sum they have contracted to pay for the Church, they have expended about 200 pounds in the purchase of the land necessary and in making stone fences, so that should the Board be prevented from remitting the 250 pounds granted, the Committee would be placed in the unpleasant situation of being unable to fulfil their engagement with the Contractor for building the Church." He concluded, "The Committee in undertaking this good work, have been influenced by no other motive than that of affording an opportunity of moral and religious improvement to *a very dense, poor and ignorant population of Somersetshire colliers*." [my italics] (ICBS 1109 fol 11/12, Lambeth Palace Library)

Shortly before the church opened, the Revd Batchelor had to eat "humble pie" in a letter to the Board of the ICBS dated 1 June 1831: "I am requested by the Committee … to inform you that the form which you were kind enough to send promising the 250 pounds voted to them has been inadvertently mislaid, so that the money cannot be drawn until you are kind enough to send another form." (ICBS 1109 fol 17, Lambeth Palace Library) Their reply has not survived, but presumably they obliged, because the grant was duly made.

Meanwhile, in June 1829, **George Newnham** had "applied for the office of officiating minister", and the Committee recommended his appointment to the Vicar of Kilmersdon, who held the gift of the living (and is still Patron). Thus it was that when Holy Trinity was formally opened on 19 July 1831 and consecrated by the Bishop of Bath and

Coleford vicarage, now the "Old Vicarage"

Wells, the Revd George William Newnham became its first clergyman. At this stage there was still no accommodation for him. Bids had been sought for the building of a clergyman's house, the cost of which was not to exceed £400. Plans submitted by Thomas Thatcher were eventually approved, with some minor changes in June 1830, at a total cost of £540. It was not until Christmas 1832 that Newnham was able to move into what was then called the "Rectory Manse".

The official opening and consecration of Holy Trinity on 19 July 1831 must have been a great day for Coleford. On 31 July 1831, *John Bull* reported, "On Tuesday the New Church at Coleford was consecrated, on which occasion a large concourse of persons was attracted to witness the interesting ceremonies. The Lord Bishop of the diocese, attended by the Chancellor and the Registrar, was met on his arrival at the church by the committee, the officiating minister, and upwards of twenty clergymen in their robes ... The church, which has been chiefly built by private subscriptions, aided by a grant from the Church Building Society, is a neat gothic structure, capable of containing about 500 persons, 400 of which are declared free and unappropriated for ever." The Bishop preached on Leviticus, chapter 19, verse 30, "Ye shall keep my sabbaths and reverence my sanctuary—I am the Lord."

> **George Newnham** was a graduate of Corpus Christi College, Oxford, although his degrees were not distinguished (2nd class Classics and 3rd class Maths and Physics). He was ordained deacon in 1831 aged 24, and priest in 1832, by the Bishop of Bath and Wells.

The Revd Batchelor made his last entry into the Minute Book of the Church Building Committee following the opening of the church. "Here ended the Secretary's calligraphic labours—the Church was opened to a large congregation of sick and poor and consecrated by the Bishop, who preached, the appointed Minister reading the prayers, on July 19 1831. The collection amounted to £100." (The Minute Book subsequently became a journal in which several incumbents, though not all, made notes and comments about the parish.)

In a document dated 27 September 1831 (ICBS 1109 fol 15, Lambeth Palace Library) the following declaration was made: "We the undersigned Minister and Inhabitants of Coleford in the Parish of Kilmersdon, and Surveyor of the Church, do hereby certify that the work has been completed in a substantial and workmanlike manner, according to the plan and declaration submitted to the Incorporated Society for promoting the enlargement, building and repairing of Churches and Chapels; that by such building of a Church 502 sittings have been obtained, and of that number 408 are free and unappropriated; that a Schedule of the number of the free sittings, and a plan describing their situation in the church, signed by the Minister and Churchwardens, have been entered in the parish Registers and hung up over the Minister's pew; and that an Inscription, in the subjoined form, has been placed in a conspicuous part of the Church over the entrance." The declaration was signed by G W Newnham, Minister; John

Lambert; David Padfield Flower and George Gait, Inhabitants of Coleford; and John Sperring, Surveyor. The plan of the sittings was entered into the first Baptism Register and is reproduced in chapter 10. The copy over the Minister's pew has long since disappeared, possibly in 1885 when the seating was reordered. But the Inscription was placed in the church porch where it remains today. The wording followed the prescribed form of the ICBS.

This Church was erected in the year 1831, it contains sittings for 502 persons, and in consequence of a Grant from the Incorporated Society, for promoting the enlargement, building, and repairing of Churches and Chapels; 408 of that number, are hereby declared to be free and unappropriated for ever.

G.W. NEWNHAM   Minister.
JOS[H] BRITTEN. ⎱ Church-
BENJ[N] CANDY. ⎰ wardens.

1831 Incorporated Church Building Society inscription in the church porch

The church building may well have been completed, and the church in use, but there were still some problems. The vicarage took another eighteen months to complete, possibly due to lack of funds. This begs the question: where did the Revd George Newnham live during that time? The only clue lies in further correspondence with the ICBS, written this time by Newnham, and headed "Chilcompton". Given that the Revd Batchelor, Stipendiary Curate of Chilcompton and Babington, was Secretary of the Church Building Committee, it may be that he saw Newnham's homeless plight and allowed him to live at Chilcompton until his vicarage was built.

There are two letters from Newnham to the ICBS, and they underline the poverty of the situation. The first letter is dated 27 February 1832: "Gentlemen, You have already granted on Behalf of Coleford Ch and Parsonage the sum of £250. But in order to clear off their debt, after the utmost prudence, the Committee will be obliged to take the last £100 reserved out of the sums subscribed for the endowment—unless further aid can be obtained. The benevolence of the neighbourhood is exhausted—and for double duty and the cure of 1400 souls the present stipend is unavoidably under £50 from the non-letting of the 100 pew sittings. At the same time the poverty of the place renders unlikely the letting of many more, and entails a heavy expenditure on the clergyman. The house will be habitable in the course of the summer. Cases have occurred of a second benefaction from your funds, and as the poor curate I would submit to your

judgement, Gentlemen, whether this be not worthy of admission into the number."
(ICBS 1109 fol 18/19, Lambeth Palace Library)

This cry from the heart went unheeded, and on 12 April 1832 Newnham wrote
again. "Gentlemen, I pray you forgive my pertinacity in again submitting to your
consideration the case of Coleford Ch. I find upon enquiry that the parish of Monckton
Combe with a total population of 1500 has received a grant of £300 for a church
containing only 350 free sittings—and that Redcar North Riding of Yorkshire containing,
with an adjoining hamlet, 1200 souls, has received, towards a church containing also
only 350 free sittings, £300 at first, and a subsequent grant of £100. Suffer me,
Gentlemen, with all deference, to urge the still more pressing necessities if not claims
of my poor Curacy of Coleford nr Frome. The population of the 3 hamlets united is
barely under 1400—the free sittings are 408. Those of the remaining 86 which are let
scarcely bring in £25 per Ann which with the Vicar's £20 [i.e. the Vicar of Kilmersdon]
constitute my whole salary—Fees none—The Church is yet unpaid for—the Committee
deeply involved—and they have already expended £200 or £300 subscribed towards
this poor endowment. This surely ought to be considered as a debt yet unpaid. Again
Gentlemen, I beg you to consider, whether you can refuse to hear and answer so loud
an appeal to your generosity …" (ICBS 1109 fol 20/21, Lambeth Palace Library)

There are no replies on record to either letter. Perhaps the Board of the ICBS objected
to Newnham's enquiries into other parishes, or maybe they did not like the suggestion
that a second grant was a "debt unpaid". Whatever the reason, Newnham's plea went
unheeded and a second grant was not given.

3

FOUNDING A COMMUNITY

THE REVD GEORGE NEWNHAM had been ordained deacon but was still not a priest when he came to Coleford to take charge of the new church of Holy Trinity. At that time candidates for ordination, upon graduating from university, presented themselves to their bishop who, after examining them on godly learning, would duly ordain them. Despite the lack of theological or pastoral training, it was not unusual in the 1830s for a newly ordained man such as Newnham to be put in charge of a church. What is unusual is that he threw himself devotedly into his parish rather than spend his time in country pursuits, as did so many rural clergy at that time. By the time the Committee responsible for bringing the new church into being met for the final time in June 1833, George Newnham had been ordained priest and was already hard at work. Fortunately for us, he recorded his achievements in the parish records shortly before his departure from Coleford, thus providing a fascinating insight into the congregation at the new parish church of Holy Trinity, and also of the early reluctance of the local people to take advantage of the services offered.

He writes: "The first funeral was performed the day after the consecration the first grave being a child's* in the south-west angle of the cemetery. Many interments taking place in the neighbouring churchyards of Leigh, Mells, Holcombe, Stoke, Kilmersdon, and the burial ground at the Wesleyan meeting, on account of lying near relations, the funeral duties are sometimes incredibly light as the Register books will testify—a circumstance particularly agreeable in the winter season especially as the "saints" were appropriated to the Wesleyan earth and the sinners left to the consecrated clay. The same cause or a similar one, caused after the first rush to the new church, a scarcity of baptisms, added to the partial enforcement of the _th [sic] canon forbidding parents to stand as sponsors. The baptismal service was always read after the second lesson in the afternoon service and to avoid lengthening the services oftener than could be avoided, the people were invited to come monthly, of which notice was always given on the previous Sunday. In the event of no children being presented at the month, the people were invited to come on any succeeding Sunday that was desired, from which again the month was reckoned. Private baptism has always been administered with reluctance from the delay of parents to bring their children afterwards to Church, notwithstanding the promise. Special defaulters: G Brice, Jas. Sheppard, John Gerrard." (D/P/Coleford 8/3/1, p71–72)

*7-year-old James Hamblin was buried on 20 July 1831.

Although the Revd Newnham's account leaves out the canon number, he was in fact referring to the 31st Canon. (Canon Law relates to the laws of the Church as distinct from Civil or Criminal Law. All clergy are obliged to observe Canon Law.) Six children were baptised on the first Sunday: Sophia Brice, Marianne and Martha Widcombe, Clara Young (base-born) [i.e. born out of wedlock], William Jeffreys and Marianne Adams. In 1831 there were twenty-four baptisms, and thirty-three in 1832, before numbers tailed off year by year to just eleven in 1836.

With the building of the first church school in 1834, people gradually turned more to Holy Trinity and less to neighbouring churches for their spiritual nurturing. The Revd Newnham also helped cement the church in the social life of the community, starting traditions that continue to this day. For instance, the annual garden fete to commemorate the anniversary of the foundation of Holy Trinity was first celebrated in 1832, before the vicarage was occupied, when a collection was made for the Sunday School. At the time of writing this is continued in the annual Summer Fair.

The Revd George Newnham had arrived in Coleford a newly married man of twenty-five and had only been in office three years when tragedy struck: his wife Helen Maria died. A memorial was placed on the south side of the sanctuary with the inscription:

The Newnham memorial on the south wall of the sanctuary

NEAR THIS HOLY PLACE
WHICH IN LIFE SHE LOVED TO FREQUENT
LIETH THE BODY OF
HELEN MARIA
WIFE OF THE REVD G. W. NEWNHAM.
SHE FELL ASLEEP IN JESUS
AUGUST 28 A D 1834
1 THESS. IV 13–18

In 1982, **Jack Coles** noted:
When the sanctuary floor was being relaid some years ago, they found two small coffins, and we assumed that she might have died giving birth to stillborn twins, as there is no record in the baptismal register of these children being baptised.

At that time it was unusual for stillborn babies or unbaptised infants to be given any type of funeral, and presumably the Revd Newnham took his dead babies and quietly buried them in the church sanctuary, a rare and compassionate act on the part of the bereaved father.

Despite this personal tragedy, the Revd George Newnham's achievements were considerable. By the late 1830s, funerals and baptisms had become a regular part of church life. However, it seems that funerals sometimes presented problems, as he recorded: "The conducting of Burials has been a frequent source of painful collision and complaint. By degrees Sunday funerals were confined to a time before morning service from 9–10. The penalty upon coming late being the not carrying the coffin into church. Ultimately from the example of the near parishes of Babington and Chilcompton it has been resolved to forbid them altogether except in peculiarly urgent cases." (D/P/Coleford 8/3/1 p85)

George Newnham was a diligent visitor but found that many of his parishioners did not understand the ways of the Church of England, still less the stately language of the *Book of Common Prayer*. Thus he noted, "The *Office for the Visitation of the Sick*, I am ashamed to say, I have not used a dozen times during my ministry here, partly from the vulgar, dispiriting prejudice among the people against 'praying by a book.'" (D/P/ Coleford 8/3/1 p83)

But as more members joined the congregation, a new period of spiritual development was embraced. "Confirmations being almost unheard of has [*sic*] been but little regarded by Coleford people. The lists of those confirmed at Kilmersdon in 1834 (and Shepton) and at Mells in 1837, and Midsomer Norton in 1840 are to be seen at the beginning of the Baptism Registration Books. Some of them have conducted themselves satisfactorily since, others as schismatics or heathens." (D/P/Coleford 8/3/1 p79)

The pattern of Communion services in these early years was typical of many parishes in the 1830s where the sermon took precedence over the sacraments. The revival of sacramental worship began after the spread of the Oxford or Tractarian Movement which emphasised the importance of the sacraments. Thus the Revd Newnham wrote, "The Communion was at first celebrated but quarterly—but afterwards six or seven times a year dividing it into portions of eight weeks as nearly as might be taking Easter, Whitsuntide, the anniversary July 19 (or near it) and Christmas Day or the New Year as fixed points. At first the Methodists used to attend in token of good will, but on finding that our plans, schools etc. necessarily clashed and afterwards that their fixed morning meeting interfered, they withdrew—at least the leaders. The sermon was generally omitted on Communion Sundays. The administration [of Holy Communion] was at first by repeating the words to each individual, subsequently to twos, and latterly to the whole assembled at the rail. Notorious evil livers have been occasionally passed by." (D/P/Coleford 8/3/1 p73)

The new church at Coleford was fortunate in being presented with a handsome silver Communion set at the time of its opening in 1831. The chalice bears the inscription "Presented to Coleford Church by Jane Paget, Widow, of Newberry House. 1831". Instead of a paten (for holding the bread to be consecrated), there is a tazza (which looks like a paten with a foot, i.e. rather like a cake stand). This is contemporary with the chalice and bears the same inscription. There is also a paten but it has no inscription, is heavier in weight, and may be a later addition. A wine flagon completes the set and bears the inscription "Presented to Coleford Church by Jane Paget, Widow, of Newberry House. 1844". All four pieces have a sunburst design, in the centre of which is the

The Oxford or Tractarian Movement began on 14 July 1833 when the Revd John Keble preached a sermon before the Assize Judges in the University Church of St Mary the Virgin, Oxford, condemning the interference of the State in Church matters. Soon after this, a number of Oxford clergymen, led by John Henry Newman, Edward Bouverie Pusey and others, began to publish a series of tracts covering all aspects of religious and spiritual life. As a result of these tracts (there were ninety in all), many clergy and lay people began to have a deeper understanding of the sacraments and a direct result was the more frequent celebration of Holy Communion. The movement suffered a serious setback in 1845 when Newman became a Roman Catholic, but by this time the message of the tracts had reached a wider audience. Those clergy who followed the teachings of the Oxford Movement were sometimes known as **Tractarians** or **High Churchmen**. Later, when the followers began to put increased emphasis on ritual they were sometimes called **Ritualists** or later still, **Anglo Catholics** to distinguish them from Roman Catholics.

A direct result of the tracts was the revival of interest in medieval architecture so that churches built after the 1850s looked very much like those dating from the 13th–15th centuries. This gave rise to the so-called **Gothic Revival** and the building or restoration of many churches by Victorian architects.

symbol IHS with a trefoil design piercing the "H" and three nails below. Mrs Paget was a generous benefactor to Holy Trinity, and had been one of the original subscribers to the church building fund. At the time of writing this book, the Communion set given by her is still used at Holy Trinity at Christmas, Easter and the Dedication Festival.

Robed church choirs were rare in the 1830s, and there was no regular choir at Holy Trinity during its early days. The Revd Newnham believed this gave him greater flexibility in deciding when any singing should take place, generally having three separate "singings" during a service. The first singing would be a hymn; the second a psalm; and the third another

The Paget silver given to Holy Trinity at the time of its consecration

hymn. Hymns were taken from *The Cottage Hymn Book*, which was adopted at Holy Trinity owing to its "cheapness and general simplicity". During the afternoon services, the psalm followed the second response, a custom which Newnham said he had learned while attending St Mary's, Oxford, although if he could start over again he would have moved the psalm to the "parochial place after the third collect". (D/P/Coleford 8/3/1, p87) There may have been an informal choir which would have sung from the gallery, because in his history of Kilmersdon, Lord Hylton noted that "Mr Newnham gratefully acknowledged the help of G Padfield, the leader of his choir" (p99). George Padfield's memorial is over the church door and records his death on 7 April 1874, aged 68.

George Padfield's memorial in Holy Trinity

The Revd Newnham's notes go on to describe other church work in those formative years, including a five-shilling charge for the Churching of Women, which money was used to supply baby linen for the use of needy families. The linen was kept by Martha Padfield.

Also, Newnham was sensitive to the poverty of his parishioners. "Collections have always been very small owing partly to the great poverty of the place, partly to the weakness of my powers as an advocate—strangers having been but rarely called in." (D/P/Coleford 8/3/1 p89)

The Paget silver The style of the pieces in the Communion set reflects the way in which Holy Communion was administered in 1831. Both the tazza (a small plate with a foot) and the paten are large when compared with their modern counterparts. This is because a loaf of bread, rather than small wafers, would have been used at this time, thus requiring what was in effect a large plate. When the priest was about to administer the consecrated bread he would break it into small pieces, having already broken the loaf in two during the Prayer of Consecration. Probably the need for an extra "plate" is reflected in the addition of a matching silver paten at a later date. The bowl of the chalice is tall and deep because at this time the priest would give the chalice into the hands of the person receiving the consecrated wine. This method of administering the wine inevitably meant that more was consumed than the chalice would hold, hence the need to replenish the chalice from wine contained in the flagon. (Many a chalice has been inadvertently drained by an overzealous communicant!) The later (and present day) practice at Holy Trinity of using unleavened wafer bread and the minister holding the chalice has resulted in fewer mishaps. (Some churches still use ordinary bread rather than unleavened wafers.)

The annual sermon collection was used to aid the work of the Sunday School.

A degree of flexibility regarding service times was also required. "Some brethren have counselled the having [*sic*] of an evening service in lieu of afternoon, but from reluctance to exchange a formed congregation at an hour when no other place of worship was open for a questionable one in apparent opposition to the Methodists, and inability to give a third service, the experiment was never tried. There might also be some difficulty in lighting." (D/P/Coleford 8/3/1 p101)

Newnham's attempts to take the Church to the people of Coleford included midweek services, lectures and activities for the children. "Wednesday evening service was commenced from the opening of the Church but given up mid-winter. At times it was interrupted by indisposition. The congregation varied from 20–40, and in consequence the scanty supply of 12 or 14 candles was thought sufficient. In the Winter of 1838/9 the service was held in the schoolroom for the convenience of light and warmth; it would have been earlier tried but from the disapprobation of the Ordinary [i.e. the Vicar of Kilmersdon who opposed the idea], and the fear of approximating Methodism." (D/P/Coleford 8/3/1 p103) The Wednesday evening service was not resumed in the spring of 1839 because of the "bodily inability" of the minister.

> Although **John and Charles Wesley** had been prolific hymn writers, the hymn books now familiar to us did not appear until the mid 19th and early 20th Centuries. The *Hymnal Noted* (1852 and 1854, published in two parts) was the first major hymn book, followed by *Hymns Ancient & Modern* (1861) and the *English Hymnal* (1906). *The Cottage Hymn Book* may have been a fairly local publication.

The Revd Newnham also made valiant attempts to engage his flock in other ways, including through missionary lectures. Poor attendance meant that monthly meetings gave way to quarterly meetings, but even then numbers remained very low unless the lecture coincided with the Wednesday evening service. Nor was the school room the only place, other than the church, where Newnham conducted services. "Cottage lectures used to be given at the groups of Kilmersdon Common, Upper and Lower Lypeat [*sic*], in the houses of invalids, while health lasted, with an audience varying from three to ten. Their interruption was often a cause of upset, particularly when (as in the case of Dan Plummer's house at Upper Common) they occupied the place of an abandoned prayer meeting." (D/P/Coleford 8/3/1 p105) Such gatherings had also taken place at John Langley's or M Bryant's cottage at Lypeate, or Mar. Ashman's in Dunch Lane.

As the Revd Newnham's health deteriorated, these cottage gatherings ceased. The death of his young wife, and his own failing health, meant that despite good solid congregations, he was forced to give up many of his additional activities by the spring of 1839. By then he had regular morning congregations of thirty, and about one hundred (excluding teachers and children) at the afternoon services, and the number of scholars and teachers at the Sunday School had exceeded those on the Wesleyan lists. The infant school, opened in 1834, had settled into a steady routine by 1839. At first progress had been impeded by staffing problems and epidemic diseases amongst the children. A special club had been established for the Sunday School children to encourage saving through the purchase of tickets that could be redeemed for clothing and books. The articles thus redeemed were chosen by the Revd Newnham so that they were "in better keeping with the station of the wearers". (D/P/Coleford 8/3/1 p111) Clubs had also been established for women and for men. These had been less successful than Newnham might have hoped; the former was "left to spinsters and widows", while few men were willing to submit "to the bondage of Church regulations".

The Revd Newnham cared for the material needs of his parishioners in addition to their spiritual needs. He noted that "It has been a custom during the 8 [*sic*] winter months to brew soup weekly for about 16 to 20 people distributed on Tuesdays: Eliz. Bryant and Eliza, Martin—Vag End; Thomas Robbins, Mary Pratten, ? Vranch, Bett Widcombe—Church Street; John Clark, Grace Watts—Violet Alley; ? Hamblin—In field; Eliz. Lottle—High Street; Eliz. Brooks, Jane Purl, ? West—Grove; Ann Robbins, Mary Hill—Greyhound Hill; Mary Hamblin, Chr. Coles." (D/P/Coleford 8/3/1 p127)

When he was succeeded by the **Revd John West** in 1840, George Newnham handed over a sound foundation on which Holy Trinity's second priest could build, although he was conscious that he had made little progress in catechising, which he felt to be beyond the ability of his Sunday scholars. Unlike his wife Helen Maria, who died so young, the Revd George Newnham, despite his frail health at Coleford, married twice more and lived a long and fulfilled life. After leaving Coleford in 1840, he went to Shaw in Wiltshire but only stayed until 1842. From there he moved to Combe Down near Bath and stayed until 1877, having also the neighbouring parish of Monkton Combe from 1845 until 1863. Sometime after his death the following inscription was added to his first wife's memorial in Holy Trinity:

ALSO

THE REV[D] GEORGE WILLIAM NEWNHAM,

DIED AT CORSHAM, WILTS. DEC[R]. 21ST 1893,

AGED 87 YEARS.

In 1982 **Jack Coles** noted: "I happened to be in church a couple of years ago when a man came in who said he was the great-grandson of the first vicar. He had married twice more, one wife being very wealthy, and [he] had thirteen children." The truth of this is borne out in the Census returns through which we can follow the Revd Newnham's life after he left Coleford to become vicar of Combe Down (1842–77) and Monkton Combe (1845–63).

The **1851 Census** records George Newnham, aged 44 years, living at Monkton Combe near Bath and married to Catherine, aged 31 years, whose place of birth was Midsomer Norton. They had three children: Lewis, aged 5; Charlotte, aged 3 and Margaret, aged 2. Also resident in the Parsonage at Combe Down was

Charlotte Cox, nurse, aged 31; Sarah Small, 22; Elizabeth Bravis, 28; and Charlotte Bryant, 17, all servants.

By the **1861 Census** George Newnham was 54, still living at Monkton Combe, and was widowed once more. His son, Lewis, was 15; but there is no mention of Charlotte and Margaret, who would be too young to have left home, so presumably they had died in the intervening decade. But there were other children from this second marriage: Ashby, aged 10 and probably born some months after the 1851 Census; Ernest, aged 6; Ella, aged 5; Helen K, aged 3; Annie, aged 2; and two babies, Henry and Frederick, aged 6 months. It is likely that Catherine Newnham died after the birth of the twin boys, a tragic repetition of the fate of George Newnham's first wife, though by no means unusual. Also resident in the Parsonage were two nurses, both widows: Elizabeth Pemberton, aged 54, and Charlotte Cox, still with the family and now aged 40. Also, Sarah Phillip, cook, aged 34; Matilda Baker, housemaid, aged 20, and Emily Baynton, nursemaid, aged 17.

In the **1871 Census**, the 64-year-old George Newnham was still Vicar of Combe Down, and had married for the third time. His wife, Harriet, was born at the Cape of Good Hope and was 51 at the time of the Census. By this time the older children (Lewis, now 25, and Ashby, now 20) had presumably left home. There was a 13-year-old daughter Kate H Newnham, who was probably Helen K, as recorded in 1861, and also, Anne S (Annie) was now 12. But there was no mention of Ernest who would have been 16, though he might have been away at school; nor was there any mention of Ella who would have been 15, nor of the twin boys who would have been 10. There seems to have been one child of this third marriage: Caroline, aged 6, who was described as a scholar along with her half-sisters Kate and Anne. It was probably George Newnham's third wife Harriet who was "very wealthy", having a ladies' maid, Elizabeth Warron (or Warren), aged 30 (also described as a domestic servant), resident in the vicarage at the time of the Census. Other servants were: Matilda Biggs, teacher, aged 32; Mary Nusser, children's maid and domestic servant, aged 60; Susan Long, parlour maid, aged 24; Ann Williams, cook, aged 39, and Ruth Maxey, housemaid, aged 16. Also resident at the time of the Census was Charlotte Greaves, Harriet's sister, who is described as a clergyman's wife.

All in all, by 1871 George Newnham was in a far more prosperous position than the "poor curate" of 1832 who had entreated the Incorporated Church Building Society to increase its grant to Holy Trinity because the living was so impoverished.

By the time of the **1881 Census**, George Newnham had retired to Corsham in Wiltshire, and while he was described as "married" he and Harriet were apart on Census day, and possibly living apart. There was no mention of Caroline, his daughter by this marriage, who would have been 16. But the elderly clergyman (now 74) had two of his older children at home—Frederick, now aged 20 and described as an Oxford undergraduate, and Sophia A, who was probably the same as Anne S, and now aged 22. There was no mention of Frederick's twin brother, Henry. He may have died in infancy, or may simply have been resident elsewhere.

There were three servants—Ann Benjamin, cook, aged 35; Sarah Hunt, parlourmaid, aged 26; and Alice Williams, housemaid, aged 18. Harriet Newnham was now living as a lodger at 2 Belgrave Villas, Fisherton Anger, in Wiltshire. Now aged 61, she was described as a clergyman's wife and was accompanied by her former "ladies' maid" Elizabeth Warren, now simply described as the widow of an army sergeant. It seems that Harriet had come down in the world.

In the **1891 Census** George Newnham was still living at Corsham and was described as a widower. By now he was 84 years old and had the company of his daughter, Ella, now aged 35. There were three servants, Rosa Smith, cook, aged 32; Elizabeth Brown, parlourmaid, aged 32; and Annie Norman, housemaid, aged 20.

4

A GOOD FOUNDATION

By contrast with funerals and baptisms, the Revd George Newnham never conducted a wedding in Holy Trinity. Marriage services were not initially included in the rites of passage contemplated for the new church, and couples continued to travel to Kilmersdon, the mother church of the parish, to wed. There was some delay in applying for a licence to conduct weddings, and it was not until 12 February 1842, when Holy Trinity became a separate parish, that the licence for the Solemnisation of Matrimony was finally granted to Holy Trinity. Even when it was gained, there was concern at the "imprudent haste" with which many couples rushed to the altar, including the first couple to be married at Holy Trinity, John and Harriet Edgell. John Edgell, son of coal miner Adam Edgell, was recorded as an underage coal miner and Harriet, daughter of naval mariner Thomas Pratten, as an underage knitter, when they were married on 12 March 1842. The ceremony was performed by the **Revd John West**, Newnham's successor, and witnessed by Benjamin Martin, the Parish Clerk, and John Button. Their first child, Charlotte, was baptised on 8 May 1842, only two months later!

A further benefit of Coleford becoming a separate parish was that the stipend of the incumbent was raised to £120 a year. The same licence outlined the bounds of the new ecclesiastical parish, which was carved out of the parish of Kilmersdon, served by the mother church, "… the District within and part of the parish of Kilmersdon of which District the limits and boundaries are and shall be as follows (that is to say) the District commences at the north East Corner of a piece of land within the said parish of Kilmersdon belonging to John Moore Paget Esq which piece of land is No. 310 on the parish map and is bounded by the road leading from Mells to Lypeat [*sic*] on the North and by the parish of Babington on the East and thence through the centre of the said Road passing by Cherry Garden to Lypeat [*sic*] and from thence continues through the centre of the same Road to the North East corner of a piece of land in the said Parish of Kilmersdon belonging to Francis Craddock gentleman which said piece of Land is No. 884 on the Parish Map and is bounded by the said last mentioned Road on the East and by the road leading from Kilmersdon to Holcombe on the West, through the centre of the said last mentioned road to the part where the same meets the parish of Holcombe and from thence along the boundary of the said Parish of Kilmersdon against the parishes of Holcombe, Leigh on Mendip and Babington to the North East Corner of the said first mentioned piece of land belonging to the said John Moore Paget."

Like Newnham before him, the Revd John West was to suffer personal tragedy while in office, when he and his wife lost their only child, Anne Margaret West, aged 17 years. Anne was buried by the Revd William Batchelor, Curate of Babington (and of Chilcompton), and a memorial tablet was placed on the north wall of the sanctuary. (See transcription overleaf.)

The West memorial on the north wall of the sanctuary

The **Revd John West** is an unsolved mystery. *Crockford's Clerical Directory* for 1860 lists a John West, ordained by the Bishop of Llandaff in south Wales as deacon in 1827 aged 24, and priest in 1828, but there is no mention of Coleford in his entry. He is listed in the *Alumni Oxoniensis* as being Rector of Asholt in the Diocese of Bath and Wells from 1832 until his death on 29 April 1888. Clergy still held livings in plurality in the 1830s, but it is unlikely that this is the John West who was at Coleford because Coleford would have been listed with Asholt.

The **1841 Census** lists John West at Asholt, which is near Cannington, beyond Bridgwater—a long way from Coleford. His wife is listed as Elizabeth West, while the name of John West's wife on the memorial to their daughter Anne Margaret West, who died in 1842 (see transcription overleaf), is Mary. No other John West is noted in any of the clergy listings.

Livings in plurality In the 18th and early 19th centuries it was common for a clergyman to be the **incumbent**, i.e. vicar or rector, of several parishes which might be in different parts of the country. He would live in one parish and employ a curate, i.e. an assistant priest, in the others, for a very small stipend (wage). The incumbent might visit these parishes once a year, but rarely more than this. Any fees from weddings and funerals and other income would go to the incumbent, many of whom grew very wealthy, while the curate would live close to poverty. The Barchester novels by Anthony Trollope and the novels by Jane Austen were written at this time and reflect church life. Today, clergy often have more than one parish, e.g. the benefice of Coleford with Holcombe, but this is a different system from that of 200 years ago. Nowadays the incumbent of the **benefice**, i.e. the group of parishes, lives and ministers within it.

BENEATH

REST THE EARTHLY REMAINS OF

ANNE MARGARET,

THE ONLY CHILD OF

THE REVD JOHN WEST AND MARY HIS WIFE.

SHE ENTERED UPON THIS WORLD OF TRIAL

28TH SEPTEMBER 1824.

HER PURE AND PIOUS SPIRIT

DEPARTED IN THE FIRM FAITH OF CHRIST

26TH MARCH 1842.

THEIR HOPE IS FULL OF IMMORTALITY

FOR GOD PROVED HER

AND FOUND HER WORTHY FOR HIMSELF.

By the middle of the 1840s, Holy Trinity had earned itself a place in the village community that it served. When the **Revd Robert Hayman Whiteway**, the third incumbent, arrived in 1846, the original school had proved sufficiently successful to become overcrowded, and new premises were sought adjoining it. The Revd Whiteway himself donated the land on which the new school was built, indicating that he had private means.

An insight into the life and worship of Holy Trinity may be gained from the Articles of Enquiry sent to the Churchwardens of every parish in the diocese in preparation for the Bishop's three-yearly Visitation. No returns were submitted during the Revd John West's ministry in Coleford, nor in the early years of Robert Whiteway's, but in 1851 the Churchwardens (Thomas Brice and Francis Craddock) sent in a detailed reply. (D/D/Va 5/8 1851) The questions, some of which were "quaint" to say the least, were identical for every parish. So we learn that the Easter Vestry meeting to appoint the Churchwardens was held on Easter Sunday rather than Easter Monday and that the Clergyman appointed one Churchwarden and the parishioners the other. The church fabric, i.e. the building, was in good repair (as it should be for a church only 20 years old), but there were no funds for repairs arising from gifts of benefactors. Regarding the churchyard, we learn that it was sufficiently fenced in and the Churchwardens were asked, "Is it kept free from all profane uses, particularly from being made a playground?" Answer: yes. "Are pigs and cattle excluded? Note that churchyards are fenced for the express purpose of keeping off this profanation. Indeed, sheep are the only animals that are at all suited to such a pasture." Answer: yes.

Next the Churchwardens were questioned on the quality of ministry exercised by the priest. "Does your Minister, properly habited [i.e. wearing the correct robes], perform the Services of the Church, as prescribed by the Book of Common Prayer, without adding thereto, diminishing therefrom, or altering in any respect? Audibly, distinctly and in a devout manner? At due and seasonal hours?" Answer: yes. We learn, too, that there were services in the morning and afternoon, that a sermon was preached, and that the Holy Communion was administered ten times a year. Oddly, given the fact that the Revd Whiteway gave the land for the new school, the question about whether the Minister instructed the children of the parish in the Catechism at Afternoon Service went unanswered. But the answer was a firm yes to the question, "Does he visit the sick readily and diligently and attend upon his parishioners who desire it, or have need of instruction?"

The Churchwardens were able to affirm that there was "a suitable reading desk for the Minister, a comely and decent Pulpit with Cloth and Cushion, two surplices kept in good repair and clean, a Bible of the largest size free from note and comment, a Book of Common Prayer for the Minister, also for the Clerk, clean and well bound. There was a decent Font of stone, Communion rails entire, firm and in good order. There was a proper Table for the Holy Communion, covered at the time of Divine Service with a cloth of silk or other decent stuff, and with a fair linen cloth at the time of ministration [of Holy Communion]".

Regarding other matters, the Churchwardens could answer yes to several questions:

The **Revd Robert Whiteway** was certainly no scholar, having graduated from Worcester College, Oxford, with a 4th class degree in Literature and Humanities. A Devon man, he was ordained deacon in 1839 and priest in 1840. He came to Coleford in 1846 and stayed until 1865. He was Rector of St Helen's, Ipswich, 1866–72, and of St Clement's, Ipswich, 1866–77. His last parish was Eynsford, Kent from 1877—he is in the *Clergy List 1882* as vicar of Eynsford, but there is no mention of him in the 1898 edition.

The **1851 Census** records Robert Whiteway, aged 34, living at the vicarage in Coleford with his wife Sarah Whiteway, aged 28. They had two children, Augustine aged 3 years, and Sarah aged 1 year. There were four servants, a possible indication of the Revd Whiteway's private means. These were Anna Sturman, a widow aged 51, described as a nurse and servant; Ann Jeffs, aged 35, cook; Eliza Lacy, aged 23, housemaid; and John Silcox, aged 30, footman.

By the **1861 Census** Robert Whiteway was 44 and Sarah 38. Their family had increased to four with the addition of Emma Frances aged 9 and Constance aged 8. There were now three servants: Marianne Savioz, aged 41, a Swiss-born governess; Martha Padfield, aged 22, housemaid; and Sarah Ann Moon, aged 19, cook. Robert Whiteway may have been the benefactor to the school, but his children had their own governess.

In 1862/63 Robert Whiteway was absent from the parish for several months, but correspondence in the *East Somerset Telegraph* in March/April 1863 seems to suggest that this was due to a parish exchange with the Revd J R Cotter, who took duty at Coleford during that time. In 1865 Whiteway left Coleford to become Rector of St Helen's, Ipswich.

"Is there a decent Metal Basin or Plate to collect alms at the offertory? Is there a Flagon with a cover? And a Chalice or Cup? And a Paten or Metal Plate for the Bread? Is there a fair linen cloth for covering what remains of the consecrated elements? And are they diligently cleansed after every Communion, and not employed to any other use? Are there Hassocks, Mats or Cushions in sufficient number, and in due repair, for kneeling at the Communion, and at other Services of the Church? Are the bells and bell frame safe? Is your Church regularly, and from week to week, swept and kept free from dust, dirt, and everything that is noisome and unseemly, at the charge of the Parish?" These questions may seem odd, or even slightly insulting, but many churches at this time did not have decent and seemly Communion vessels and altar linens. Indeed it was not until the teachings of the Tractarian Movement had become more widespread that services were held regularly at all, and in many churches the books, vessels, linens and general state of the building were in varying stages of decay.

The church did not at this stage own a funeral bier, and the question "Do you take care that due order is observed during the time of Marriage and Burials?" received no answer. Also, we are told that the Ten Commandments were displayed, but not the table of degrees within which marriage is prohibited.

At the time of the 1855 Articles of Enquiry (D/D/Va 7/9 1855), many of the answers were the same, as were the two Churchwardens. By this time Churchwardens' Accounts were being kept, and while they could affirm that the Parish Clerk [Benjamin Martin] "is of honest conversation and sober life", they left unanswered the question whether the Churchwardens attend Divine Service regularly. By 1855, Holy Communion was held on the first Sunday of every month.

There was a change of bishop by the 1858 Visitation (D/D/Va 8/8 1858), the new bishop being Robert, Baron Auckland. By this time the Easter Vestry meeting for the election of Churchwardens and presentation of their accounts was held on Easter Monday, and the Churchwardens were Francis Craddock and James Green. Church Rates were now being levied "in order to sustain or add to, or improve, or restore … the Church, Churchyard and Church goods". The Churchwardens were diligently keeping their accounts, and attended Divine Service "regularly to see due order kept, and to assist at the several ministrations". They also affirmed that they "prevent idle persons from abiding in the Churchyard or Church porch". The Parish Clerk was still a man of honest conversation and sober life, was competent to perform his duties, and was paid £5 a year. The Sexton was also affirmed as doing his duties diligently and punctually. Repairs were being carried out so that the water carried from the roof would "not injure the Walls and Foundations". And the dead could now be transported to their resting place on the parish bier.

By 1861 (D/D/Va 9/8 1861) Francis Craddock had been joined as Churchwarden by William Ford, but their replies were unchanged.

All in all, Holy Trinity was in good order during the ministry of the Revd Whiteway, but in 1862/3 he was away from Coleford for several months. He was temporarily replaced by the Revd J R Cotter, whose arrival prompted criticism of Whiteway's style in a letter to the *East Somerset Telegraph* of 28 March 1863. The writer signed himself "An Episcopalian", i.e. a member of the Church of England. (Had he been a Methodist or other nonconformist he would probably have signed himself "A Dissenter".)

He wrote, "A few months ago a change of ministers in the Established Church took place at Coleford, and the first Sunday after the event witnessed a well-filled Church, and the opinions formed of the new minister's capabilities were of no ordinary character; he was, indeed, considered by the majority an able and excellent preacher. During the short stay of the new minister (the Rev J R Cotter, BA) he has, by his earnest and excessive labours, succeeded in making himself deservedly popular among the inhabitants of this place. To say nothing of Mr Cotter's labours as a minister of the glorious gospel of Christ, too much praise can scarcely be given to him for his exertions in endeavouring to benefit the inhabitants of the neighbourhood by presiding at public meetings, and more particularly by taking a prominent part in rendering the Prince of Wales's Wedding Day one of marked importance in the annals of Coleford. Never before have we seen less party-spirit in the Church, as exhibited on that memorable day by the excellent treat the children received belonging to all the schools (both Church and dissenting). If Mr Whiteway, the absent clergyman, had been here, we venture so far as to say that we could not have expected it. Considering the time Mr Cotter has been with us, I have no hesitation in saying that he has won the esteem and respect of the majority of the parishioners. The rev. Gentleman is shortly about to leave us, to give place to our *own* clergyman (the Rev R H Whiteway), and I am certain that his departure will be a source of regret to many; and, for a testimony of the respect and esteem we have for him, I would earnestly recommend that a valuable present be made to him by the friends and inhabitants of our village."

This was very embarrassing for the Revd Cotter who was quick to take up the cause of the absent clergyman on behalf of the congregation, responding with a letter the following week in the *East Somerset Telegraph*, 4 April 1863. His reply also suggests that the Revd Whiteway was looking after his own parish while he was in Coleford. Clergy exchanges were not unknown, although they were usually on a more permanent basis. He wrote, "I cannot refrain from expressing my regret that you have suffered my name to appear in a letter published in the *Somerset Telegraph* last week. What the writer says of myself may have been kindly intended; but I would assure 'Episcopalian' it savours too plainly of flattery to be at all gratifying, and becomes really painful, when I am forced to believe, in considering the animus of the letter, that there must be some petty spleen in the mind of the writer against the clergyman whose long and faithful labours in Coleford are justly appreciated by the well-judging portion of the inhabitants, and to whom I am happy to have committed the pastoral care of my own parish, during the time of my residence here." There was a postscript: "The Revd R H Whiteway was, as you are aware, a subscriber to the treat given to the children on the 10th."

The same issue of the newspaper carried a reply to "Episcopalian" from Noah Rogers Spicer of Coleford. He wrote, "If ever a column in the *East Somerset Telegraph* was tarnished by any written communication, it was by 'An Episcopalian' … [His] letter carries its own condemnation … and neither would it be worthy of a reply were it not as much to vindicate the Rev J R Cotter, as to show that it emanated from some private spleen towards the Rev R H Whiteway. Of course any person of respectability or education, who knows Mr Whiteway, will, by reading the letter, at once see such to be the case. 'An Episcopalian', what an unworthy member! Who would so wilfully try to hurt the feelings of a clergyman who always faithfully preaches the gospel. I do not … believe him to be a churchman nor a dissenter … There are worthy churchmen and worthy dissenters, but that individual can be neither … Oh! the hypocrisy for such a man to talk of the 'glorious gospel of Christ'. 'An Episcopalian' as he calls himself can be nothing better than an ignominious and dastardly fellow. I am willing to reply further to his letter, provided he will come out in his true colours."

The following week, 11 April 1863, "An Episcopalian" sent a lengthy reply, but declined to reveal his true identity. He wrote, "Surely, Mr Editor, I am not deserving all the buffeting which I received at the hands of … Mr N R Spicer, last week. It seems that the remarks made in my letter—which were kindly and affectionately intended towards the Rev J R Cotter—have met with a great offence from one or two of my brethren in the Church." He then tried to excuse himself by saying that he merely wanted to draw attention to the Revd Cotter's caring ministry, and that he "deserved a lasting token of our respect". He continued, "… but for the sentence which referred to Mr Whiteway, the letter would, doubtless, have passed without any public comment; but I can assure the rev. Gentleman, and also Mr Spicer, that it was out of no *spleen* towards Mr Whiteway, as they have chosen to term it. Having been one of the sheep of his flock for a number of years, and having had the pleasure of being personally acquainted with him, far be it from me to speak disrespectfully of Mr Whiteway's labours as a minister of Christ's gospel; but what I affirmed in my former letter, I considered no 'spleen', but merely a friendly hint, kindly intended. If I have indulged in any word or sentence against him, I am very sorry. In thus endeavouring to do a benevolent action, I am afraid I have subjected myself to the displeasure of Mr Cotter, and the disrespect of a few of my fellow members of the Church of England …"

The correspondence came to a halt after this but clearly "Episcopalian" had a grievance against the Revd Whiteway. However, as we have seen, all seemed in order at Holy Trinity, and the Revd Whiteway was a good benefactor to the school. He stayed at Holy Trinity for another year or two before moving on to his next parish in Ipswich in 1865.

In 1864 only William Ford signed the Bishop's Articles of Enquiry. (D/D/Va 10/8 1864) There was a new question: "Do you take such measures as the law prescribes to prevent tippling in public houses and houses for the sale of beer on the Lord's day; especially during the hours of Divine Service?" Answer: yes. This question reflects a nationwide concern about the ill effects of alcohol. By the 1860s the Temperance Movement was gaining ground and indeed Coleford was to have its own Temperance Hall in 1865.

Coleford in the 1860s was a thriving community, benefiting from the expansion of the local mines. New houses were erected, particularly in the Highbury area, to

The **Revd Joseph Rogerson Cotter** was born *c.* 1823 in County Cork, Ireland, and was ordained deacon in 1845 and priest in 1846, serving at Killaloe. (At this time the Anglican Church in Ireland was not separate from the Church of England.) He then served at Corfe Castle in Dorset 1852–56; as Rector of Winterbourne Houghton in Dorset 1857–77; and St Mary Magdalen, Colchester, from 1877. He may have been a great-great-great-uncle of Clarissa Cridland, whose mother's family had the surname of Cotter. Clarissa's great-great-grandfather was the Revd William Laurence Cotter, born in Queenstown, County Cork, in 1844, who was Rector of West Coker in Somerset 1880–98. Joseph Rogerson Cotter may have been the brother of William Laurence Cotter's father as they both originated in County Cork at roughly the same time. (It is difficult to trace Irish family records because a fire at the Dublin Record Office in 1922 destroyed many records, so that there are missing links in the chain.)

accommodate the expanding population that fed the demands of the coal mines for labour, and the village experienced something of an economic boom. These years saw a number of changes in the village, with the building of a new Primitive Methodist Chapel (1863), a new Wesleyan Chapel (1865), and the arrival of a new vicar at Holy Trinity (1865).

The **Revd Thomas Pomeroy Leigh Yewens** was to be the longest serving of Holy Trinity's clergy. He was the first vicar of Coleford to have been to a theological college, having studied at St Bee's College in Cumberland.

The Revd Thomas Yewens quickly settled into the village, working closely with the Methodist ministers at the Primitive and Wesleyan Chapels, and taking part in ecumenical activities such as open air services to mark local pit disasters (*East Somerset Telegraph*, 30 June 1866), and helping to found a Bible Society. It is perhaps surprising, then, that he had to defend his record regarding his relationship with the Methodist Chapels when he was accused of telling the children at the Church School "that it is a wicked thing for anyone to go to Chapel". He wrote to the local paper rebutting the claim, as the best way of getting his message to the widest number of people (*East Somerset Telegraph*, 22 July 1869).

Founded in 1816 by the Bishop of Chester (The Right Revd G H Law), **St Bee's College** in Cumberland was an early attempt at theological training for candidates who were unable to have a university education. The college course lasted two years and the students were residential. **Thomas Yewens** was ordained deacon in 1846 and priest in 1847, serving in the Dioceses of Lichfield, Bristol, Chester and Salisbury before coming to Coleford in 1865. This was to be his final parish, and in 1896 he retired to Cheltenham. He died on 8 March 1899 and his death was briefly reported in the *Somerset and Wiltshire Journal* of 18 March.

Indeed the strength of Yewens' relationship with the Methodist Chapels was evident some fifteen years later, in 1883, when he got married. [See box below regarding the Revd Yewens' marriages.] His bride, Bessie, was the daughter of the Revd George Shutte of Torquay; and when the happy couple arrived in Coleford, the Churchwardens and congregation and members of both chapels greeted them. A silk gown was presented to the bride, and an illuminated address signed on behalf of the parishioners and friends was given to the happy couple. The *East Somerset Telegraph* of 10 February 1883 noted the occasion as "… the cheerful and spontaneous act of an attached people in grateful remembrance and in practical sympathy with a long and faithful ministry extending over a period of varied difficulties … believing that her [Mrs Yewens'] presence will materially strengthen your ministry, and promote the work of the Church".

The first detailed record of the Churchwardens' Accounts is given in 1869 (even though the Churchwardens were presenting accounts at the annual Vestry meeting as early as 1855, these do not seem to have survived). The first entries in 1869 identify

The **1871 Census** records the **Revd Thomas Yewens** as aged 53 and living at the vicarage with his first wife, Caroline, aged 64. No children are recorded, though given the ages of Thomas and Caroline Yewens, they may have had children, now grown up and living away. As well as a visitor (Caroline White) at the vicarage on Census day, there was a Curate, the **Revd Francis E Horwood B A**, aged 24, and described as a boarder. This is the first evidence of Coleford ever having a curate.

The **Revd Francis Horwood** graduated from St Mary Hall, Oxford, in 1870 and was ordained deacon in the same year and priest in 1871. He served as curate at Coleford from 1870–72; and curacies at St Philip and Jacob, Bristol, 1873–75; at Wordsley, Worcestershire, 1875–77; Holy Trinity, Leicester, 1877–79; Kingsthorpe, Northamptonshire, 1880–84; and Hungarton, Leicestershire, 1887–93. The last edition of Crockford's Clerical Directory in which he is listed is the 1918 edition, when his position was Rector of South Crowton, Leicester.

St Mary Hall, Oxford, where Francis Horwood took his degree, was one of the last Academic Halls founded in medieval times, and gradually superseded by the Colleges. By the 19th century the few remaining Halls provided a less expensive means of studying at Oxford. Francis Horwood was one of the last generation to study in a Hall, for in 1877 they began to be absorbed into the college system, though St Mary's struggled on until 1902.

By the **1881 Census** the Revd Yewens, now aged 63, was a widower, living alone at the vicarage except for one general servant, Ellen Edgell, aged 20, who may not have been resident.

The **1891 Census** records the 73-year-old Thomas Yewens living with Bessie his 43-year-old wife, to whom he had been married for eight years. Their one general servant was Zipporah Plummer, aged 26.

Edmund Candy and John Holbrook as the Churchwardens (both farmers), and were witnessed by the Revd Yewens, Joseph Webb (another farmer), James Ashman and George Brice. Income from the Church Rates contributed to the costs of running the church, while the vicar's stipend was augmented by income from pew rents and Queen Anne's Bounty. (For information on pew rents, see chapter 10; for information on Church Rates see right, and for Queen Anne's Bounty, see the box in chapter 2.)

Regular expenditure included lighting, organ tuning, payment of the organist and of the person who pumped the organ. Such expenditure indicates that an organ had been installed before 1869 (the first entry for organ tuning), the church clock before 1870 (when repairs costing £1 5s were carried out), and that the two surplices which had been in use since 1851 were in need of mending at a cost of 5s 6d. The original plans for Holy Trinity included a clock on the church tower, but this was dropped to save money. The date at which the clock was added is unknown.

> **Church Rates** By Common Law every parish was liable for the upkeep of its church and churchyard, the rate being decided at the annual Easter Vestry meeting. During the 19th century there was a movement to abolish the compulsory Church Rate, and this became law in 1868, when it was replaced by a voluntary rate. But some parishes, especially those with little or no endowment, still clung to a compulsory rate. In Coleford the rate varied from 2d to 3d in the pound over the last quarter of the 19th century, rising from £32 5s 7d in 1879 to as little as £6 0s 5d in 1893 (the year of the miners' lockout). In 1894, with many of Coleford's miners still out of work, a voluntary rate only was levied, raising £4 11s 7d.

In 1878 a dispute arose over the tolling of the bell at funerals. A series of anonymous letters appeared in the local newspaper supporting the differing sides of the argument after a pauper went to the grave in silence because there was no money to pay for the tolling of the bell. The Church and the Poor Law Guardians were criticised for their unchristian approach, but as one defender noted, the pauper was buried in a decent and respectful manner, brought out in a hearse with bearers supplied, and according to the *East Somerset Telegraph*, 19 October 1878, the vicar gave a "solemn and impressive service".

During the Revd Thomas Yewens' ministry at Coleford, the gallery was taken down and the church re-seated. By the 1880s there was a growing trend towards abolishing pew rents and making church interiors more congenial for sacramental worship. Even though the Revd Yewens was on co-operative terms with the local Methodists, he may also have been more high church than his predecessors, and this being so, would have subscribed to this school of thought. Details of the actual changes made to the church interior in 1885 will be found in chapter 10. The *East Somerset Telegraph* of 10 January 1885 informed its readers that the work was in progress. This necessitated the closure of the church for several months, and the 11 April issue ran an advertisement informing all that Coleford Church would be reopened "on Tuesday next, April 14th with a Public Tea and Entertainment".

The *East Somerset Telegraph* of 18 April 1885 described the opening day: "The church during Tuesday was thrown open to the public, and during the afternoon there were a large number of visitors. The tea took place at 5 o'clock, and shortly after the schoolroom was crammed to its utmost capacity with a large and respectable company. Trays were given by Mrs Yewens, Mrs Robbins, Mrs Foxwell, Mrs Ford, Mrs Walsh, Miss James, Mrs King, Mrs Hamblin, Mrs Martin and Mrs Jones, Mrs E and Mrs Alfred Bryant, also G Terry Esq., 5s, Mrs J W Yewens 7s, a Friend 5s, Mrs Batey 5s, and a Friend 2s 6d. In addition to these Ladies, Mrs Fortescue Horner, of Mells Park, and the Misses Minnie and Clara Robbins assisted at the tea tables. At 7 o'clock an entertainment consisting of vocal and instrumental music was given in the large schoolroom opposite. The vicar, the Rev. T P L Yewens, presided. The Mells Choir, assisted by Mr Derry, organist of Frome, sang some capital glees, which were thoroughly appreciated. J W Knowlden, Esq., of Holcombe, also sang three capital songs accompanied by the Rev W E Whitaker of Holcombe. Mr C Evans, without whom an entertainment in Coleford would hardly be complete rendered very valuable assistance in giving two pianoforte selections and in addition a novel performance on the ocarina." [An ocarina is an egg-shaped wind instrument with a protruding mouthpiece and six to eight finger holes, producing an almost pure tone.] "Messrs Knowldon and Treasure also contributed greatly to the amusement of the audience by the performance of an amusing trio, which was loudly redemanded [*sic*]. The performance was shorn of some of its attractions on account of the inability, through death and sickness, of two performers (Messrs Bissex and Ridler) being unable to be present. The room was crammed to excess, and many thanks are due to the performers who so kindly contributed to the evening's entertainment." The Revd George Newnham had also been present and had assisted at the entertainment.

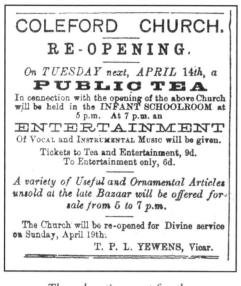

COLEFORD   CHURCH.

RE-OPENING.

On *TUESDAY* next, *APRIL* 14*th*, a
PUBLIC TEA
In connection with the opening of the above Church will be held in the INFANT SCHOOLROOM at 5 p.m.   At 7 p.m. an
ENTERTAINMENT
Of VOCAL and INSTRUMENTAL MUSIC will be given.

Tickets to Tea and Entertainment, 9d.
To Entertainment only, 6d.

A variety of Useful and Ornamental Articles unsold at the late Bazaar will be offered for sale from 5 to 7 p.m.

The Church will be re-opened for Divine service on Sunday, April 19th.

T. P. L. YEWENS, Vicar.

The advertisement for the reopening of the church in 1885

On Sunday 19 April, the first since the church had reopened, the Revd George Newnham preached. The *East Somerset Telegraph* of 25 April 1885 tells us that he preached twice that day. "In the morning the Church was almost filled, and at the evening service numbers were unable to gain admission, the aisles and every available spot being occupied. Collections were made at the close in aid of the renovation fund." The re-seating of the church and the loss of the gallery meant there were far fewer seats (about 200), and one wonders whether there were any disgruntled parishioners amongst those who either didn't get a seat, or had to stand in the aisles.

It was while Thomas Yewens was vicar that smallpox hit Coleford. The first case was reported in the *Somerset Standard* of 19 November 1887. "A case of small pox [*sic*] has come under the care of Dr Kenrick of this place who after taking every precaution to isolate and confine the infection communicated with the Medical Officer of Health for the district. Bills are placarded about the village, advising all to be re-vaccinated. On enquiry, we find the disease has not as yet spread further, and that the patient is doing well. It is to be hoped that the strongest means taken will effectively stamp out the malady in the district."

However, there were further cases and an appeal for help was made to the Sisters of the Society of St Margaret at East Grinstead. Despite initial suspicion, the Colefordians soon accepted the Sisters, who proved themselves fearless in the face of infection.

The *Somerset Standard* of 11 February 1888 reported that "Smallpox has again made its appearance [in Coleford]. In one case a little girl is under the care of the parochial medical officer; in the other a man is attended by Dr Kenrick. It is hoped the disease will be as effectually dealt with as were the previous cases. The medical officer of health for the Frome Union, and the Sanitary Inspector have visited Coleford with a view to the isolation of the small-pox patients. The Board of Guardians have, we understand, given instructions for inquiries to be made for a cottage, and also for a nurse, so that a system of isolation of infectious and contagious diseases may be established. This is much needed in this populous mining village and neighbourhood."

The temporary isolation hospital was situated at the bottom of the hairpin bend opposite the Kings Head, and is now a private house. The *Somerset Standard* of 14 April was able to report that the worst was over: "We find that the smallpox cases in the temporary hospital here, have been reduced to two, both of whom are convalescent. Of the total of 19 cases, some very virulent types have occurred, but not one single death has taken place, thanks to the very efficient nursing of the Sisters from East Grinstead, and to the care and attention of the medical officer, Mr Kenrick."

Even so, the disease continued its affliction amongst the poor and it was not until mid-May that the Sisters returned to East Grinstead, as reported in The *Somerset Standard*

The Society of St Margaret is an order of Anglican nuns, founded in East Grinstead, Sussex, in 1855 by the Revd Dr John Mason Neale, to nurse the sick poor in their homes. Word soon spread and there were requests for help with nursing from far and wide, especially when epidemics struck communities. It is not clear whether the Revd Yewens had asked the Sisters for help, or whether this was the request from the Poor Law Board of Guardians referred to below. Even so, Sisters were still relatively new in the Church of England (the first communities to be founded since the Reformation date from the 1840s), and many people regarded them with suspicion as being a concession to Roman Catholicism.

of 19 May. "We are pleased to find the dreadful scourge of small-pox has all but left this village there being now only one convalescent patient left in the temporary hospital. The medical officer in charge anticipates advising the closure of the hospital in a week or ten days. The sisters of S Margaret's, East Grinstead, who so devotedly and charitably nursed the patients, and to whom so large a share of thankfulness is due, left Coleford on Monday last amidst the general regret of the inhabitants, to whom they had much endeared themselves. A pleasing incident is that the inhabitants are making a subscription which will be sent to S Margaret's to be devoted to some charitable purpose."

The smallpox epidemic had also touched other local communities including Midsomer Norton, where it was followed by diphtheria and a number of children died. The East Grinstead Sisters stayed approximately eight weeks, and later they published an account of their time in Coleford which gives us a truer picture of the seriousness of the outbreak (there was a death despite the denial of the local newspaper), and also of the grinding poverty of the people of Coleford at the time.

"Coleford is a poor mining district seven miles from Frome; dissent being as much one of its chief features as coal—its only Church being shut up from Sunday to Sunday. Even on Good Friday, there was no service at Church or Chapels: only tea drinking at the latter. The feeling against our coming was very strong, and the Coleford cottages being built back to back, with no back doors and with gardens in front, our neighbours had every opportunity of watching our proceedings, and made the utmost use of their eyes. 'The Sanitary Inspector' and Dr and Mrs Parsons helped us to arrange the house which was to be our temporary hospital. It consisted of two small cottages not too conveniently placed; as everything, including water, had to be fetched from a distance. The Coleford doctor was anxious to get his patients into our Hospital at once. We had no ambulance: but there was no difficulty in getting the first patients in, as they consisted of … a girl of twelve years; and her father, also getting better, and able to walk with some assistance. The mother was too ill that day to be moved, but was brought to us two days after. Sister M stayed in and got beds ready, &c. for fresh patients, while Sister B set off with Dr Kenrick to fetch a boy [of fourteen] who had been ill a fortnight … [He] was not only very ill, but very heavy; our only possibility of conveying him to the hospital, was to place him in a chair and carry him sedan fashion. The road was very rough and rutty, and the half trodden-in snow rendered it in many places uncertain and slippery, and stiles at intervals did not improve matters!

"One of our very bad cases was that of a … father of eight children. His wife had been nursing him, and she, poor thing, though she had done her very best, had by no means alleviated the awfulness of the disease … When asked if he would like to go to the Hospital, he just gave one look at Sister B, and then calmly said, 'No thank ye, Missis: I'd rather bide where I be.' The doctor … suggested taking him out for a drive the next day; and … the drive ended in the patient being safely landed in our Hospital. It afforded some excitement in the village for the gig, lent by the doctor, allowed only room for the patient and his driver, and as the former had to be put in lengthways, his driver (Sister B) could only manage her steed by kneeling in front of him, the owner of the gig running on foot behind. The poor wife had been frantic at our taking her husband off, thinking he must die on the road, and declared she would rather have seen us take him to the Churchyard. Her astonishment therefore two days after was all the more satisfactory, when on seeing the improvement that ordinary care and attention had wrought on his poor sores, she exclaimed, 'Well Missis, you have done well by him.' And so we were fairly launched in our work; other cases followed … In all we had fourteen …

"Our last patient was the husband of one of our first women; he had been left in charge of four children, no woman near to help. His wife recovered, but a fortnight after she was out again, the man fell ill. He had lived a dreadful life, which no doubt aggravated the disease, and he died at the end of the week. He was perfectly wild with delirium, but in his quieter times said more than once, 'no more beer, no more baccy.' Whether in penitence or regret, it would be hard to say … His funeral was a rather difficult matter: he had been a man over six feet high, and his coffin was so big and so heavy, that it had to be left at first in the garden, as the men were afraid to come nearer, and we had to carry it into the house and carry his body down to it. Everybody was much too frightened to give any help. Instead of the ordinary hearse, the coffin was laid on a truck used for mending the roads, which we covered with a white sheet. This was propelled by two men in front, and one behind, while the Sisters followed after, as they were quite uncertain whether they might not have to put the coffin into the grave themselves: which, however, happily, was not required of them. Great was the alarm of the inhabitants, as the procession passed along: and it was not lessened by the sight of the sanitary inspector, going along in advance, and sprinkling disinfectant powder on the road all the way. He ended the process by throwing some of it on the coffin after it had been lowered into the grave. The scare was very great during the whole time. Our coals, for instance, were brought from the pit by the miners, and thrown out on the road, for us to get in as best we could. But gradually the feelings of the people underwent a total change, and their gratitude became as intense as their dread of us had been … The simple loving gratitude of these poor mining folk touched us the more because they had been so very much against the idea of Sisters coming to nurse them. The whole of our patients were dissenters."

When the Sisters left, a man wrote them a farewell note, saying, "My Dear Sisters, As you have finished your work with us and are about to leave us we thank you with all of our hearts for your kindness to us as a people and we pray that the smile of the Almighty rest upon you where ever you go. God has blessed the work in your hands and he will bless you also for labouring among the poor people in Highbury."

Queen Victoria's Golden Jubilee was kept in Coleford as a great day of jollification and feasting. The *Somerset Standard* of 25 June 1887 gave a lively description of the day, and while Holy Trinity was not directly mentioned, no doubt church members enjoyed it as much as anyone else. "The Jubilee was celebrated in Coleford on Tuesday, the 21st instant. The day being so beautifully fine the festival passed off in the most pleasant and satisfactory manner. Upwards of 1,000 people assembled at the schools at one o'clock when about 500 children, accompanied by the teachers of the various schools, members of the Jubilee Committee, Foresters, Oddfellows, Shepherds and other Friendly Societies, with their respective banners and emblems marched in through the village, headed by the East Mendip Brass Band. Returning to a field the children were regaled with a bread-and-butter and cake tea; and the adults with a meat tea in the church school-rooms. A very happy evening was spent in the field, and prizes awarded to successful competitors in racing, jumping, hammer-throwing, cricket ball throwing, and other athletic sports. Dancing and other enjoyments were also indulged in, ending with cheers for the Queen and the National Anthem."

In 1894, fifteen members of the church choir, "through the munificence of the vicar, Churchwardens and friends", embarked on the earliest known choir outing, to Weston-super-Mare. An unidentified press cutting records that the weather was good until about 3 pm, when a downpour spoiled the rest of the day. "The one hundred and one pleasures and attractions of the delightful watering place were duly patronised and appreciated, and a sumptuous dinner and tea was heartily partaken of at Huntley's celebrated restaurant … Though the Revd and Mrs Yewens were unable to attend Mr Albert Foxwell, the parishioners' Churchwarden … was indefatigable in his efforts to make everyone happy, and the outing proved a success." The report concluded: "We are pleased to note the establishment of a choir, which seems a step somewhat in the right direction, and we trust the meeting will be a forerunner of annual excursions and more friendly unions."

As mentioned above, the Revd Thomas Yewens retired in 1896, and Holy Trinity's fifth priest, the **Revd William Arthur Dwight**, arrived in Coleford in the same year.

The earliest surviving daily Service Register dates from the Revd William Dwight's time, and on his first Sunday, 21 June 1896, there were sixteen communicants at the 11.00 am service. He noted that he had read the "39 Articles of Religion" and the "Declaration of Assent", required of all new clergy, and that on the following day he had begun daily Matins in the church. In October at the Harvest Thanksgiving he noted "choir in cassocks and surplices for the first time" and also that the psalms were sung and that there was an anthem, *The Harvest is the end of the World*. The Churchwardens' Accounts show expenditure of eight

The Revd William Arthur Dwight

shillings in 1896 for the new choir hymn books and music; and eleven shillings for new cassocks for the choir. (D/P/Coleford 4/1/1) The Register shows special events in church; for instance, on Saturday, 22 May 1897 there was a confirmation by the Bishop with twenty candidates. Queen Victoria's Diamond Jubilee was marked by a special service on Sunday, 20 June 1897.

In 1898/9 "knelling stooles" [*sic*] were purchased at a cost of £14 4s 10d. The Revd Dwight also brought with him an enthusiasm and zeal for fundraising to support various causes. In his first full year as incumbent, he raised £20 13s 3¼d for "charity and special use", which was disbursed at his discretion. He also established a series of special mid-week addresses during Lent and special collections for Easter gifts to the church—in 1897 thirty-five subscribers presented a new cross and vases. A year later came candlesticks, enabling altar candles to be used for the first time on Easter Sunday 1898, and in 1899 new hymn books. Outside, a new weathercock was installed on the church tower. It was carried to the church by W Edgell at a cost of 1s, it was installed by Seward Edgell for £1 4s 3d and gilded in situ by Sam Read for 7s 6d. (D/P/Coleford 4/1/1)

A Communicants' Guild was formed and also a Benefit Society, the latter to help the poor. Daily Evensong was begun in November 1898. In the same year four services were held on Christmas Day, at 8.00 am (seventeen communicants), 10.30 am, 11.30 am (fifteen communicants) and 2.45 pm. Despite all this enthusiastic activity, the Revd Dwight preached his last sermon at Holy Trinity four years later, on 8 July 1900, before moving on to Buckland Dinham.

The **Revd William Dwight** was a graduate of Keble College, Oxford, which had been founded to commemorate John Keble, one of the founders of the Oxford or Tractarian Movement (see box in chapter 3), and Dwight brought with him all the influence of this revival. After leaving Oxford, William Dwight studied at Wells Theological College (founded in 1840), before being ordained deacon in 1891 and priest in 1892. He spent his entire ministry in the Diocese of Bath and Wells: as Curate of Mells 1891–6, as Vicar of Coleford 1896–1900 and finally as Vicar of Buckland Dinham. According to the 1912 edition of *The Clergy List*, he was still at Buckland Dinham in that year.

The Revd Dwight was an American, born in Massachusetts, and the **1891 Census** describes him as "a student of theology". On Census day the 23-year-old ordinand was holidaying at Freshwater on the Isle of Wight with his mother, Anna, aged 54. Possibly this was a pre-ordination break before being made deacon.

In the **1901 Census** the 33-year-old Revd Dwight was married to Edith, aged 36, and they had recently left Coleford for Buckland Dinham. William Dwight's 64-year-old mother was living with them (as she had done at Coleford), and there were no children.

- 5 -

A NEW CENTURY

On 16 September 1900, the Revd Joseph Henry Wade, previously curate at Islip, Oxford, "read himself in as incumbent". He became Vicar of Coleford from 1900 and stayed until 1914, and he was also briefly in charge of the neighbouring parish of Babington from 1908 to 1910. In later years, many of the older people in the village would remember Joseph Wade as the outstanding vicar of Coleford. Indeed, he was so popular that when he died in 1944, thirty years after leaving the parish, the congregation at Holy Trinity mourned his passing as if the intervening years had never happened.

The Revd Joseph Wade continued to build on the work done by his predecessor, and one of his first tasks was to start a parish magazine, the first issue of which was published in January 1901. This was not the very first parish magazine, Wade having noted in the January 1901 edition that "this leaflet is intended like its predecessor to be a parochial newspaper. It will be a monthly record of local Church events … To those who are genuinely interested in their Church these things cannot lack interest, so we hope that this new magazine will find a place at those firesides where the old was always welcome, and that it will make for itself many fresh friends." He also had a wider vision for the new venture: "We may claim S Luke as one of the first Christian journalists. The world was his parish and the Acts of the Apostles the first parish magazine."

The Revd Joseph Wade

The February 1901 edition paid tribute to the late Queen Victoria and commented: "A memorial service was held here as elsewhere simultaneously with the Royal obsequies at Windsor. A large number of people gathered together to pay a last tribute of respect to their departed monarch. We have never seen the Church so full."

Easter gifts included a brass ewer for the font in 1901, and a new organ was purchased and first used on 12 November 1901. The Revd Dwight's mother had contributed £5 to the organ fund, which,

The **Revd Joseph Wade** graduated from London University in 1884 and then went to theological college at St David's College, Lampeter, until 1887. His ordination as deacon in 1887 and priest in 1888 was followed by curacies in Chester and Oxford dioceses. He came to Coleford in 1900 and his final parish after leaving Coleford was at Kingsbury Episcopi in the Diocese of Bath and Wells, from 1914–25, after which he retired from ministry.

The **1901 Census** records Joseph Wade, aged 40, living at the vicarage with his wife, Alice Josephine, aged 41. Any children they may have had had left home by this time. There were two servants at the vicarage: Mabel Gibbs, aged 15, housemaid, and Florence Moore, aged 14, kitchenmaid.

Sometime during the Revd Wade's ministry, Ron Brewer's grandmother, Florence Barnett, was a servant at the vicarage. She earned £8 a year plus meals and accommodation, and (unlike many servants at the time) was given Thursday afternoon off so that she could visit her family in the village.

As well as being a conscientious parish priest, Joseph Wade was also a prolific writer. He jointly wrote several books with his brother, the Revd Canon G W Wade of St David's College, Lampeter: *Somerset* (Little Guide), 1907; *Monmouthshire* (Little Guide), 1909; *Rambles in Somerset*, 1912; *South Wales* (Little Guide), 1913; *Herefordshire* (Little Guide), 1917. He also wrote a number of books in his own right: *Cathedral Cities of England and Wales* (Little Guide), 1924 (dedicated to the memory of his wife, Josephine, who died in 1914); *Rambles in Cathedral Cities*, 1925; *Rambles in Cornwall*, 1928; *Rambles in Devon*, 1930; *Rambles in Dorset*, 1931; and *Rambles in Shakespeare Country*, 1932. He died in 1944.

Books written by the Revd Joseph Wade

when the Revd Wade arrived in the village, already stood at £58 0s 2d, but raising the money for the new organ was no easy task. In the parish magazine of October 1901, Wade wrote, "An organ in all respects exactly what we are looking for, has been offered to us at the very reasonable price of £170. Towards this sum the owner has kindly offered to contribute £20 … The organ may be purchased immediately for £100, leaving the remaining £50 to be raised within twelve months … Our total reserves now amount to £64. This will be supplemented by what we hope will prove a generous Harvest Offertory. We shall have to raise about £30 in solid cash within the next month if the instrument is to be ours. Who will help us to secure this sum?"

The following month we hear the good news that the organ had been secured though the debt had not been fully paid off. Mr Bray had offered to play the organ for two years and donate his fee to the organ fund. The new organ, which had come from Frank Beauchamp, was removed from its previous home at Norton Hall by Messrs Giffen and Stroud of Bath. A special wooden platform was laid in the south-east corner of the church to act as a foundation for the organ, and choir stalls were rearranged on top of this to accommodate the choir and a reading desk. The £10 cost for this work, done by Charles Hamblin, was paid for by the Vicar as a thanksgiving gift. The old organ (which was a Sweetland organ) was sold to Radstock's Wesleyan Chapel Schoolroom for £7 10s, money that was put towards the cost of a new organ stop. The parish magazine for December 1901 reported that a cyclone preceded the first service using the new organ on 12 November: "The blast howled round the corners of the Church as if all the organs in creation were waiting to be blown; and it says something for the interest which the parish as a whole took in the event, that so large a congregation braved the fury of the elements." The organist of Wells Cathedral gave a recital at 3.00 pm followed by Evensong at 7.00 pm at which the former vicar, the Revd W A Dwight, preached. Between the organ recital and Evensong there was a parish tea party.

Two years later, in 1903, the Revd Wade oversaw fundraising for a vestry and storeroom at the west end of the church. This is now the choir vestry. (See chapter 10 for more details of restoration work carried out during the Revd Joseph Wade's incumbency.)

Over the years, Holy Trinity has played an integral part in the day-to-day life of the community, and has also reflected national events through special services. The opening years of the 20th century witnessed a number of these, including the memorial service for Queen Victoria on 2 February 1901, when the church was filled to capacity (already noted), a service to commemorate peace with the Boers on 2 June 1902, and a service to mark the coronation of Edward VII on 7 August 1902.

The parish records noted the great thunderstorm that devastated the area on 13 May 1906: "A thunderstorm of unusual severity broke over the village this evening just as the people were coming to the six o'clock service. The thunder was for 1¾ hours directly overhead and the lightning was unceasing. The rain fell in sheets. All the roads were flooded to the depth of several feet where ever the water could collect, and people had some difficulty getting home from the various places of worship. The church escaped serious injury, though the water fell in buckets-full through the trap door in the tower and great damage was done at the lower end of Coleford by torrents sweeping away walls and gardens. One house in Highbury and another at Lypeat [sic] were struck by lightning."

Writing in the June 1906 edition of the *Coleford Parish Magazine*, the Revd Wade described the storm: "It was a day of flood and flame … We had not many at Church, but the few who … did face the mutterings of the gathering storm, did not know to what they were committing themselves … We were in for a cataclysm … With every tick of the clock lightning of every fantastic shape and colour looked in at every window … and the thunder crashed overhead with the deafening roar of some terrific explosion. Every moment we expected the Church to be struck, and the tower to fall tumbling about our ears. The only thing that happened was a cascade which descended through the trapdoor of the tower, and transformed the floor of the baptistery into a brimming lake. Beyond the temporary discoloration of our spick and span walls, the Church has received no damage. At the conclusion of the service the congregation scampered away like lamplighters; we never saw the Church emptied so quickly … People who had not prayed for years are reported to have sunk upon their knees on the highway in sheer terror, thinking that the 'crack of doom' had come." The Revd Wade's comment about the flooding of the baptistery confirms that the original font was under the tower.

Catastrophic thunderstorms were not the only examples of extreme weather conditions, with deep snow and ice frequently accompanying wintertime. The two photographs show typical winter scenes.

*Right: View of the church path under deep snow
(undated, but showing the chimney built in 1909)*

*Below: Church Street under deep snow with the school
on the left, looking across to the church (undated but
likely to be the early 1900s)*

Local events included the 75th anniversary of the dedication of the church on 19 July 1906. A parish mission from the Church Army Van was held to coincide with this. The Church Army had been founded in 1882 by the Revd Wilson Carlisle as the Church of England's answer to the Salvation Army. A fleet of horse-drawn caravans inscribed with Bible texts took to the roads in order to evangelise the rural parishes. Such a mission, led by Captain Webb, came to Coleford in July 1906, and by kind permission of Mr F Candy was allowed to park in his field opposite the school. Open-air services were held, plus "Magic Lantern" services in the school, as well as special Sunday services that culminated in the 75th anniversary of the church's dedication on Thursday 19 July. Reflecting afterwards in the August parish magazine, the Revd Joseph Wade admitted that while the open air services had been fairly successful they had not made a significant difference to numbers in the congregation.

In July 1907 the dedication festival was kept, in the words of the Revd Wade, "with a service and a subsequent frollification … What our old parochial log book calls 'a simple fete at the manse' we now entitle a 'Garden Party at the Vicarage' … We made, we think, a happy selection in procuring for our preacher for the day our former vicar, Mr Dwight. The Garden Party was a brilliant function. The weather might have been made for the occasion … We scored a record attendance, and overtopped in numbers even the exceptional success of last year. We must have had as many as 140 seated around the tea-tables … We cannot speak too gratefully of the extremely loyal way in which everyone worked to make the festival a success … Mr Fred Lambert, as master of ceremonies, engineered everything with beautiful precision." Following this success, the Sunday morning congregation was disappointing, and in the evening a thunderstorm deterred many from coming to church.

1907 Dedication Festival garden party with the Revds William Dwight and Joseph Wade

Members of the congregation were also involved in diocesan events. On 22 June 1909 seventeen of them joined the Revd Wade at the diocesan Millennium celebrations in Wells. This would have been a major event for those who went, for they were joined by the Prince and Princess of Wales, and heard a sermon from the Archbishop of Canterbury, before travelling on to Glastonbury where the ruins of the Abbey were handed into the safe keeping of the Bishop of Bath and Wells.

While Holy Trinity had long been a focal point of village life, space for church social activities increasingly became a problem. Finally, on 20 February 1908, an iron building was erected in the vicarage gardens, and opened by the Rural Dean, the Revd L G G Horton of Wellow. Officially called the Church Lecture Room, it was known more affectionately as the "Bug Hut". The iron building had been purchased from Mr Foulkes of Norfolk Villa, Frome, for £30 and was erected by volunteers— W Edgell, Fred Lambert, W White, T Barnett, W Emblin, and O Plummer. With the addition of a porch, the total cost of the new building was £40 14s. When the Bishop came to Coleford to confirm twelve members of the congregation on 10 March 1908, he inspected the new building and complimented those gathered on the work. The Church Lecture Room was extended by 14 feet in May 1909, making it 34 feet x 14 feet 11 inches, and the inside and outside were decorated. The increased space made a significant difference, and by October 1912 the room was open as a clubroom four evenings a week, and boasted its own billiard table. The billiard table was finally disposed of twenty-five years later, as it was no longer used and deemed to be in the way in the Church Room.

There was a thriving branch of the Church of England Men's Society at Holy Trinity, and in November 1913 they held a special service in church and had a collection for the Welsh Mining Disaster Fund. About eighty men attended and £1 3s 4d was raised for the appeal. William Marchant Jones (choirmaster) sang *The Toilers*, and Fred Lambert, H and P Hamblin and C Jones sang *Nearer, my God, to Thee*. The preacher was the Revd E D Lear, Rector of Mells.

In 1914, a number of capital funds were set up, including an organ fund (£100), to cover the costs of tuning, repair and choir music; a fabric insurance fund (£52 10s), for the insurance of the church building; a churchyard maintenance fund (£52 10s), the interest from which was to be used for the upkeep of the churchyard; a Sunday School fund (£67), for Sunday School expenses; and a fabric repair fund (£30). These funds were overseen by a Financial Council, a lay council, elected each year, but members could be re-elected. In 1914 the Chairman was Mr W G Hamblin and the Secretary was William Marchant Jones. Under a new system of church finance, each church had to raise a levy payable to the diocese. This was the beginning of what is now known as "the Parish Share" of the Diocesan Common Fund. In 1914 Holy Trinity had to raise £4 1s, and in order for there to be enough income to pay this as well as the church running costs, a sum of £10 needed to come in from collections and fundraising events. The Financial Council was an unofficial body: the Church of England Assembly (Powers) Act 1919, as a direct result of which Parochial Church Councils came into being, was still some years away.

Early in 1914 the Revd Joseph Wade announced his impending departure, saying, "You need a younger and more vigorous man for your leader, who will … bring to the work fresh enthusiasm and wider vision." That may well have been true, but how wrong he was to be about the qualities of his successor. When the Revd Joseph Wade left at the end of April 1914, he bequeathed a thriving community to his successor, with a solid financial basis, but this would all be undone in a very short time.

Shortly before the Revd Wade left Coleford, the parish magazine recorded under the title "At the other side of the World" a series of articles by Mr Arthur Moore, a Coleford man who had gone to Australia as a missionary. The parish magazine for March 1914 contains a short item with the news that Arthur Moore was to enter upon three years' training at St John's College, Armidale, New South Wales, leading to ordination. The Bishop of Grafton and Armidale had asked for financial help from Mr Moore's home parish to cover the costs of his upkeep. In response, the Coleford branch of the Church of England Men's Society undertook to raise the £10 required for the books for his course. Unfortunately, the parish magazines were not kept after Joseph Wade left the parish, so we do not have a local record of his progress. However, Arthur Moore was ordained after completing his studies and he never forgot the kindness and support of his home parish. After his death, funds were bequeathed to Coleford church for prizes for the Choir and Sunday School—the Canon Moore Memorial Prize Fund and the Canon Moore Sunday School Fund. Holy Trinity still benefits from the interest from these funds.

Canon Moore Arthur George Moore was a Coleford man who went to Australia as a missionary in 1913. He trained for the priesthood at St John's College, Armidale, and was ordained deacon in 1916 and priest in 1917. He was Curate of Casino 1916–18, Vicar of Nimbin 1918–20, Vicar of Mullumbimby 1920–24, and Vicar of Lismore 1924–28 and Rector of the same parish 1928–33, all in the Diocese of Grafton. In addition, he was Rural Dean of Lismore from 1926. In 1928 he was made Canon of Grafton Cathedral. Canon Moore returned to England in 1934 and became Vicar of

St Barnabas' Sunderland 1934–38, and St Luke's, Oseney Crescent, New Kentish Town from 1938. (St Luke's was an important church, designed by Basil Champneys between 1868 and 1870. It contains some fine stained glass by Philip Webb and William Morris. It is now redundant and in the care of the Churches Conservation Trust.) Canon Moore died in London on 16 April 1947 and is buried in Coleford churchyard.

The grave of Canon Moore

Soon after Joseph Wade left Coleford, his wife, Alice Josephine, died. She had been a great support to him in his parish ministry and was well loved by the congregation. In addition to the duties expected of clergy wives in those days, Mrs Wade was also the organist at Holy Trinity. A credence table for holding the Communion vessels was later given in her memory, inscribed:

IN MEMORY OF
ALICE JOSEPHINE WADE
ORGANIST 1904–14

This is still in regular use and stands in the sanctuary near the altar.

Credence table in memory of
Mrs Alice Josephine Wade

6

TROUBLED TIMES

THE REVD JOSEPH WADE's successor, the **Revd (John) Henry Evans**, who had been the Vicar of St Katherine's, Frome and Woodlands, was installed on 22 June 1914.

With a track record of little more than two years in each of the previous parishes in which he had served, the Revd Henry Evans' lack of rapport with his parishioners in Coleford was probably due more to his personality than his high churchmanship, Coleford by this time already being more "high" church than "low". By 1916 he had introduced Holy Communion on most days and there were usually four or five communicants.

But it soon became clear that the new incumbent was out of tune with his flock, and by 1916 he had reached a state of open conflict with his congregation. The official parish records, overseen by the vicar himself, offer little help in understanding the problem, preserving only a press cutting as an indicator of the difficult parishioners whom Evans believed he faced. On 25 February 1916, the *Morning Post* reported on the "Vicar's challenge to critics": "The Vicar of Coleford (Somerset) in his current monthly magazine, referring to the fact that clergymen may not act in a military capacity, asks how it is possible to show anonymous letter writers and others that the clergy are neither cowards nor shirkers. He proceeds, 'After much thought and deliberation the vicar of this parish has hit upon the following measures to meet his own case: In school, college, and curate days, he was supposed to defend himself ably in the "boxing ring" and does not remember being beaten in fairly equal conditions. He is now ready to put on gloves with any of these unknown persons if they will reveal their

Like Joseph Wade, the **Revd Henry Evans** had studied at St David's College, Lampeter, where he gained his BA, and later studied at Oxford University. He was ordained deacon in 1898 and priest in 1900 and served firstly as a curate at Merthyr Tydfil from 1898–1901. A number of curacies followed, all in different English dioceses and none lasting more than two years. Two of his curacies were at churches which followed the Oxford Movement— St Gabriel's Pimlico and St Paul's Oxford. After leaving Coleford, Henry Evans became a Chaplain to the Forces from 1917–20. Following the Great War, he became Vicar of Haselbury Plucknett until 1927, and finished his active ministry in the Diocese of Leicester.

identity in public further. Further, in order to relieve any likely miner-recruit who may have a conscientious reason, as, for instance, the support of a widowed mother, he is not ashamed or afraid but willing to take his place in the mine and give the wages to the dependent if piecework can be arranged which will not interfere with clerical duties.'"

No parish magazines for the period after the Revd Joseph Wade have been found, so it is fortunate that the other side of the dispute is preserved in copies of letters written by William Marchant Jones. (Preserved by his son, Richard, these were made available to Julie Dexter in 1991 for research on the history of Coleford.) In direct response to an article in the *John Bull* magazine, similar to that which appeared in the *Morning Post* and other national papers, William Marchant Jones wrote, "Mr Evans, by reason of his pugilistic challenges has made himself an object of national interest and I would therefore suggest to you that you send a commissioner to this place to find out exactly what sort of man he is. The population of Coleford at the last Census was 1291 and since the outbreak of war and before compulsion came into force the village had supplied 85 to the forces. All the others are working in the coalmines here and risking their lives daily for that which is necessary to the nation for carrying on the war. We have raised for the Belgians about £100 … (As well as further unspecified amounts for the Prince of Wales Fund.) Mr Evans has certainly helped but owing to his unpopularity his share has been a very minor one … To say that there are 'Peace at any Price' people and Pro Germans in this village is to cast a foul slander on a community who have tried to do their bit and is merely a red herring to detract your readers' attentions from his vapourings about fighting anyone who would doubt his pluck. I confidently assert he cannot give the name of one Pro German in the whole district."

He continued, "Allow me to give you one or two details (I could give you dozens) of Mr Evans' attitude to his fellow men. A year ago some of us got up a concert for Belgium and realised £15. Mr Evans persuaded us to allow him to quarter a Belgian family at the vicarage with the money. Accordingly, M Wecky and his wife and two daughters arrived there. In Belgium he was the station master of Turnhout and they were refined middle class people. Some weeks after their arrival I had them to my house and they used my bathroom. It was their first bath since leaving Belgium. They were made to enter and depart the vicarage through servants' quarters. Their supper one night consisted of one onion each with bread and cocoa. Their w.c. was in the garden and the floor was below level and consequently was covered with water 3 inches deep in wet weather. M Wecky had to put bricks for the ladies to step on. M Wecky cleared out as soon as possible and we as a committee refused to sanction others going to the vicarage. We now send out collections direct to Belgian headquarters."

The grand façade of Turnhout Station, Belgium, built c. *1905*

Indeed, so strongly did William Marchant Jones feel about events and the impact of the Revd Evans that in November 1915, after twenty-four years service, he resigned from the church choir. His letter to the vicar also takes up the cause of Fred Lambert, a pillar of Holy Trinity: "Mr Lambert devotes his spare time to visiting the sick, poor and needy. He is a welcome visitor in more than one home where never a clergyman enters. He went unbidden to these places in the first instance from a sense of duty. He continues them because of the amount of good he is able to do thereby. I only hope the rebuff he has received from the quarter from which he had the right to expect the greatest encouragement, will not check him in his good work. In saying that, such actions as his are far more acceptable to me than making the sign of the cross or bowing to the east. I am voicing the sentiments of the majority of Church people in Coleford."

William Marchant Jones as a young man

In his letter to *John Bull* William Marchant Jones noted that Fred Lambert was a "hardworking conscientious God-fearing Christian. He is universally liked and respected. He was lay reader at Church and suffered Mr Evans' eccentricities until long after the rest of us had left the Church in disgust. At last finding argument and remonstrance all in vain on a certain point Mr Lambert stayed away from one service by way of protest and went to the Wesley Chapel. At night the Vicar prevented him reading the lessons as usual and told him to resign from all his official duties. He said it was punishment for encouraging schism but we all know that it was to get rid of the star that outshone the sun."

He continued, citing other examples of the detrimental impact Evans had on Holy Trinity and the people who worshipped there: "Mr Evans has finished our Sunday school and gets the children to Church. He says the children must be taught by the minister only. Sunday schools are fundamentally wrong and Sunday school teachers are well meaning people who do more harm than good by reason of their inexperience and want of training. Fees for headstones have risen from 7/8 to 25/–. He took a fee from a woman here a year ago and now is trying to bully the woman into having it moved again. The Church of England Men's Society, which was a strong body when he came, has died a natural death after he publicly stated he did not believe in that organisation. The choir has dwindled to five boys and the collections now amount to two-thirds of the running expenses of the Church. One of his chief complaints against the Parish is that the people do not come to him to confess their sins. The Bishop has been making inquiries into the matter but owing to the lapse of time we have lost hope."

The vehemence with which William Marchant Jones wrote his resignation letter was made clear not just from the tone, but from the tearing of the paper where he underscored his name in the copy. By the time the press reports appeared in early 1916, many long-standing members of Holy Trinity had ceased to attend church, often

Fred Lambert Owing to the lack of parish records for this period, it is impossible to know whether Fred Lambert returned to Holy Trinity after the trouble caused by the Revd Evans. But it seems likely that he may have done so because his son, Alan (born 1907), is on the choir photograph taken with the Revd E R Oxby in the 1920s. During the incumbency of the Revd Joseph Wade, Fred Lambert was closely involved with the Church of England Men's Society, often giving talks on spiritual matters to the members as well as contributing theological articles to the parish magazine. **Frederick James Lambert** was born in 1874, and as well as his church interests he was a member of the Coleford football team. He is shown on the 1908–09 team photograph when they became champions of the Paulton and District League and winners of the Frome Tournament Cup.

Fred Lambert (centre, middle row)

Fred Lambert had followed his father in working at the local mines and progressed from a 16-year-old labourer at the time of the **1891 Census** to being a Colliery Weigh Clerk at the time of the **1901 Census.** His grandchildren, Chris Lambert and Wendy Perry, think he may have progressed to become Manager at Vobster Quarry. The fact that he owned a car would indicate that he had a better job than many of his contemporaries. His grandchildren remember him later in life, still reading his Bible daily, and saying Grace before meals. He had three children—Fred junior, who was killed at Vobster quarry; Alan (the father of Chris and Wendy), who they believe played the organ at Holy Trinity; and Dorothea, who, like many other young people, pumped the organ for a time.

Fred Lambert died on Christmas Day 1945, aged 75 years, and is buried in Holy Trinity churchyard.

finding spiritual comfort at one of the chapels which served the village. This is evident in the Service Register where the numbers of communicants were now below a dozen. W M Jones himself was worried about the impact that publishing his letter might have on his business as a newsagent, not least because he believed that Evans had support among local clergy who were only aware of his side of the dispute.

Given this state of affairs, it is perhaps not surprising to find that the Revd Evans departed the village shortly afterwards, the strong community bequeathed him by the Revd Wade left in disarray. One of his last tasks was to hold a special service of intercession on 27 September as part of the "National Mission for Repentance and Hope", which had been called by the Church of England "to arouse the conscience of England and especially the Church of England, with regard to the grave evils which exist amongst us, and are threatening the well-being of the Nation". Services in connection with the Mission had also been held in June, and from 6–10 October the parish was visited by the "Bishop's Messenger" for the Mission, the Revd George T Steacy. Evans' final Sunday was on 5 November 1916, a note in the Service Register declaring "Vicar's last Sunday".

Before leaving the Revd Evans' ministry behind, mention must be made of the measles epidemic of 1916. No parish magazines exist from that time, but the Service Register for Sunday 30 January notes that the Sunday School was closed due to measles. Deep snow for much of February made life extremely difficult, and the number of communicants was reduced to less than half a dozen. In Holy Trinity churchyard a gravestone tells a tragic story. It marks the spot where three children lie buried, all victims of measles. The inscription reads:

SACRED
TO THE MEMORY OF
ARTHUR CHARLES
GEORGE NELSON
AND ANNIE LEAH
INFANT CHILDREN OF
PTE. HENRY JOHN HASKINS
(RIFLE BRIGADE)
AND ANNIE MAY HIS WIFE
WHO DIED AS THE RESULT OF AN
EPIDEMIC OF MEASLES FEB 1916
ERECTED BY PUBLIC SUBSCRIPTION.

The grave of the Haskins children who died in the measles epidemic in 1916

Arthur Charles Haskins was 2 years old; Nelson George Haskins was aged 18 months; and Annie Leah Haskins was aged 4 months. They were all buried on 1 March 1916. The grave is still in good repair and the inscription easy to decipher unlike many nearby.

The new Vicar of Coleford was the **Revd Herbert Francis Gane**, whose first Sunday was on 7 January 1917.

Unlike his predecessor, the Revd Herbert Gane was a low churchman, but despite the hopes that came with the appointment of a new priest, it seems that he did not get on with his congregation. Still in a state of shock from the strife that had rent them asunder, the people of Holy Trinity had to regroup, and a priest whose long years overseas had left him out of touch with the church at home, at a time when clergy were thin on the ground because of the war, was likely to be of little help. It is probably also true to say that while the Revd Evans had been too Anglo Catholic for Coleford, Herbert Gane was far too Low Church. One of the changes made by the Revd Gane was to stop the almost daily Eucharist that the Revd Evans had started. The pastoral situation was slow to improve, perhaps because Gane himself was unpopular with his parishioners and may not have been suited to the rigours of parish life.

The Minutes of the Annual Vestry Meeting in 1917 reveal that the question of the inadequate lighting of the Church was raised, and it was agreed to provide shades for the lamps in order to throw the light downwards. The lighting was provided by oil lamps, and "on the motion of Mr [W M] Jones it was resolved to ask the Church Council to consider the advisability of raising Funds to relight the Church with Acetylene Gas". However, the 1918 Vestry Minutes record that "the present time was not opportune to undertake any new scheme of lighting the Church ... A trial had been made on some lamps with shades but the resulting improvement in light was not sufficient to justify the expense". (D/P/Coleford 9/1/1)

There are no parish magazines or other documents to tell us about the social life of the Church during the Revd Gane's short stay in Coleford. But there is one exception—a photograph of a choir outing at "Heaven's Gate", Longleat, taken on 18 July 1917. There we see the Revd Gane in an ill-fitting

The **Revd Herbert Gane** trained at the Church Missionary Society College in Islington, an institution founded in 1826 to train men for the overseas missionary work of the CMS, an evangelical missionary society dating from 1799. He was ordained deacon in 1906 by the Bishop of London to serve in the Colonies, and priest in 1907 by Bishop Oluwole for West Equatorial Africa. He served at various mission stations in West Africa from 1906 until January 1917 when he came to Coleford. After leaving Coleford, Herbert Gane returned to the CMS in an administrative role, followed by positions in a number of parishes in various dioceses where his average stay was five or six years. The 1947 edition of *Crockford's Clerical Directory* lists him amongst those whose address was "temporarily unknown".

The Revd Herbert Gane and parishioners at the choir outing to "Heaven's Gate", Longleat, July 1917

jacket, surrounded by men, women and young children in their "Sunday best" and an assortment of hats and flat caps. A soldier, home on leave, holds the hands over his shoulders of two women.

From August 1919 the Revd Gane's initials appear less frequently in the Service Registers. Interspersed with them are other signatures from neighbouring clergy, mostly for Evensong. At 8.00 am on Sundays there was often no congregation, and communicant numbers at 11.00 am were often as few as ten or eleven.

The War had taken its toll on the village, and in February 1920 a Faculty was granted "To place an Alabaster War Memorial in the Parish Church of Coleford". On 18 June 1920 there was a Service of Dedication of the War Memorial in Holy Trinity. In addition to the Revd Gane's signature in the Register, there is J Turner, the Minister of the Primitive Methodist Chapel, and E Braham, the Minister of the Wesleyan Chapel. No record was made of numbers attending, but presumably there was a large congregation. The handsome alabaster memorial bears the names of the fallen: George Mudford, Arthur Wilkins, Arthur Ashman, Cephas Thompson, Gilbert Cullen, John Cosh, Seth Lane, Charles Futcher, Walter Cullen, Fred Ford, Percy Lay, Frank Button, Mark Whale, Charles Lane, Fred Melling, Stanley Edgell, Gilbert Trussler and Fred Treasure. Stanley Edgell's family had a memorial erected in the Primitive Methodist Chapel, and when it eventually closed, the memorial was brought to Holy Trinity where it may be found on the west wall inside the church.

In addition to the memorial in memory of the fallen, there is also a framed manuscript list of all the men from Coleford who served in the Great War (see the appendix to this chapter).

Herbert Gane's stay at Holy Trinity was prolonged only until a more permanent replacement could be found. His final service was on 26 December 1920, when there were only four communicants at the 11.00 am service of Matins and Holy Communion. There may have been more in the congregation who did not receive Holy Communion.

Left: The War Memorial in Holy Trinity

Right: The list of the men of Coleford who served in the First World War

The **Revd Edward Rome Oxby** went to St Aidan's Theological College, Birkenhead, in 1910 and was ordained deacon in 1911 and priest in 1912. In 1917 he gained his BA at Oxford (2nd Class Honours in theology) and MA in 1920. He served several curacies in different dioceses before coming to Coleford as Vicar from 1921–27. His previous post had been as curate at St John's Midsomer Norton from 1920–21. After leaving Coleford he served in several parishes in Bath and Wells until 1944 when he became a college chaplain in Rochester diocese. He combined parish ministry with lecturing at Wells Theological College from 1935, and became Diocesan Inspector of Schools from 1936. For these extra ministries he was rewarded with the title "Prebendary" (i.e. non-residential Canon) of Wells Cathedral from 1939. He was still in active ministry in 1947 when he was listed in *Crockford's Clerical Directory* as Chaplain of Huggen's College, Northfleet near Gravesend.

The Revd Edward Rome Oxby

The New Year was to bring a new priest when the **Revd Edward Rome Oxby** came to the village to help Holy Trinity and its people back onto their feet.

The Revd Oxby's first Sunday at Holy Trinity was 13 March 1921 (Passion Sunday), and there was a "Service of Introduction" at 3.00 pm, when the preacher was the Archdeacon of Wells (the Venerable Walter Farrer). Rebuilding the parish can have been no easy task. While the memories of the Revds Evans' and Ganes' ministries were fading, the community was in the grip of a post-War depression, the miners struggling against wage cuts and longer hours, and the coal mines, which had provided the economic foundation of the community for so long, nearing closure. Despite these difficulties, the Revd Oxby oversaw changes that marked a rebirth for the parish church. These changes included the decoration of the church, and the Service Registers have a note that "on the 7th and 8th Sundays after Trinity Matins was said in the School and Evensong in the Churchyard, owing to the closure of the Church for re-decoration".

The early 1920s saw the establishment of the Parochial Church Council (PCC), giving the laity a share in parish decision-making. The Easter Vestry meeting was retained for the election of the Churchwardens. At a joint meeting of the Vestry and PCC in 1922, it was agreed that they would elect the Churchwardens annually.

By 1924, the number of regular communicants was on the increase for the first time in a decade. New heating apparatus was installed, maintenance of the churchyard had

An important development in Church government had taken place in 1919. The **Church of England Assembly (Powers) Act** (known as the Enabling Act) conferred legislative powers on the Church Assembly. In 1921 the Church Assembly used its new powers to establish **Parochial Church Councils**. The duty of these Councils was "to co-operate with the incumbent in the initiation, conduct and development of Church work both within the parish and outside". Most of the powers formerly possessed by the Vestry and Churchwardens relating to church finances and the maintenance of the church building were transferred to the new PCCs, whose members were elected annually.

A modern picture of the font installed in 1924

improved and a new credence table was given. This credence table may have been the one given in memory of Mrs Wade. It is likely that the new heating apparatus replaced the old stove near the church door with a solid fuel boiler and hot water pipes going round the walls, referred to by Phyllis Coles. In 1903–04 the church had been extended at the west end on either side of the tower to make a choir vestry and a coal store. This coal store became the stoke hole for the new boiler, and many a verger has got up in the middle of the night to stoke the boiler for Sunday morning. The old stove near the church door was dispensed with, and in its place a new font was installed. (There is no documentation to prove that the new font was acquired in 1924 but all the circumstantial evidence suggests this, especially as Ron Brewer's grandmother remembered as a young woman seeing the old font lying broken up in the churchyard.)

The progress made during this period was significant in re-establishing the sound worshipping community that the village had known before the Great War. The success of Revd Oxby's work and those who supported him in it is evident in the success of the choir, which won a number of competitions during this period, including first and second place at the Midsomer Music Festival in 1925/6. By this time William Marchant Jones was Choirmaster once more. Though the Revd Oxby was soon ready to move on (the standing Churchwardens were returned to office in April 1927, to ensure some continuity in the running of Holy Trinity until the appointment of his replacement), he had paved the way for a new vicar and left a revitalised congregation.

A modern photograph of the church tower,
showing clock and weathercock

K Moore, G M Jones, M Ellison, D Gibbs, H Willis

L Morse, F James, W Perkins, T James, W Crosby, F Filer, W Wilmot

R Morse, W Hamblin, S Lambert, E Steeds, G Mounty, A Lambert, P Hamblin, W Bird

P Button, W Wilmot, E Cullen, W M Jones (*Choirmaster*), Rev E R Oxby (*Vicar*), W G Hamblin (*Organist*), M Goddard, O Spear, F Hamblin

R Witcombe, F Burton, G Moore, F Perkins, L Withers, E Horler, H Coles, W Morse

The award-winning thirty-voice choir c. *1926*

APPENDIX TO CHAPTER 6

In grateful Recognition of the Men of Coleford who served during the Great War.
1914–1918.

Richard Allen, CPO, [Chief Petty Officer] RN
Arthur Edgell, FC Stoker, RN
Fred Hounsell, Seaman, RN
Charlie Wilkins, Corpl., Naval Brigade
+Arthur Wilkins [Wilkinson] DCM, Corpl., Life Guards
John Ward, Gunner RFA [Royal Field Artillery]
Donald Green, Corpl., Wiltshire Regt.
John Young, Pte., Wiltshire Regt.
Albert Spiller, Pte., Somerset LI
Leofwin Plummer, Corpl., Somerset LI
Tom Chambers, Pte., Somerset LI
Charles Connock, Pte., Somerset LI
William Hamblin, Pte., Somerset LI
James Ward, Pte., Somerset LI
Albert Trim [Trimby?], Pte., Somerset LI
Stanley Higgins, Pte., Somerset LI
William King, Pte., Somerset LI
Benjamin Moore, Pte., Somerset LI
Sidney Turner, Pte., Gloucestershire Regt.
William Horler, Sergt., Somerset LI
William Boyce, Bugler, Somerset LI
Edmund Boyce, Seaman, RN
James Chambers, Sergt., Somerset LI
Victor Chilcott, Pte., Somerset LI
+George Mudford, FC Stoker, RN
Wm. Ayling Goddard, LYA, RN
Arthur Goddard, Capt., Indian Army
Fred Prangley, Pte., Gloucestershire Regt.
Hedley Harding, Sergt., North Som. Yeomanry
John Cullen, Sergt., Somerset LI
Clifford Jones, Sergt., Grenadier Guards
George Hamblin, Pte., Devonshire Regt.
Charles Rideout, Corpl., Machine Gun Corps
Thomas Edgell, Farrier ASC [Army Service Corps]
+Mark Whale MM, L/Corpl., Machine Gun Corps
Tom Elliott, Sergt., Somerset LI

Frank Moon, FC Stoker, RN
William Edgar Ford, Seaman, RN
Bertram Leonard Ford, L/Corpl. Machine Gun Corps
Alexander Candy, Pte., Somerset LI
Tom Ashman, Pte., Somerset LI
William Paget, Pte., Somerset LI
Walter Dredge, Pte., Somerset LI
Fred Plummer, Pte., Somerset LI
Robert Cullen, Pte., Somerset LI
Albert Ashman, Sergt., Canadian Artillery
Fred Steeds, Lieut., Somerset LI
+Percy Lay, Pte., Somerset LI
Arthur Rideout, L/Corpl., Somerset LI
+Cephas Thompson, Pte., Somerset LI
Reginald Hilary, Sapper, RE [Royal Engineers]
Tom Hayes, Pte., Royal Irish Rgt.
Fred Marsh, Pte., Somerset LI
+Gilbert Cullen, Pte., Somerset LI
+John Cosh, Pte., Somerset LI
+Fred Ford, Bombardier, RFA [Royal Field Artillery]
Harry Haskins, Rifleman, Rifle Brigade
Albert Angell, Gunner, RFA
Philip T Jones, Surgeon Capt., RAMC [Royal Army Medical Corps]
Fred Pearce, Gunner, RFA
Isaac Turner, Gunner, RGA [Royal Garrison Artillery]
George Rideout, Pte., Somerset LI
+Gilbert Trussler, Pte., Somerset LI
Stanley Price, Pte., Somerset LI
Walter Horler, Pte., Somerset LI
Richard Blacker, Pte., Somerset LI
Oliver Cosh, Pte., Somerset LI
+Charles Lane, Corpl., Somerset LI
William Bunny, Sapper, RE [Royal Engineers]
Arthur Moon, Gunner, RFA
+Seth Lane, L/Corpl., Somerset LI
+Charles Futcher, Pte., Somerset LI
Raymond Gilson, Pte., Somerset LI
William Hawkins, Pte., South Wales Borderers
Arthur Wiltshire, Pte., Royal Marines
Clarence Turner, Seaman, RN
Godfrey Harding, Pte., Warwickshire Regt.
Willoughby Harding, Pte., NZMC [New Zealand Medical Corps]
+Arthur Ashman, Pte., Grenadier Guards
+Walter Cullen, Pte., Somerset LI

+Frank Button, Pte., Welsh Regt.

Mark Willmot, Pte., Somerset LI

Herbert Chivers, Pte., Machine [Gun] Corps

Frederick Merritt, L/Corpl., Wiltshire Regt.

Cyril Edgell, Pte., Royal Marines LI

Harry Coombes, L/Corpl., Royal West Kents

William John Williams, Pte., Durham LI

Stephen Cradock, Pte., King's Own Yorks. LI

Eric Adams, Gunner, RGA

Clifford Wilkins, Driver ASCMT [Army Service Corps Motor Transport]

Herbert Ashman, Sapper, RE

Harry Coles, Pte., Somerset LI

Charles Uphill, Corpl., RGA

+Stanley Edgell, Pte., King's Company, Grenadier Gds.

George Horler, Sergt., RAMC

Albert Percy Hamblin, Farrier, Royal Naval Div.

+Fred Melling, Pte., Royal Berkshire Rgt.

Cecil Plummer, Pte., Machine Gun Corps

Jesse Edwards, Sapper, RE

Gilbert Coles, Driver, ASCMT

Ernest James Church, Gunner, RFA

Albert Starks, Pte., Somerset LI

George Witcombe, Pte., Somerset LI

Ernest Steeds, Gunner, RGA

John Moore, Pte., Yorkshire LI

Walter Bryant, Pte., RAMC AIF [Australian Imperial Forces]

Christopher Bryant, Pte., AIF

Ernest Gillard, Gunner, RGA

Edward Gillard, Pte, Royal Irish Regt.

Gilbert Gillard, Gunner, RFA

James Carpenter, Gunner, RGA

William Candy, Pte., RAMC

Reginald Candy, L/Corpl., Wiltshire Regt.

William Bryant, Pte., Devonshire Regt.

William Futcher, Pte., Somerset LI

Chaffey Cullen, AC, [Air Craftsman] RAF

Oliver Rossiter, AC, RAF

George Dowding, Pte., Grenadier Guards

Albert Trimby, Pte., Oxford and Bucks Regt.

Albert Moore, Corpl., Coldstream Guards

Albert Thompson, Pte., Coldstream Guards

Walter Thompson, Gunner, RGA

George Price, Pte., Machine Gun Corps

Stanley Gillard, Gunner, RGA

Frederick Cosh, Pte., Somerset LI
+Frederick Treasure, Pte., Somerset LI
Gilbert Plummer, Pte., Machine Gun Corps
Bert Hamblin, Pte., Somerset LI
Albert Wrintmore, Pte., Somerset LI
Frederick Sheppard, Pte., Somerset LI
Reginald Witcombe, Pte., Somerset LI
Edward Treasure, Pte., Machine Gun Corps

The original framed manuscript, now in the church hall, gives the initials of the regiments in which the men served, but in some cases the full description has been added for present day readers of this book. It will be apparent that while many served in the Somerset Light Infantry, others served in a wide variety of army regiments, plus a number in the Royal Navy, and two men served in the newly formed Royal Air Force. A number were gunners in the Royal Field Artillery and in the Machine Gun Corps, both of which were machine gun detachments, and others served in the Royal Garrison Artillery operating heavy field guns on bombardments of the German trenches preparatory to attempts by the infantry to take the trenches by force. A smaller number were Sappers with the Royal Engineers. These men, who were probably coal miners in civilian life, were deployed underground digging tunnels for the men to live in underneath the allied trenches, or in some cases digging underneath the German trenches and laying mines to explode along the enemy front line. There were several members of the Royal Army Medical Corps, some of whom may have been field ambulance drivers, a non-combatant role, but one which was highly dangerous because these men would frequently go onto the battlefield to rescue the wounded, often at great risk of sniper fire and shell fire. Amongst the RAMC listed was Surgeon Captain Philip Jones, son of the Coleford doctor, who lived at Coleford House. Two brothers served in the Australian Imperial Forces. Of the 132 Coleford men who went to serve King and Country in the Great War, 18 were either killed in action or died from their wounds. The list gives a much clearer picture of the way in which the village was depleted of its young men as the War progressed. The list is not in alphabetical order, and is probably compiled from the order in which they joined the Forces.

7

A FRESH START

THE **Revd Harry Frederick Ralph-Bowman** arrived in Coleford early in 1927 and stayed for nineteen years. The length of his ministry in Coleford brings him within the memory of many people still living in the village.

Described by Jack Coles as a great preacher, the Revd Ralph-Bowman was made a Fellow of the Philosophical Society of England—which was felt to be a tremendous honour for a country parish like Coleford. The Revd Ralph-Bowman had initially trained for the Baptist ministry, but had never felt totally at home with the strict Calvinism of that denomination, and in 1914 he became Minister of an independent Chapel in Wandsworth. When the Great War broke out he applied unsuccessfully to become an "Other Denominations" Chaplain, and so he went to work as a Civil Servant in the Ministry of Munitions. In 1921 the family moved to Somerset where he became the Organising Secretary of St Dunstan's Society for the Blind, a charity that cared for ex-Servicemen blinded in the War. During these years, he became friendly with the Rector of Old Cleeve, who offered to sponsor him for ordination in the Church of England. He subsequently studied at Wells Theological College, and was ordained deacon in 1924 and priest in 1925. He became curate of Twerton-on-Avon from 1924 until the end of 1926 when he came to Coleford. At that time the living, including the vicarage, was worth £350, and the population of Coleford was 1,270.

One of the more prosaic matters he had to deal with early in his tenure was the

---

The **Revd Harry Frederick Ralph-Bowman** was the son of a grocer from Walthamstow in Essex, and after leaving school aged 14, he worked for the grocery firm Kearley and Tongue, later to become the International Stores. He was encouraged by a Baptist Minister to train for ministry and after studying at Spurgeon's College and Regent's Park College, he was appointed Assistant Pastor at North Street Baptist Chapel in Wellington, Somerset. In 1910 he went to Newport in South Wales where he was responsible for building a new chapel in Llanthewy Road. He met his future wife, also a Baptist, when he was a student taking services at Billericay, having cycled out from Walthamstow. There were three children from the marriage: John, who lived just four hours; Murray Peter (known as Peter) who became an Anglican priest; and a daughter, Pamela.

knotty problem of church crockery! Through the winter of 1929–30 concerns were raised about church crockery going missing. This resulted in the PCC Secretary taking an inventory of stock, and making up the omissions. By March 1930 he was able to report that fifty-two cups and saucers, forty-nine small plates, nine large plates, thirty-five spoons, two sugar basins, two cream jugs and six odd saucers were safely held under lock and key. Some things never change! Clearly this did not end matters, as in October 1933 the PCC agreed that anyone wanting to borrow church crockery or other items for events should apply directly to the vicar.

Early in his ministry at Coleford, the Revd Ralph-Bowman suffered a nervous breakdown. His son, Peter, has left an account of this traumatic experience. "Father was in his stall in the chancel; the choir was standing, waiting for him to intone the Creed. We were halfway through matins. No sound came—he stood, opening and shutting his mouth … and slowly, helplessly, he flapped the white sleeves of his surplice, begging to be returned … to the world of speech. Nobody moved, nobody knew what to do or how to help him. We all waited until … he stumbled … between the pews of dumb worshippers; his quick breath the only sound in the hush. Mother and I, fearful and ashamed, follow him across the church-yard, down the narrow path between the high laurel hedges to the vicarage and into the study where he lay weeping in the chair … But he could speak. It was a nervous breakdown and the nerve specialist asked him what he would like to do. 'A long sea voyage.' Father organised for himself two trips from Tyneside to Mediterranean ports as assistant purser in a cargo vessel."

The Service Register gives evidence of when this breakdown took place. On Sunday, 27 October 1929, the initials "HFRB" appear at the 8.00 am Holy Communion Service and at 11.00 am Matins, but not at Evensong, when the service was taken by R Fielding. With the exception of Matins on 24 November 1929, the Revd Ralph-Bowman's initials do not reappear in the Register until 27 April 1930 (the Sunday after Easter).

As 1930 drew to a close, the vicar, whose health was now restored, began to look ahead together with the PCC to the centenary celebrations the following summer. On 27 November, the PCC also agreed to set up a Commemoration Fund to mark the church's centenary. The object was to finish the windows recently installed (see chapter 10), provide new curtains in the vestry, cover the costs of new surplices and cassocks (being made by the Women's Club) and, if there was enough money left over, erect a new lectern. In April 1931 surplus Centenary Funds were used to pay for a new altar cloth, made by Miss Celia Perkins, and "artistic work around the altar", at the vicar's direction. The nature of this artistic work is unclear, but the undated picture of the Nativity play (see page 85) may give a clue. On the photograph the altar is curtained off, but above the curtain may be seen the top of the reredos (stone screen behind the altar), and the top of the Commandment tablets. These clearly show some decorative work, and it is possible that the Ten Commandments had been covered with this geometric pattern. This is borne out in chapter 10 where Esme Harrison recalls the Ten Commandments being replaced by "blue trellis-like windows, much to the annoyance of some of the congregation". (Also on the Nativity play photograph, the ends of the lettered banner, painted in 1905 over the chancel arch, may clearly be seen.) In 1952 the Ten Commandments were restored, thus suggesting that they had either fallen into disrepair or had been obliterated in some way. They were finally taken down (though not destroyed) in 1971.

During 1931, questions were also raised about arrangements for heating and lighting of the church room (the Bug Hut), not least because it was used by so many village groups. To help resolve this, a separate fund for the church room was set up to manage its income and expenditure.

At the Annual Meeting in April 1931, Mr H Ashman "suggested [the meeting] ought not to close without reference to the Vicar's general work during the past year. He thought it was remarkable how well all the services had been maintained and finances in the difficult times through which we had been passing. He said that the Church had enjoyed peace during that year as well as in all the years the vicar had been in office. He also referred in terms of praise to the level kept up in the matter of sermons. In many ways Coleford was a difficult parish and he thought the annual meeting was the time for members to pledge their loyalty to the Vicar. The meeting received these remarks with general acclamation".

The centenary of the church was kept on 19 July 1931 and the Bishop of Taunton preached at Evensong. The Service Register gives no indication of how many people attended, although in the morning there had been thirty-five communicants at 8.00 am. This was considerably more than the usual number which varied between six and fifteen.

1932 brought new developments as the PCC got behind an initiative to produce and sell magazines. The PCC Minutes tell us that they would contain "one page of advertisements and one page for local matters", so they were probably similar to earlier parish magazines. If more than 114 copies could be regularly sold, there would be sufficient income to do away with the need for advertisements, and if a small profit could be made the PCC hoped to include "a little picture of our church".

1933 saw the Women's Club purchase a piano for the church room, new collection bags were made by Miss Smith and new surplices for the choirmen. As today, much of the routine business of running the church was managed by the PCC, but things did not always run smoothly. In 1935 there was a major disruption to PCC activities brought on by a dispute with the Treasurer. An Executive Committee and a Financial Committee were set up to try and help resolve the problem, which appears to stem from a dispute over the parochial accounts and the refusal of the Treasurer to hand over relevant papers and records. As a result, on 25 July 1935, the Finance Committee recommended that "we issue new books to the treasurer and commence all financial matters clear as from last Easter". In doing so, they agreed to treat the papers held by him as "non-existent", and to inform the Archdeacon of their decision. After the meeting, the Vicar visited the bank to check the position in relation to the church bank accounts and a new Treasurer was appointed—Jack Coles. The dispute rumbled on and eventually the Rural Dean, the Revd Horton Starkey, was called upon to adjudicate. The PCC agreed to abide by his decision as long as the outgoing Treasurer handed

Mothers' Union banner, 1936

over to the Rural Dean all the books and records that they themselves had been unable to obtain from him.

The Treasurer wasn't the only person who came under PCC scrutiny. In September 1936 a dispute over the cost of heating bills brought suspicion on the Sexton, who was believed to be "siphoning off" wood, which was delivered to his home rather than direct to the Church. On 15 April 1937, the PCC was informed that the Sexton had been dismissed from his duties. A new Sexton, Cecil Price, was appointed in December 1937.

On a spiritual level, the Revd Ralph-Bowman reported to the annual Vestry and PCC that the work of the Church "was carried on with enthusiasm and harmony". 1936 brought a series of changes to Holy Trinity. In January the Sexton was asked to go about his duties robed. In April a jumble sale raised sufficient funds for a Mothers' Union banner, which had been dedicated at Evensong on 17 March 1936. Prayer books were purchased for the use of the congregation, and the ringing of the "Sanctus Bell" was introduced.

Later in 1936, Mrs Ralph-Bowman obtained a piano for use in the church, and a successful Nativity play proved so popular that on 21 January 1937 the PCC agreed to the presentation of a Passion play at Easter. That, in its turn, was highly praised and rewarding, adding greatly to the value of Church life, and starting a new tradition still fondly remembered by parishioners. Following a break during the Second World War, production of the Passion play was resumed in 1947 and continued until 1954.

Also in 1937, another Nativity play, *The Way to Bethlehem*, was performed in church. This took place on Christmas Day at 7.30 pm before an audience of sixty people, with repeat performances on the Sunday after Christmas and on 12 January 1938. The Nativity plays proved to be as popular as the Passion plays.

Despite such events, recruiting young members to the church was becoming

The Sanctus Bell During the Prayer of Consecration at Holy Communion the church bell would be (and still is) rung three times when the priest said the words "This is my body" over the bread, and three times when he said "This is my blood" over the wine. As the Vicar explained to the PCC on 16 April, the idea of the bell was that "those who could not take part in the service could commune spiritually at the most sacred part of the Communion Service".

*Holy Trinity
Nativity play
(undated)*

The Anglican Young People's Association, known as the **AYPA**, was founded in 1902 in St James' Church, Paris, Ontario, Canada, under the leadership of Canon James Brown. It had four principles: work, worship, edification and recreation. In 1916 Bishop Roper of Ontario commended the work of the AYPA and expressed the hope that it would spread throughout his diocese. At that time the AYPA catered for young people between the ages of 18 and 24. World War II affected membership and in 1942 it was suggested that the minimum age be lowered to 15. The result was that it became a teenage organisation and lost its appeal to the older members. The AYPA spread across the British Empire but has now died out in the UK. However, in the 21st century it still flourishes in West Africa and in the West Indies.

increasingly difficult. Matters were helped by the AYPA—the Anglican Young People's Association—the Coleford branch having been founded on 7 November 1937.

After Evensong on 13 March 1938, a special meeting was held in the church to discuss the acceptance of a new altar cross and processional cross. Members of the congregation were shown the crosses and voted to accept the gift from the younger members, which were dedicated at Evensong on 10 April 1938. Jean Chivers (née Price) recalls that the AYPA members had worked very hard to buy the crosses, saving up their ha'pennies and farthings, so that the gift was a real labour of love. The group also presented a new Gospel Book on Easter Sunday 1941. Jean Chivers remembers that the AYPA arranged a variety of social events built around their Christian faith, which attracted strong support. She was Secretary of the AYPA for a time and, like Phyllis Coles, remembers the rallies at Swindon, Stourbridge, Thatcham, and in Coleford, as well as outings and social evenings.

Jean Chivers also recalls that after a Corporate Communion on the first Sunday of

Coleford Anglican Young People's Association members
on a visit to Swindon

each month, the young people would enjoy a cooked breakfast at the vicarage. The girls would cook the breakfast and the boys would wash up. There is no reference to the AYPA in Coleford after World War II.

Mr W G ('Soffy') Hamblin, organist for many years, suffered a prolonged illness in 1937. Messages were sent wishing him a speedy recovery, while Mr Ern Steeds helped fill the gap. This informal arrangement continued until January 1939, when Mr Roy Withers was appointed as organist, and the PCC took up a collection for a gift to mark Mr Hamblin's long and faithful service.

The incumbency of the Revd Ralph-Bowman had been something of a renaissance for Coleford. The parish records are full of details of church life, such as the wearing of vestments at the Eucharist for the first time on Easter Sunday 1940. Many of the older members of today's congregation remember the church of their younger days with affection.

Bob Swallow was another young lad who became a

W G (Soffy)
Hamblin, organist
at Holy Trinity for
many years

Coleford AYPA gathering on the vicarage garden

The late **Jack Steeds** recalled one memorable Christening, when he and Ken Mounty were told to fill the font, but they were unsure where to get the water. Eventually they filled it up to the very top from the outside tap. Afterwards the Revd Ralph-Bowman called Jack outside the church and asked him where he had got the water. Upon being told he said, "I came to Baptise the baby, not b— drown it!" Jack lost the job. Jack's career as choirboy was equally unfortunate: "I used to flick papers at the others in the choir. One day the Vicar said, 'John Steeds, will you stop playing around!' Granny Steeds pulled me out of the choir and into the pew with her." Jack was also one of the boys who pumped the organ and frequently fell asleep so that no sound came out! But Jack seemed undeterred and told his stories with relish. In adult life Jack became a popular and highly talented musician and entertainer. The Jack Steeds Accordion Band was in great demand throughout the locality. Jack never married, but later in life was a carer for his sister, Olive Perkins, with whom he lived in the family home opposite the Kings Head. Olive and Jack regularly received Holy Communion at home. Olive died in September 2004 and Jack died in August 2008.

Jack Steeds (left) in November 2007 with Dennis Chambers

Dennis Chambers recalls: Membership of the Church choir did not come easily, would-be choristers having to undergo an audition. On my first day as a chorister I was very nervous because my parents were in the congregation, and my dad had said I hadn't got to let him down. We came out of the vestry and we were singing as we went up the aisle. I was looking down at my book to make sure I didn't make a mistake and I never saw the step until it was too late. Over I went, and didn't I catch it when I got home!

Bob Swallow as a choirboy

choirboy at about this time. Later Bob would become Sexton, and at the time of writing is still a member of Holy Trinity.

The impact of the Second World War cannot be escaped. Unlike their parents and grandparents during the First World War, the parishioners had the presence of the Revd Ralph-Bowman to see them through the dark days, and his notes in the Service Registers reveal how much activity was focussed on Holy Trinity: "Dunkirk Evacuation—National Thanksgiving" (9 June 1940); "Chain of Intercessions for 2 hours by AYPA" (1 August 1940); "London Air Raid 10 victims" (22 September 1940); "Home Guard Church Parade" (All Saints' Day 1941, the first of many); "British

Mike Wells recalls: I joined the choir in 1942. The Priest was the Revd Ralph-Bowman, and later the Revd Bernard Adams. The Choirmaster was W M Jones. The lay reader was Mr Jack Coles, my uncle.

At Christmas we all had a carol solo to sing. I sang the page in *Good King Wenceslas* and W M sang the king. I sang this part until my voice broke. I was all right on the Thursday Choir practice night, but by Sunday I could only croak.

I left the choir in September 1952 to join the Royal Air Force. The Revd Adams presented me with a leather-bound Bible which I still have. I also received the Canon Moore prize: a book entitled *Somerset Churches* by Arthur Mee. My sister Ann also received this prize.

I remember going to Wells Cathedral for the Royal School of Church Music Summer Festival. All the choir were members of that society and were allowed to wear a badge designed like a treble clef sign.

During the spring of 1944 the American Army was camped in Mells Park opposite Halecombe Quarry. One of the Americans came to church one Sunday for Evensong. All the choirboys were curious, as we had never seen a coloured man before. After the service, my Uncle Jack found him waiting outside. He told Uncle Jack that he had put nothing in the collection and handed him a ten-dollar bill, asking if it was enough. My uncle said that it would be quite all right. Our coloured friend came to church right up until D-Day, when the Americans moved out. We never saw or heard from him again.

Mike Wells as a choirboy

Legion Women's Branch Dedication of Banners" (14 December 1943); "National Day of Prayer, Church Parade of Public Bodies" (St George's Day 1944); "Memorial Service for Harry Perkins, RAF" (Evensong 1 October 1944). And on 8 May 1945, "United Service of Parish to give thanks for Victory over Germany." This took place at 7.00 pm following a Children's Treat in the schoolyard. On the following Sunday, which was a Day of National Thanksgiving, there was Evensong and a Church Parade of the British Legion and others. On 19 August there was a "Day of Thanksgiving for Victory over Japan and the End of the War". Thirty people received Holy Communion at 8.00 am that day.

Eight men from the village died on active service in World War II. These were Edward Parfitt, Harry Perkins, John Phillips, Bob Seymour, Kenneth Seymour, Fred Steeds, John Taylor and Arthur John Lay. Their names were added to the War Memorial inside Holy Trinity. Unfortunately, no record was kept of the men and women of Coleford who served in H M Forces during World War II.

In 1946 the annual Vestry meeting reflected on the events of the immediate past, as the vicar thanked "all workers for the services they had rendered during the past year which had been one of stress and strain owing to the war. While the number of helpers in all departments of the work of the church has been depleted week by week on account of the Call to Arms, many who remained found the burden was bearing in the demands of continued life which was a drain upon their strength. The work of the Church had gone on and all ecclesiastical service had been maintained by members in meetings and congregations had suffered accordingly. He urged them to persevere with prayers … to the end."

The Revd Harry Ralph-Bowman left Coleford in 1946, his last Sunday being on 23 June. He became Rector of South Poole, near Kingsbridge in Exeter diocese, having exchanged livings with the previous Rector of South Poole, the **Revd Bernard Norton Adams**, who was instituted on 16 August 1946.

Robin Thompson recalls: I had to join the church choir like the rest of the young lads in 1942. The vicar at that time was the Revd Ralph-Bowman. The Choirmaster was Mr Ern Steeds followed by W M Jones. He used to work for Coleford Co-op as a roundsman and the organist was Mrs Jo Carpenter. The lay reader was my uncle, Mr Jack Coles. The Sexton was Mr Cecil Price. At that time we didn't have any choir practice because of the war.

On one memorable occasion at Sunday morning Matins when we came out of church at 12 o'clock, a plane had been shot down near Holcombe at Brickhouse Farm. The pilot was parachuting down and we thought he was going to land in Ashill but the wind took him and he landed in Mells Park. Some of the Home Guard got on their bikes and rode to Mells Park to arrest him, but when they got there the Home Guard at Mells had already arrested him.

The Churchwardens at that time were Mr E Lambert, Douglas Witcombe, George Mounty and Simeon Kurton. In about 1945 Mr W M Jones took over as choirmaster, and in 1946 Norman Button took over playing the organ, and from then on choir practice started on Thursday nights—prompt at 7.00 pm until 8.30 pm. The men who had taken part in the war came back into the choir, and so then all the choir stalls were filled. The cross bearers were Fred Plummer and John Turner. Sunday School had to be attended every Sunday and at this time the vicar changed the service from Matins to the Family Eucharist at 9.30 am. The church was almost always filled for that service and also for Evensong. About that time the vicar, Mr Adams, decided to improve the vicarage lawn, which we boys were instructed to give a hand with. We decided to get it ready for playing stick cricket and he used to allow us to play this on the lawn because there was no playing field; our playground was the street. On another memorable occasion we were kicking a ball in and out of the vicarage gates on a Sunday morning after family Eucharist, waiting for the vicar to come and tell us we could go down and play on the lawn, when the elders of the Methodist Chapels stopped and watched us as, much to their disgust, we were kicking a ball about on a Sunday! A delegation from the chapels went round to see the vicar, but we never found out what was said because as they left to go their chapels the Vicar told us to come round and start our game of cricket. After cricket, we had our Sunday dinner, and then attended Sunday School in the afternoon. We then went home for tea before going back to the church for Evensong.

In 1946 my parents moved to South Norwood to take up the offer of a job for my father at Croydon Airport. My Uncle Jack came up with us, and to make sure that I was still going to be a choirboy, he introduced me to the vicar at St Aldhelm's Church in Thornton Heath … After about twelve months, I was sent back to my grandparents in Coleford because those in the London school didn't understand the country language. I was glad to get back to Coleford because as we went to the church school we had to attend church on Ash Wednesday and Ascension Day, after which we were allowed to go home for the rest of the day. Our school teachers were Mr and Mrs Evans. He used to play the organ for the school services and his wife used to conduct. My Uncle Jack used to put on the Passion plays at Easter and he also used to put on different plays, mostly religious or Christmas themes, which we performed at Stoke St. Michael, Mells Barn and Leigh-on-Mendip.

In 1948 my parents returned from London. My father returned to the quarry; and unfortunately, in 1949, one of the choir members, Wilf Morse, was killed on his motorcycle. The same year Cecil Price [Jean Chivers' father], the Sexton, was killed at New Rock Colliery. Albert Nicholls took over as Sexton and then Dennis Cornish. One occasion my sister, Marie, and myself went up to help my mother and father finish off cleaning the church. While we were there, we decided to play the *Dambusters March* together on the organ. After a bit, looking in the mirror on the organ, we spotted the vicar sitting in the church. We immediately stopped playing as we thought we were in big trouble, but much to our relief he said, "Carry on, I'm enjoying it."

In about 1953 they created two jobs, one as verger and the other as Sexton.

Uncle Jack Coles nominated me for the job of verger and the job of Sexton was taken by Fred Plummer. My own parents used to clean the church once a week on a Friday. On Sundays I used to have to go to church for 8.00 am Communion, the 9.30 am Family Eucharist and Evensong. At that time I had a job at Ham Farm, Kilmersdon Common, for about a year, and then I decided, with the rest of my mates, to go to work at Norton Hill Colliery. When there was a funeral at Coleford Church, I was allowed to come back to light the fires to warm the church and generally help the vicar with his duties. Most weddings were held on Saturdays in those days so that my duties could be carried out without having to take time off from work.

In 1954 a new vicar, the Revd Sutters, arrived in Coleford. I carried on my duties as verger until 1959 when I got married and had to resign from the job, the reason being there wasn't a house available in Coleford for us to live in.

APPENDIX TO CHAPTER 7

LIFE AT THE VICARAGE IN THE 1930s

THE Revd Harry Ralph-Bowman's son Peter became a priest and officiated at services at Holy Trinity from time to time. He died on 13 January 1997, aged 83. His autobiography, titled *Ah-Yes: An Introspective Retrospect*, was published posthumously in 1999. In it he recalled some of the hardships and discomforts of vicarage life, though compared with many of the villagers who were suffering real poverty due to bad pay in the mines, poor housing and the increasing threat of further mine closure, Peter Ralph-Bowman's life was privileged. Peter, who was nearly 14 at the time of the family's arrival, recalled in his autobiography living conditions in the vicarage.

"Coleford Vicarage, in ample grounds, was a sort of Georgian affair in Bath stone, and my mother once again, after so many years, had a maid in the house. Girls leaving school were happy to have £24 a year, a bedroom of their own, good regular food, a warm kitchen and the chance of a hot bath. At the time we had no electricity and no piped water—rain-water tanks for the bathroom, topped up in dry times by a force-pump, and a stand-pump in the kitchen met domestic needs.

"Father's income from the Ecclesiastical Commissioners was £400 if the population exceeded a thousand—which by his computation it always succeeded in doing. In those days he had to pay the rates on the house and suffer a dilapidation annual deduction of £20. We had no motor till 1932 … no telephone, electricity or mains water till the mid 30s. Father and I bicycled, Mother took the twice-weekly bus to Frome …"

Holidays for the vicarage family consisted of the exchange of house with another clergyman in return for Sunday duty. "Such a holiday," wrote Peter Ralph-Bowman, "meant a lot of work for Mother, in preparing her house for occupation by strangers." Usually the exchange was a success, but sometimes less so. "Sometimes Father hit on an eccentric. Harmless in the case of the bachelor who left hundreds of spent matches to mark spots in the garden where he had lain in a deck-chair, smoking … Painful, in the case of a man who wrote daily complaints. Some examples, 'Where is the coal shovel?' (it being mid-summer). 'Is there a spare key for the back door? We walked last evening, leaving by the back-door as the key of the front-door is so cumbersome. My wife mislaid the key … My wife managed to climb in through the down-stairs lavatory window which, I am sure you are aware, has a defective catch … My wife … received a severe shock from the electric cooker. It might have been fatal. We called in the electrician on your list. He seems a duffer to me and could find nothing wrong. I told him to send the account to you and we dare not use the stove. A good job that there is plenty of coal in the outhouse; we managed to force the door, so we can use the range. Unless a new key is provided for the back-door, we shall have to lug the coal through the house via the front-door … My wife … fell down the steps at the front-door this morning … She was struggling with the coal bucket … She bruised her coccyx grievously. Good job it wasn't a parishioner! … We nearly called in the doctor but [my wife] had previously noticed the brandy in the side-board fortunately.'"

So having lost the back-door key, insulted the electrician, burned the winter coal supply and consumed all the brandy, could there possibly be any more problems? Indeed, yes. "'A dray-man called today with crates of bottled beer from Rode Brewery. I told him not to deliver during our stay. Such a bad example to the young people, [my wife] says … I wish we could get milk delivered. I complained to the man at the Rectory gate about the uncleanliness of his product and he has refused to supply us … Your friend, as he claims to be, the local bobby, is rather impertinent. He called to report complaints about our dogs. I think I told you we were bringing three bull-terriers … I sent the constable away with a flea in his ear … Your church-warden's wife called today, not to see if we were enjoying ourselves but to allege that our dogs have killed three of her ducks—prize-winners and pedigree and all that of course. She had the brass nerve to say that in a like case the Rector would have paid up cheerfully. Maybe he would, I said, but I shan't … Finally she went away … but not very gracious … The Vicar of Whatley called yesterday. Said he didn't know you were away. Stayed for hours, eyes everywhere and asked himself to tea … I hope you will write to any other clerical friend who might come snooping around … Our eldest nephew was nearly killed yesterday. My brother and his family (three boys) have joined us for the rest of our stay. I complain sometimes of their boisterous behaviour but banisters … ought to stand the weight of a boy of fourteen. I think you should ask the Diocesan Surveyor not to repair them but to replace them with something sturdier.'"

The Revd Ralph-Bowman remained unperturbed by all these letters; nor did he reply to them. Instead, to prove he had received them, he pinned them all to the wall of the main bedroom in the vicarage where he was staying so that the sender would find them on his return.

8

A BRAVE NEW WORLD

IN 1946, in the aftermath of war, the village welcomed its new vicar, the **Revd Bernard Norton Adams**, to Coleford.

The Revd Bernard Adams wrote detailed annotations in the Service Registers, providing additional information on many aspects of life at Holy Trinity, but he did not record marriages and funerals in the daily Service Registers, there being separate Registers for these. Inducted as the tenth Vicar on 16 August 1946 at 7.30 pm, he noted in the Service Register that the "Service was followed by a delightful social gathering in the Miners' Welfare Institute". In his first Christmas at Holy Trinity, the Revd Adams noted: "On Xmas Eve at 6 pm the Christmas Candle was lit and blessed and from an illuminated Christmas Tree gifts were presented to the members of the Children's Church."

The **Revd Bernard Norton Adams** graduated from Selwyn College, Cambridge, in 1901, and was ordained deacon in 1904 and priest in 1905 in Salisbury Cathedral. His first post was as an Assistant Master of Melksham High School, 1901–05, combined with the curacy of Melksham, 1904–06. He was Chaplain and Assistant Master of Bishop's School, Salisbury, and Chaplain of Fisherton Asylum, 1906–07, and then moved north and served as Assistant Master at Stockport Grammar School, 1907–19, combined with the curacy of St Mary, Stockport, from 1916–19. Livings in Chester diocese followed from 1919–29 after which he moved to Winchester diocese as Vicar of Ecchinswell with Symondton 1929–31. He had already spent over forty years following his vocation and came to Coleford after he exchanged livings with his predecessor. The exchange took Harry Ralph-Bowman to South Poole (with Chivelstone) in 1946, where Bernard Adams had been incumbent since 1931. Bernard Adams served the remainder of his ministry in Coleford, before retiring to Dunster in 1954.

The Revd Bernard Adams

He also introduced the Midnight Eucharist in 1946, and there were sixty-nine communicants (ninety-seven communicants including eighteen at 9.00 am and ten at 11.00 am on Christmas Day). Summing up his first few months in Coleford, the Revd Adams noted in the Service Register that over his first sixteen weeks there had been 439 communicants, nine baptisms, eight marriages; and no funerals. He added, "Community singing was held after Evensong once a month. A Bible Class for Boys and a Boys' Club were both started. Regular Choir practices were held and the singing improved greatly with Mr W M Jones as Choirmaster and Mr Norman Button as Organist. Parochial Church Council meetings were held regularly each month. The Children's Church was started in September and there are now 57 on the Register. The Women's Guild raised nearly half the money required for New Cassocks. At Christmas a Christmas Tree and lighted Candle were placed between the Choir Stalls on Christmas Eve and presents were given to the members of the Children's Church. At Midnight the Holy Communion was celebrated and the number of communicants was the largest on record. In spite of bad weather in December the numbers at Church remained very good and collections had doubled."

Coleford Children's Church

Martin Chivers' Children's Church membership card

1947 Passion play entry in Service Register

Jack Coles

Jack and Dorothy Coles with Stuart, Hilary and Margaret

Soon after his arrival the Revd Adams started the *Coleford Parish Magazine* and he had hoped that the whole village would contribute to it, but it received very little support. No issues have survived in the church records, and a copy loaned for this book reveals a rather dull publication with much "churchy" language and very little else! It is not clear whether the magazine died out during the Revd Adams' ministry at Holy Trinity, but certainly his successor, the Revd John Sutters, began a new publication.

During Holy Week 1947, a Passion play was performed in church, thus reviving a pre-War custom which was to continue until 1954. As well as the Revd Adams noting the event (which raised £7 17s 9d towards new choir cassocks) in the Service Register, all the cast signed the Register. The vicar noted: "On the Wednesday in Holy Week and on Good Friday Evenings *The Drama of the Passion* was very reverently and excellently given by those whose names are written on this page, & Mr Norman Button added to the reverent effect by his devotional playing & his choice of the music."

Post-War village life included the difficulty and inconvenience caused to Churchwardens when the Archdeacon made his Visitations during the afternoon. In 1950 a letter was sent pointing out that it would be easier for the Churchwardens if such meetings could be arranged to take into account their day-time jobs. Despite this, Jack Coles remained a steadfast member of the church, both as Treasurer and as

Churchwarden. His support for the vicar and dedicated work for Holy Trinity and the people who worshipped there are regularly mentioned in annual reports.

The post-War years also saw some bereavements. On Sunday, 7 August 1949, Evensong was held as a Memorial Service for Wilfred George Morse, who died aged 30 and who had been a chorister at Holy Trinity for over twenty years; 112 people were present. And a few months later the Revd Adams noted in the Service Register that "on March 6th [1950] Mr Cecil Price who had been Sexton of this Church for 13 years was killed in the New Rock Colliery. RIP"; 163 people were present at Evensong on 12 March which was held as a Memorial Service. Cecil Price had been Sexton since 1937 and was Jean Price's (now Chivers') father. (Cecil Price's wife, Vera, was to have a long widowhood, dying on 14 December 2002, aged 97 years. Her funeral service was conducted at Holy Trinity by the Revd Valerie Bonham on Monday 23 December.)

The war had brought many changes to the village and as a new generation grew up, numbers attending Holy Trinity slowly began to dwindle. At the end of June 1951, the Revd Adams noted in the service Register that "Communicants fell from 577 to 416, a deficit largely accounted for by the slackness of the younger people". Even so, the choir was still flourishing under the direction of William Marchant Jones.

At the end of 1952, the Revd Adams noted: "Once again records were broken and for the first time in its history the Church Collections came to over £300. Of this £117 was given to special objects. The year was unfortunate in that part of the organ was flooded and £94 damage was done. On the other hand the Gift day realised over £62 & enabled us to repair the Church Path. During the year, through the generosity of Mr W M Jones the Sanctuary floor was renewed, and the Ten Commandments restored.

The wedding of Sybil Plummer and Dennis Hodges

F H Plummer, I L Webb, T J Turner, J Mason, E H Coles, J E Ashman, K A Mounty
K B Chaffin, M E Edgell, B I Rossiter, P M Mason, P Coles, V J Mascord, P M Witcombe, M S Plummer
B Rossiter, M Plummer, K Witcombe, W M Jones (*Choirmaster*), Rev B N Adams (*Vicar*), N Button (*Organist*), M Wells, M Fricker, P Barnett
A Fricker, S Coles, D Price, R Logan, W West

The Choir in 1951

Also during the year we received the splendid gift of the Cathedral altar rails … At the end of year we were once more without a Sexton." It is not clear whether the two small coffins referred to by Jack Coles (see chapter 2) were found on this occasion, or at a later time when further work was done.

On Saturday, 4 April 1953 (the day before Easter Sunday), Sybil Plummer married Dennis Hodges at 2.00 pm. (Sybil's daughter, Liz Smith, has recalled her mother saying that she preferred two o'clock weddings: "'Tis a proper time," Sybil would say.) Sybil's brother, Gordon Plummer, was best man, and Mary Brotherton was one of the bridesmaids. No doubt the village children carried out the old wedding custom of tying the church gates and not allowing the bride and groom to leave the churchyard until the groom had given them pennies. This old custom seems to have died out in recent years.

By 1954 William Marchant Jones, the Choirmaster, was also noting the falling numbers, as he reported the difficulties he was having recruiting new adult members to the choir. The situation would not have been helped by the interregnum, as from the spring of 1954 a series of priests stood in for the Revd Adams during a time of illness. These include the Revd H J Sutters, the Revd J R Alford and the Revd Haworth. Bernard Adams' final service at Holy Trinity was on 25 July 1954.

An Oxford graduate and an Anglo Catholic (after ordination he preferred to be called Father), **John Sutters** had trained for the priesthood at St Stephen's House, an Oxford theological college, and was ordained deacon in 1939 and priest in 1940. Fr John Sutters combined curacies in Oxford diocese together with lecturing at St Stephen's House until 1949, when he moved to Ripon. A hospital chaplaincy combined with Chaplaincy of Ripon Grammar School, and a minor canonry of Ripon Cathedral, took him up to 1952. In 1952 he came to Bath and Wells as Priest Vicar of Wells Cathedral and Chaplain of Wells Theological College until 1954, when he came to Coleford. In 1957 he contributed to *The Oxford Dictionary of the Christian Church*, a major reference work which has gone through several editions and is still in print. He served the parish of Coleford from 1954 until July 1961 when he became Vicar of Highbridge in Somerset (1961–73), and Assistant Master of King Alfred School, Highbridge (1961–71). He then moved to St Margaret's-on-Thames in London diocese (1973–80) and retired to Oxford in 1980. He died in February 2003.

Fr John Sutters and his wife, Muriel

Shortly before the Revd Bernard Adams left the parish, major boundary changes came into force by an Order in Council [i.e. the Queen's Privy Council], dated 5 February 1954. At that time the parish of Babington extended as far south as Hippy's Farm, Coleford Green. It also included Goodeaves Farm and Stock Hill, although at this time The Crescent was the only housing development between the two farms along the main road. The Order in Council took all the area belonging to Babington parish south of the disused Newbury branch line of the railway and gave it to Coleford parish. In return, Coleford gave up to Babington a portion in the area of Newbury House.

As the year progressed, preparations for the installation of the new vicar included work on the vicarage garden. Finally, on 17 December, the accounts show the hire of the Miners' Welfare Institute opposite the church for the reception to welcome the new vicar, **Fr (Herbert) John Sutters**, after his induction service on 17 December 1954 at 7.00 pm.

The Parish Communion Movement In the 1950s a movement in the Church of England sought to encourage the Sung Eucharist as the main Sunday service instead of Matins or Morning Prayer. This "Parish Communion" movement aimed to make the Eucharist more accessible to the whole congregation. Previously Holy Communion would be attended by just a few people—those who were confirmed and would receive Holy Communion, but non-communicants had not been encouraged to attend. The Parish Communion Movement marked a major shift in how parishes worshipped because it encouraged the whole congregation to attend. Today it forms the normal pattern for Sunday worship, but it might help us to understand the reasoning behind Fr Sutters' notice to the congregation about fasting. This rule about fasting before Communion has now been relaxed.

During his time in Coleford, Fr Sutters oversaw a number of changes, partly reflecting developments in the wider Church and partly his own disciplined routine of regular Eucharist and Daily Office. So it comes as no surprise that at the beginning of 1955 he noted in the Service Register that "Morning and Evening Prayer are said daily, with Litany on Wednesdays and Fridays". He reintroduced the daily Eucharist (at which there were usually two or three communicants) but the Passion and Nativity plays ceased.

A telephone was installed at the vicarage in May 1955, and in December carol singers raised £6. Also in December, a Verger was appointed. This was Robin Thompson whose memories of Holy Trinity appear in this book.

One of the biggest challenges for the congregation came with the introduction in February 1955 of the Parish Eucharist, for which new prayer and hymn books were purchased in 1956, paid for in three separate instalments.

A typewritten notice filed by Fr Sutters in the Service Register states:

Beginning on Sunday, 27 February, the first Sunday in Lent, the main Sunday morning service will be the Parish Eucharist at 9.30 am each Sunday. All members of the Children's Church and Sunday School are asked to make this their regular Sunday morning worship: it is the service our Lord Himself gave us, and all Christians should make "The Lord's Service on the Lord's Day" a fixed rule.

I hope parents will come with their children: and babies, even if in prams and even if vocal, will be welcome. It is meant to be the gathering (weekly) of all Church people of all ages, from one week to 100 years old!

Those who have been confirmed may receive Holy Communion at this service, if properly prepared. If you mean to receive, do not have any food or drink till afterwards. If you do not wish to receive Holy Communion every Sunday, you may join the service without doing so; but I hope that those who are confirmed will soon form the habit of receiving each Sunday.

All Church people, children as well as grown-ups, are urged to COME REGULARLY TO THE LORD'S SERVICE ON THE LORD'S DAY.

Children's Church in junior and senior classes continued to meet on Sunday afternoons, in addition to attending the Parish Eucharist.

July 1955 saw the introduction of a new parish magazine to be known as the *Coleford Parish Paper*. Writing in the first edition Fr Sutters wryly commented, "A parish paper can help the life of a parish considerably—*if* it is well managed, and worth reading. If this one isn't, tell me!" Clearly he had a sense of humour because his final note was: "Note to Conservatives. Please don't let the colour [red] of this month's cover stop you buying this Parish Paper; we shall have a blue one before long!"

Looking back over the first six months of his ministry at Holy Trinity, it is clear that Fr Sutters loved his parish and the people in it. He wrote in the first issue of the *Coleford Parish Paper*, "You have indeed made me and my family welcome since we came here last December: Here are just a few memories of this happy six months—the unfailing support of the daily Eucharist—the friendliness and welcome in your homes—the *increase* in congregations in the worst patch of snow and frost—the power of prayer in the Three Hours silent Watching on Good Friday—the heartfelt fervour of that full Church on Easter evening—those lovely Sunday Evening Baptisms with you all to witness and pray—the happy family parties I have been bidden to at weddings—the Church

Colin Turner's Children's Church membership and Chorister card 1953

Council on its knees in Church and then so ready to help with everything when we get to business—the crowds at the Ascension Day Sung Eucharist—the deeply Christian courtesy and sympathy of one or two who have felt it their duty to question or criticise— the first little trickle of penitents coming to seek God's peace in Sacramental Forgiveness—the Tuesday mornings in the school with the children—thank God and thank you—and now to do even better." Looking ahead, Fr Sutters expressed the hope that by the end of his first two years he would have met all the families in the parish.

The choir was a thriving body, far larger than that of many village churches at the time. In 1955 the head choirboy was Colin Turner, who in 2009 is still a faithful member of the congregation, and Church Treasurer. In 1956 he was succeeded as head choirboy by Stuart Coles.

In October 1955 several parishes in the deanery [i.e. a grouping of local parishes] were holding a week-long Mission of Spiritual Renewal to be conducted by the Village Evangelists, a volunteer organisation of clergy and laity dedicated to help in village mission work in this country. The mission took place from Sunday 23 October until the following Sunday, with good numbers coming to all the services throughout the week. This mission was aimed at the regular church members, but three years later a further mission was aimed at the whole parish. Fr Sutters had hoped to follow the 1955 mission with one a year later, but all the potential leaders were already engaged elsewhere. Meanwhile the spiritual life of the congregation continued to be deepened by the frequent services and also by informative articles about the Christian faith in the monthly *Coleford Parish Paper*.

Towards the end of 1955 Fr Sutters applied for a Faculty for an aumbry for the Reservation of the Communion for the Sick. This Faculty was granted and the Sacrament has been reserved at Holy Trinity since that time.

On Christmas Day 1955 a new white cope (a ceremonial cloak worn in processions), which had been given anonymously, was blessed at a service of Evening Prayer and Carols; 100 people attended. The cope is still in use at Holy Trinity.

Commander and Mrs Jones of Coleford House hosted the Garden Party on 16 June 1956 in aid of the Church Restoration Fund, as they had done for many years.

1956 saw the 125th Anniversary of the Dedication of the Church. Writing in the *Coleford Parish Paper*, Fr Sutters remarked, "In past years we have not kept the day itself, but only a neighbouring Sunday. The 125th year seems a good occasion to make more of our Church's birthday, and beginning on the eve to keep the day itself as well. So please all come and start off the festival on Wednesday evening, and give the Bishop of Taunton a real Coleford welcome—including Coleford singing—on his first visit. I have put down three Eucharists for the day itself, and I do hope that all of you who can will come to the Altar then as well as making the Sunday of the festival, July 22, a real Corporate Communion of *all* our people." The Eucharists on the day were at 6.30 am, 7.30 am, and 9.00 am. The service on the eve of the festival was Evening Prayer with a sermon from the Bishop of Taunton, who also blessed the new aumbry. A note in the Service Register for 18 July 1956 (Eve of Dedication Festival) tells us that "Perpetual

The aumbry

An **aumbry** is similar to a small safe and is set into the sanctuary wall near the altar. The consecrated bread and wine of Holy Communion, sometimes known as the Blessed Sacrament, is kept there. A white or gold veil is placed in front of the door of the aumbry, and there is a white lamp over the altar to denote the presence of the Sacrament. The only time when the Blessed Sacrament is not reserved is in Holy Week from the end of the Maundy Thursday Eucharist until the First Mass of Easter.

Reservation of the BLESSED SACRAMENT began after this Service [9.30 Holy Communion]".

During the service on the Eve of Dedication, there had been a procession, and incense had been used for the first time. Some people had *feared* it would be used regularly while others *hoped* it would be! So in the August *Coleford Parish Paper* Fr Sutters wrote an article about the use of incense in worship with reference to its Biblical foundation, but ended by saying that while it was not the last time incense would be used at Holy Trinity, it would not feature on a regular basis.

Barbara, in middle age

Barbara Ackroyd at the time of her arrival in Coleford

In the *Coleford Parish Paper* for December 1956, Fr Sutters welcomed a new arrival to the parish and congregation who was to prove a real asset to Holy Trinity over the coming years. Miss Barbara Ackroyd, the new Diocesan Moral Welfare Secretary, had moved to Kilmersdon Common from St Agnes in Cornwall where she had been the Matron of a Mother and Baby Home.

The end of 1956 marked the retirement as Choirmaster of William Marchant Jones. This was not the first time he had resigned, but he had indicated his intention to retire to Fr Sutters soon after the latter's arrival. He had agreed to remain for a time but now felt the time had come to give up. Fr Sutters wrote in the December 1956 *Parish Paper*:

"I cannot but acknowledge with the deepest gratitude Mr Jones' help and friendship in my first two years … In more than one matter of policy we have differed; sometimes I have been glad to defer to his guidance, sometimes he has loyally accepted my decision to follow a line he would not have chosen himself. But we have always worked happily together, with mutual respect … For the Choir, his resignation is the end of an age. His first connection with it was over sixty years ago as a boy … I hope that he will feel able to sing with the Choir still as often as possible … We still have him with us—let us hope for many years to come."

On Sunday, 5 May 1957, Mr Jones was presented with a leather-bound Prayer and Hymn Book, an illuminated address and a gift of money. The choir had already presented him with a travelling clock. Fr Sutters remarked in the June *Parish Paper* that "so well had the secret been kept that 'WM' was caught out, at a loss for words—an event which not even the oldest present could ever remember happening before! With characteristic generosity, Mr Jones asked that the cash part of the gift be added to the money we are raising to renew the Church service-books."

The *Coleford Parish Paper* for January 1957 records the death on 2 December 1956, after a short illness, of George Mounty, former Churchwarden and village postman. His funeral took place in Holy Trinity on 6 December and the church was full and the choir was in attendance. Two days later there was a Requiem at which nine people received Holy Communion. Fr Sutters paid tribute to him in the January *Parish Paper*: "Every household in the village feels a sense of personal bereavement in no longer seeing Mr Mounty going up and down on his bicycle with the letters, and no longer hearing his cheery greeting … There cannot have been many people so universally liked … quiet, helpful, and good humoured, always ready to lend a hand, never pushing himself. He was one of the best friends and colleagues a parish priest could have had: I shall never forget talking over plans with him when I first came, and seeing him look me straight in the face and say, 'I'm going to back you up …' As Churchwarden and a member of the PCC he was conscientious and thorough: and we shall miss his fine tenor singing … But it is his regular and steadfast presence in Church and at the Altar that we remember as the heart of his life."

George Mounty's life and dedication to Holy Trinity is commemorated by the oak lectern from which the lessons are read every Sunday. An inscription reads:

George Mounty 1898–1956
Churchwarden & Chorister
"The Righteous shall be had in everlasting remembrance."

The temptations of the modern world began to impinge on parish life in the 1950s, and in the March 1958 issue of the *Coleford Parish Paper* Fr Sutters addressed the problem of what he called "Saturday night and Sunday morning": "A new difficulty in the life of this village … is affecting young people who belong to the Church. A dance every Saturday night makes a lie-in every Sunday morning a much stronger temptation than before." The dances were held in the newly opened Royal British Legion Memorial

The **Community of the Resurrection** is an Anglican Religious Order for men, who specialise in mission work both at home and overseas, particularly in Africa. They also train candidates for the priesthood at the College of the Resurrection, adjoining the Community House at Mirfield in Yorkshire. Historically, members of the Community, such as Trevor Huddleston, were closely involved in the fight against apartheid in South Africa. Both the Community and the theological college still exist at Mirfield along with work in South and West Africa. Retreat conducting, spiritual direction and leading parish missions still constitutes an important aspect of the Community's work in the UK.

COLEFORD PARISH CHURCH
invites you to a

MISSION

from

February 23 to March 2, 1958

The LORD BISHOP of BATH and WELLS
will commission the Missioners
and preach at the

PARISH COMMUNION
on Sunday, February 23, at 9.30 a.m.

MISSION SERVICES
on Sundays at 6 p.m., Weekdays at 7.30 p.m.

Preacher :
The Revd. SAMUEL LOUNDS
of the Community of the Resurrection,
Mirfield, Yorkshire,
followed by a cup of tea in the Parish Room.

HOLY COMMUNION
Sundays 8 (said) and 9.30 (sung)

Monday, 7.30 and 9.30	Thursday, 7.30 and 9.30
Tuesday, 7 and 9.30	Friday, 7.30 and 8.30
Wednesday, 6.30 and 9.30	Saturday, 7.30 and 9.30

PLEASE TURN OVER

Leaflet for the 1958 Parish Mission

Hall, and Fr Sutters was anxious to let it be known that he thought the British Legion was doing good work for the social life of the village, because some people had been quick to condemn it outright. However, he emphasised that while it was permissible for members of the Church to attend dances, their priority on Sunday morning was attendance at the Eucharist.

"Many of you will know by now of the fine gift promised to the Church by Mr W M Jones, a stained glass window to fill the blank [window] above the south choir stalls." This notice in the May 1958 issue of the *Coleford Parish Paper* was the first many people would have heard of this gift, which was controversial because of its modern style. More details may be found in chapter 10.

The long awaited Parish Mission took place from 23 February until 2 March 1958 and was conducted by the Revd Samuel Lounds CR, from the Community of the Resurrection, Mirfield. Fr Lounds was assisted by two lay helpers, Mrs Mary Slocombe and Mrs Frances Bucknail of the Village Evangelists. The Bishop of Bath and Wells (the Right Revd [Harold] William Bradfield) presided at the Parish Eucharist on 23 February (Lent 1) and commissioned the Missioners. Mission services were held on Sundays at 6.00 pm and on weekdays at 7.30 pm and were well attended, with between 38 and 102 people present.

Despite the success of the Parish Mission, numbers at Holy Trinity continued to dwindle, with only six candidates being presented for confirmation in 1958. Though fewer in number, those who worshipped at Holy Trinity retained an outward-looking stance, embracing the needs of the wider community. When the Wesleyan Methodist Chapel was struck by lightning in June 1958, Fr Sutters wrote to the Chapel Trustees on behalf of the PCC offering not only sympathy but also accommodation for services, a gesture much appreciated by the Wesleyan Methodists.

In May 1959 the church received the gift of six oak standard candlesticks. These were to be used primarily at funerals, when they would stand three on either side of the coffin. Mr Eric Sheppard gave the oak, a member of the congregation anonymously paid for the candlesticks to be made, and Mr Edward Manley of Chantry made them. (Half a century later those candlesticks are still in use, though they are used slightly differently. Two are placed within the altar rails and are lit at every service in addition to the altar candles, and two flank the Easter garden during the Easter season. The Easter Candle, blessed at the Easter Vigil Service, now takes the place of the six requiem candles at funerals. The Easter Candle had not been introduced in Fr Sutters' time.)

On 16 June 1959 Mrs Ellen Steeds, known to all as "Granny Steeds", died in her 100th year. She was born on 12 May 1860 when the Revd Robert Whiteway, the third incumbent of Holy Trinity was still in office, and she lived through the incumbencies of ten clergy! She spoke the Coleford dialect which, half a century after her death, is still spoken, but by a fast diminishing number of people. Her funeral was on 29 June 1959.

Granny Steeds—a Victorian survivor

Ellen Steeds was born in May 1860 and married her husband, John Steeds, when she was 15 years old. At the age of 10 years, she went into domestic service at 6d a week plus food. Her husband was a coal miner who earned 2s 6d per shift; sometimes they had to exist on 7s 6d per week. She had eight children of whom four survived her, and for sixty-four years she lived in a small cottage at Springer's Hill. Her husband died there, aged 66. To supplement the family income, she knitted jerseys for sailors at 1s 3d each. Occasionally she assisted neighbours on washing days from 8.00 am until 1.00 pm, for 6d. It was rare for her to get out of the village, and the only means was by the carrier's horse-drawn brake, which took two hours to Frome and two back, so Granny Steeds would not have made such a journey very often.

Mrs Ellen (Granny) Steeds

For some years the congregation had used *Hymns Ancient & Modern* as their staple hymn book, supplemented by the Bath and Wells Diocesan Book, commonly known as the Brown Book. Many of the hymns and tunes in the latter came from *The English Hymnal*. The Brown Books were wearing out and were out of print, and so at the end of December 1959 it was decided to buy *The English Hymnal* to use alongside *Hymns Ancient & Modern*. The books would be paid for from the "Altar Fund" so that the expense was not a further drain on the church General Fund.

In September 1959 Fr Sutters began an experimental service, as he explained in the *Coleford Parish Paper*: "I am very keen that those children, especially the younger ones, who come to Children's Church or Infants' Class on Sunday afternoons … but can't seem to get to the Parish Eucharist, should be introduced to our Lord's Service. So, as an experiment, on the 3rd Sunday of each month there will be no Children's Church or Infant's Class in the afternoon, but instead there will be a short and very simple Children's Eucharist, with explanations as we go along, *at 10.45 am*. I hope some parents may like to come with younger children, and that perhaps old people who can't come earlier may like to come then too. But I *don't* want anyone to desert the Parish Eucharist in order to come." The first Children's Eucharist took place on September 20th and there were eighteen present and one communicant (Fr Sutters). In October there were twenty-four present and two communicants, but in November only six were present and two communicants, and in December there was no congregation at all. The experiment was dropped in the New Year, but sometimes these things must be attempted even if the results are disappointing.

December 1959 had seen the 5th anniversary of Fr Sutters' licensing as Vicar, and in his letter in the January 1960 *Parish Paper*, he seemed to be disappointed at what he perceived to be his failure to bring people, especially young people, to God. But he was also able to reflect on the positive aspects—the generosity of the congregation, the daily Eucharist, the school, the Sunday worship, the choir, and the friendships he had made in church and village.

In March 1961 the news broke that Fr Sutters was to leave Coleford in July, having accepted the Bishop's invitation to become Vicar of Highbridge. This was a somewhat sudden change, Fr Sutters having previously written of his hope to follow his first five years with another five. He had already turned down the offer of two other parishes. He was at pains to explain that it was not a question of "bettering himself"; indeed, he was very upset that the suggestion had been made. But he felt that the time was now right to hand over to someone else and to take up the challenge of a new parish. Fr Sutters left the parish on 24 July 1961.

During his incumbency, Fr Sutters had endeavoured to teach about the faith and worship of the Church both from the pulpit and by means of the *Coleford Parish Paper*. Most months saw an article devoted to some aspect of Christianity, as well as containing parish news. Perhaps surprisingly for a High Churchman in the 1950s, Fr Sutters was remarkably ecumenical and was on good terms with the Methodist minister. Towards the end of his time in Coleford, he invited the minister to contribute to the *Parish*

Paper. Sometimes Fr Sutters came across as a strict disciplinarian, as for instance in his policy of no weddings in Advent or Lent (a view held by many clergy of the day), and his firmness regarding churchyard memorials. However, he was a good priest, only too aware of his shortcomings, but devoted to his parish and the people in it.

With a new decade, Coleford welcomed a new vicar, the **Revd (Frederick) Leonard Baker**, who arrived in October 1961.

The Revd Leonard Baker was instituted and inducted at 7.00 pm on Thursday, 19 October 1961 by the Bishop of Taunton and the Archdeacon of Wells. Once again the Miners' Welfare Institute had to be hired

The **Revd Leonard Baker** was born in 1906. He studied at Kings College, London and Warminster Theological College, and was ordained deacon in 1959 and priest in 1960. He served as curate of Brixham 1959–61, and was licensed and inducted as Vicar of Coleford on 19 October 1961. In July 1969 he became Rector of Heyford Warren with Lower Heyford and Rousham in the Diocese of Oxford until retiring to Newton Abbot in 1975. He died in April 1992.

for the reception following his induction service, at a cost of 15s, while 7s was spent on refreshments. Aged 55, Leonard Baker was a "late vocation", and his appointment to Coleford was his first incumbency. He wrote an introductory letter in the *Coleford Parish Paper* for September 1961, just before taking up office: "I feel very much 'at home' in coming to work among you, being Somersetshire born, it will seem quite like old times to be settling in the dear old county again … It is in praying together and working together that we can succeed."

Within the first couple of months, the Revd Baker had begun visiting within the parish, and was anxious to build up the numbers in the Sunday School. He also hoped to start a discussion group for teenagers at the vicarage on Sunday evenings. Also, it was imperative to increase numbers in the choir because some of the younger members were leaving due to the demands of further education. William Marchant Jones had temporarily stepped into the breach as Choirmaster following Fr Sutters' departure. Now, in December 1961, with the Revd Baker safely installed, he felt able to step down once more, having served in the choir for seventy years! The Revd Baker wrote in the December *Parish Paper*, "We shall continue to look forward to seeing him in his usual place on Sundays whenever he feels equal to coming."

Unfortunately, the file of the *Coleford Parish Paper* stops at the end of 1961—the magazine was certainly produced after this time, but copies were not saved, so it is difficult to gain an idea of the regular rhythm of

*The Revd Leonard and Mrs Baker
at the wedding of their son*

parish life under the new incumbent. However, the Service Registers were maintained, and these show a faithful continuity of the Sunday worship and almost daily Holy Communion. On most weekdays there were two communicants. Sunday worship consisted of the Litany (7.45 am), Holy Communion (8.00 am with an average of fourteen to twenty-two communicants), Morning Prayer (9.00 am), Parish Eucharist (9.30 am with an average of twenty-one to thirty-five communicants), Sunday School (2.30 pm), and Evensong (6.00 pm). It was the Revd Baker who reintroduced the Christmas Eve Midnight Eucharist (later called the Midnight Mass), as from his first Christmas in 1961. (There had not been a Midnight Eucharist during Fr Sutters' ministry.) On that occasion there were sixty-nine communicants (and probably more who did not receive Holy Communion). From that time onwards, the Midnight Mass has been part of Holy Trinity's tradition.

The 1960s saw a new development, funded through the generosity of long-standing church member William Marchant Jones, who enabled the purchase of the former Miners' Welfare Institute as Holy Trinity's Church Hall. For the full complicated story of the purchase of the Hall, see chapter 12.

The 1960s also saw some resurgence of activities linked to the church. Joyce Button recalls that she took up church work, joining the Mothers' Union (which marked its 40th anniversary at Evensong on Sunday, 26 February 1967), and became involved in the fete. However, it was the flowers that gave her most joy—a role she undertook first with Mollie Kelly, Nancy Seviour and Joyce Donald. As time passed, she took on the responsibility for organising the flowers, with the exception of festivals and weddings, and was helped by numerous volunteers over the years.

Under the Revd Baker improvements and renovations continued. A new radiant heater was installed at a cost of £8 18s 6d in October 1962, and in December quarry waste was tipped in the vicarage drive. As the country plunged into the freezing cold

Young Wives outing to Bristol Zoo (Joyce Wyatt, Ann Woolley, Eileen Smith)

of the winter of 1962/3, the church was not left unscathed. Throughout January, the Service Register carried comments such as "severe weather, heavy snowfall & deep drifts, weather conditions impossible, frost & cold exceptional". In April 1963, frozen pipes burst, incurring further costs as the damage was put right, so it was not until later that a new alb and girdle could be purchased. On a more domestic note, a carpet sweeper was purchased in November 1963, aiding the work of those who cleaned the church.

In 1964, the Revd Baker noted more than 4,000 communicants for the year; but despite this, the Lent discussion group had to be cancelled due to lack of support. Although the Women's Club had closed after sixty years through lack of support, a new organisation, the Young Wives, was formed alongside the Mothers' Union. William Marchant Jones outlined plans to install a coffee bar in the Church Hall to attract younger people, and Joyce Button helped re-establish the Girls' Friendly Society, which started with seventeen members and helped to make new hassocks. (Many years previously, Mrs Josephine Wade, wife of the Revd Joseph Wade, had formed a branch of the GFS.) Other efforts to attract younger people into the church included the revitalisation of the Sunday School, and a new junior choir with fourteen members.

Jack Coles continued to give faithful service to the church in many capacities. In 1965, when he marked his thirtieth year as Treasurer, he was commended for his "conscientious and capable work".

In the PCC Minutes for October 1965, the Revd Baker "spoke of the difficulty of car expenses and National Health Insurance stamps, but the Council felt no decision could be taken at the present time". Clearly he was very concerned about his finances, clergy stipends at this time being very low in comparison with other professions. So he raised the matter again at the November meeting and was met with a similarly ungenerous response. "The matter of financial help with the Vicar's car was brought up again but everyone present was of the opinion that no funds were available at the moment that could be spared for this purpose. It was also felt that this was an unusual practice except in cases where the incumbent was in charge of more than one parish." Half a century later, the PCC has a far more caring and generous attitude towards its clergy.

By 1966 the daily Communion had been reduced to twice a week, usually Wednesday and Thursday. At the PCC meeting in January 1966, the Revd Baker raised the subject of falling numbers in church—at 8.00 am there were now fewer communicants and often less than two dozen communicants at 9.30 am. He announced that on the second Sunday of each month there would be a Family Service at 9.30 am at which children would take part, and that the Parish Eucharist on that Sunday would be held at 6.00 pm. A long discussion followed! It was agreed that there would be a trial period of three months, followed by a review of the situation. In March the Revd Baker reported to the PCC that the new service had been a success, and this arrangement continued throughout the rest of his ministry at Holy Trinity.

1967 brought the purchase of materials for new albs. Repairs to the church clock were carried out by Gerhard Drescher, as well as the repayment of a loan of £125 from the Reconstructed Bath Stone Company, which was owned by William Marchant Jones. This was in connection with the purchase of the Miners' Welfare Institute (see chapter 12).

At the PCC meeting of 7 June 1967, members stood in silence as a tribute to the memory of William Marchant Jones, who had died aged 83. His funeral at Holy Trinity was reported in the *Somerset Guardian and Standard* of 16 June. The service was conducted by the Revd Leonard Baker, assisted by Jack Coles (Lay Reader), who read a lesson. Norman Button played the organ, and the choir led the singing of Psalm 122 and the hymns "We love the place, O God" and "Soldiers of Christ, arise". He was laid to rest in the churchyard. The church was full to overflowing and the list of those present took up thirty column inches in the local newspaper. A brass plaque was put underneath the window which W M Jones had given to the church in 1957. It read:

> In memory of William Marchant Jones, chorister and choirmaster
> 1884–1967. Also of his wife Mabel Mary 1882 to 1935.
> Lord I have loved the habitation of thy house.

Perhaps the biggest change at Holy Trinity came in April 1968, when the annual meeting discussed the new Holy Communion service. It was agreed that from Easter, the 1662 service from the *Book of Common Prayer* (*BCP*) would be retained for the 8.00 am service but that other services would follow the new order. The Service Register records the introduction of *Series 2* on Sunday, 5 November 1967, presumably experimentally until the decision at the Annual Meeting the following April.

New Services In 1965 a new service of Holy Communion for experimental use was authorised by the Church of England as an alternative to the *Book of Common Prayer*. This was known as *Alternative Services: Series 2*. A later Revision was known as *Series 3*; and in 1980 these, along with other services, were authorised for use as the *Alternative Service Book*, known as the *ASB*, in which *Series 2* became *Rite B* and *Series 3* became *Rite A*. These experimental services were the first attempt at modern language in worship and were initially controversial. The *ASB* has now been replaced by the greatly improved *Common Worship*.

An earlier attempt at Prayer Book revision had been made in 1927, when the *Book of Common Prayer* was fully revised and ready for use but was rejected by Parliament. (Because the Church of England is the Established Church, i.e. the State Church, matters of doctrine have to be approved by Parliament.) It was passed in the House of Lords but rejected in the House of Commons. In 1928 an amended version was prepared but it was still rejected. However, *The 1928 Prayer Book* was widely used even though it was not officially authorised, and in the early 1960s the Communion Service was issued in a small booklet known as *Series 1*. This was largely supplanted by *Series 2*.

William Marchant Jones has been part of Holy Trinity (and thus of this book) for a large proportion of its history, just as he was part of the village for many decades. He was a "self-made" man, having left school aged eleven to work in the local mines like so many other village lads of the day. He bought a shop at the Crossway and became a grocer, but was also a photographer, and tried his hand at repertory theatre. During the First World War, he commanded the Norton Radstock Divisional Special Constabulary. Between the Wars, he realised that the local dialects were in danger of extinction, so he created "Jarge Balsh", firstly as a column for the *Somerset Guardian* and the *Bristol Evening World*. Then the best were published in book form, and in 2005 some of the stories were issued on compact disc, thanks to the efforts of Robin Thompson, one of the few people who can still speak the Coleford dialect.

After World War II, with the mines closing and men coming back home needing work, W M Jones founded Reconstructed Bath Stone Ltd at Newbury and gave work to many returning servicemen.

W M Jones had a finger in most local pies! He was Chairman of Frome Rural District Council 1940–46; Chairman of Frome National Savings Association; a member of Frome Board of Guardians and Public Assistance Committee; and was involved in town and country planning. He was heavily involved with football, both locally as Chairman of Coleford Athletic, but also at County level.

He loved Holy Trinity and brought the large choir to a standard of excellence that has never been surpassed. His relationship with the various clergy blew hot and cold—if he disapproved of one he would resign, but usually came back! His gift of a new window in 1957, by stained glass artist Keith New, reflected his love of modern art and architecture. His own house, Mendip Ho, is another example of his appreciation of modernity. His final gift to Holy Trinity was in enabling the purchase of the Miners' Welfare Institute for church use.

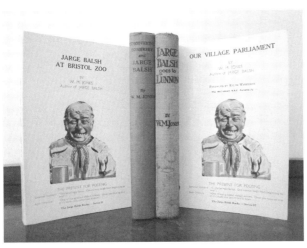

Jarge Balsh books by William Marchant Jones

The **Revd Sidney Wood** studied at Rochester Theological College, and was ordained deacon in 1963 and priest in 1964. He was curate of Kingston on Thames 1963–65. He then moved to Stokenchurch with Cadmore End from 1965–66, after which he was Rector of Heyford Warren with Lower Heyford and Rousham 1966–69. He exchanged this living with the Revd Leonard Baker, coming to Coleford in July 1969 until 1971 when he moved to Chingford in the Chelmsford diocese, having exchanged livings with the Revd Ernest Byles.

The number of baptisms increased, but the Revd Baker lamented that, of the thirty-three in 1968, only four or five were from families closely attached to the church.

The Revd Leonard Baker left Coleford in July 1969, a week before the Dedication Festival, and the services on that day were taken by Fr John Sutters, a familiar face to many of the congregation. By then many of the people who remain regular members at the beginning of the 21st century were taking an active part in the church and its associated activities. The Revd Baker was succeeded by the **Revd Sidney Gordon Wood**, who was instituted and inducted by the Bishop of Bath and Wells (the Right Revd Edward Henderson) on 25 July 1969. In fact the Revd Baker and the Revd Wood had exchanged parishes with one another, Leonard Baker moving to the parishes of Upper and Lower Heyford with Rousham in the Diocese of Oxford, and the Revd Sidney Wood moving from there to Coleford.

At the first PCC meeting chaired by the Revd Sidney Wood, it was agreed that "for the coming winter the monthly 'family service' be dropped, unless the Vicar felt it would be appropriate to have one at 11.00 am, and the Family Communion Service be continued every Sunday". At the same meeting the Minutes record that "a discussion followed re suggestions made by the Vicar for various alterations in the Church. It was agreed that this matter should be put on the agenda for the next meeting". No details of these proposed alterations were recorded, and following the discussion at the next meeting, it was decided that no immediate action would be taken.

In 1970 the Mothers' Union and the Young Wives were both dissolved, and a new inter-denominational Women's Fellowship took its place. The new group had pledged its support to the Church, although later the church affiliation was dropped. Even so, many Church members belonged to the Women's Fellowship, which continued for about thirty-five years.

1970 brought more changes, as financial support for the church and its work became an increasing problem for a smaller congregation. This was helped, in part, by the introduction of a new envelope system for weekly offerings. Early in 1970, there was an alarming deficit of over £80 in the general fund and a small deficit in the parish magazine account. The churchyard fund and restoration funds were both solvent. By hard work and an anonymous donation, the general fund was solvent by the summer, but the number of incoming bills would soon swallow up the funds, so there was no room for complacency. As a gesture of help to the Church, the licensee of the Kings

Head (Robin Thompson) offered to run a Bingo session for a few weeks and to give the proceeds to Holy Trinity.

The parish magazine was a further casualty of hard times. It had been struggling financially for some years, and in July 1970 the Revd Wood reported the high production cost to the PCC. It was decided to replace the printed magazine with a single foolscap sheet which would be delivered free to every house in the parish. This was not brought about until 1972 although in September 1971 a typewriter had been purchased.

The new Church School building in the centre of the village was dedicated on 24 September 1970. (See chapter 13 on the Church School.) Changes were also afoot in the Sunday School, details of which may be found in chapter 13.

The House of Laity of the Diocesan Synod had grasped the nettle of parish expenses, and a discussion took place at the PCC meeting in February 1971, the result of which was the decision that in lieu of paying the vicar's telephone account, a total sum of £70 be paid towards his expenses and that the situation should be reviewed in 1972.

At the Parish Annual General Meeting in 1971, "the Vicar expressed his appreciation of all those whom [sic] had contributed to the life and work of the Church during the past year. In worship there had been a satisfactory consolidation. The Family Eucharist was now firmly established and there was an upward trend in the number of people attending this service. There had been changes in the Children's work which seemed to be appropriate. The Garden party, the Dedication Festival, the opening of the new school, and the establishment of the playgroup had all been happy occasions."

With regard to the church services, the *New English Bible* had been in use since 1969, and new hymn books were purchased in 1971. Jack Coles informed the PCC at the meeting in April 1971 that after serving for thirty years as a Lay Reader, he had now relinquished his Licence. The Revd Wood thanked him for such faithful service for so many years. This was not the end of his service to Holy Trinity, merely one aspect of it, and he would continue to serve at the altar and to train boys as altar servers, as well as continuing to serve as Churchwarden.

On 19 September 1971, Festal Evensong was attended by the Lord Lieutenant of Somerset. The preacher was the Archdeacon of Wells, and the visit was deemed a great success.

Another sign of the times came with discussions about the locking of the church overnight for security reasons, although it was hoped that this would only

Church Government The Church of England has a four-tier system of government. Firstly, the **General Synod** is the Church of England's Governing Body, having replaced the Church Assembly in 1970. Next comes the **Diocesan Synod**, and then within each diocese there are a number of deaneries, i.e. groups of parishes, whose clergy and representative lay people meet together as the **Deanery Synod**. At parish level there is the **Parochial Church Council**. PCC members elect the Deanery Synod who in turn elect the members of the Diocesan and General Synods.

be a temporary measure. The church had been vandalised several times over the past few years. Keys for the church doors were purchased in 1971, and today the church is locked when not in use.

Despite financial pressure, fundraising went on apace for a variety of causes in the early 1970s. In addition to the Pakistan Flood Relief Fund, donations were made to the Kumi Uganda Mission Hospital, the Seaman's Mission, the Bible Society, the Save the Children Fund, the Church of England Children's Society, Mother Teresa's Hospital in Calcutta and the Basle Air Disaster Fund. This latter was to support the families of Axbridge and Cheddar who had been devastated by the tragic loss of many parents on a trip to Basle, Switzerland.

In November 1971 the Revd Sidney Wood dropped a bombshell on the PCC by announcing his resignation as from 31 December. He suggested that the PCC should consider an exchange with the **Revd Ernest Byles**, Vicar of Chingford in the Diocese of Chelmsford. It was agreed to ask the Revd Byles to meet the PCC at an extraordinary meeting in November. The PCC "expressed its deep regret at this news [of the Revd Wood's resignation] and wished to place on record their appreciation of all that the Vicar had done during his too brief period in Coleford". The Extraordinary Meeting to meet the Revd Byles took place on 22 November 1971, and it was duly agreed that the exchange of livings would take place. It was also agreed that it should be recorded in the PCC Minutes that "the PCC regrets the speed with which the exchange is to be effected". This is difficult to understand a generation later when it is normal for a parish to face an interregnum of a year or more, and indeed when Holy Trinity would be effectively without a priest for almost two years in 2000–01. Nor did the PCC miss an opportunity to assert its authority by asking the Revd Byles (who had not yet been appointed) "various questions re Services". The first PCC meeting of 1972, held during the short time between vicars and chaired by Jack Coles, dealt with the question of the responsibilities of the PCC, and it was stressed that everyone should give all possible support, both to the Church and to the incumbent.

The Revd Sidney Wood

One final accomplishment of the Revd Sidney Wood must be mentioned. In 1971 he produced *A Short History of Coleford Church*; but alas, no copies have survived either in the parish records, the wider village, or the Somerset archives.

- 9 -

INTO THE MODERN ERA

THE **Revd Ernest William Byles** was instituted and inducted as Vicar of Coleford on 11 January 1972 by the Bishop of Taunton.

In February 1972 it was agreed that a stencil duplicator should be purchased for producing the parish newsletter, and at the annual meeting the Revd Byles was able to thank Mr George for organising the project. An ad hoc Committee had been formed, consisting of Mr George, Mr Spearing and Mrs Bull, who had organised the purchase of paper, stencils, art insets and ink. These purchases reflect the technology of the time as copies were first typed onto a waxed stencil; fitted over a drum, which with every crank of a handle was inked; and copied onto a blank sheet of special duplicating paper, with the covers being printed separately. Then, as now, advertisements were sold to help subsidise costs.

Financial pressure on the church continued to increase. In February 1972 Mr Lambert reported to the PCC that there was £20 in the current account and £140 in the deposit account, and there were several outstanding bills to be paid. In addition, a letter had been received from the organ builders, Osmonds of Taunton, stressing the need for overhauling and cleaning, as nothing had been done for more than twenty years! Following their inspection they had valued the instrument at £6,000 and recommended necessary work on cleaning and repairs. The PCC, in addition to setting up yet another committee to consider this report, agreed that Osmonds should be asked to carry out the repairs as soon as possible and that the vicar should ask them whether they would be willing to wait twelve to eighteen months for payment of the bill of £550.

In addition to finding the money for the organ repairs, a significant increase in the Diocesan Quota (now known as the Parish Share of the Diocesan Common Fund) was anticipated, while collections continued to fall. Difficulties in maintaining an aging

Born in 1909, the **Revd Ernest Byles** graduated from London University in 1931. He trained for ordination at Bishops' College, Cheshunt, and was ordained deacon in 1936 and priest in 1937. He was curate of Brentford 1936–49, including time as Chaplain to the Forces 1940–45. Two incumbencies followed in Chelmsford diocese before he came to Coleford 1972–74, having exchanged livings with the Revd Sidney Wood. He retired in 1974 and died in Bristol in November 1992.

building were also encountered because of the Faculty system, which requires the granting of legal permission from the diocese before any major work may be undertaken on the church. This often involves significant administrative work as well as delaying urgent repair work. In the period under review there was a financial cost too.

The Revd Byles did not keep detailed notes in the Service Registers, and so any changes he may have made are not readily apparent. The 8.00 am Holy Communion had a congregation of four to eight communicants, and there were about twenty-four to thirty-six communicants at the 10.00 am Family Communion. There may have been more

> The **Diocesan Quota**, or **Parish Share**, is the amount of money paid per year by each parish towards the running costs of the Diocese, which includes the stipends of the clergy. (Those clergy who are non-stipendiary are financially self-supporting.) In addition, each parish is responsible for the running costs and maintenance of its own church building, unlike continental churches, which are maintained by the State.

present but these numbers are not recorded, nor are numbers at Evensong. Even so, these communicant numbers show a significant drop. In addition, Holy Communion was also celebrated on Wednesday and Thursday. So it is not readily apparent what it was that had dissatisfied the PCC when, at their meeting in February 1972 (less than a month after the Revd Byles' licensing), "Mr Spearing asked for elaboration on the paragraph in the News Letter referring to Church Services. A long discussion followed and it became clear that some people were not happy about changes which had been made. Certain changes were agreed upon to be made right away, and the matter should be brought to the next meeting …" At the next meeting it was decided to hold a special meeting on 15 March, and that it would be open to all members of the congregation. This meeting was not minuted, so we do not know the nature of the grievances, nor are any decisions on record. But there may be a clue in the PCC Minutes for July 1972, when "the vicar explained his reasons [not recorded] for suggesting that flowers should be in Church during the penitential seasons [i.e. Advent and Lent], but after discussion he said that as it was obvious that the members of the PCC were against this suggestion, the matter would be dropped". The suggestion (by Mrs Byles) that the church should have an Easter Candle was met with unanimous approval, and Mr Manley offered to make a tall candle stand for it. This was first used at the Vigil Service on Easter Eve 1973. And on a festive note, the PCC decided in 1972 to have a Christmas tree and appealed for decorations. Mrs Habershon provided the tree and Mary Plummer the decorations. Mary and Geoffrey Plummer still decorate the Christmas tree at the time of writing.

The winds of change were beginning to blow in the diocese, and inevitably the local parishes were to be affected. The first hint came in October 1972 when Jack Coles reported to the PCC on a meeting of the Deanery Synod. Under the heading of "Pastoral Reorganisation", it had been suggested that at some time in the future it might be necessary for Coleford and Holcombe to share the same priest.

On more practical matters, an appeal was made for a piano, and following difficulties relating to choir practice, it was announced that Mrs Byles would be undertaking the training of the choir. A new version of the Holy Communion, known as *Series 3*, had recently been approved by the General Synod and was being used experimentally by some churches. A demonstration of the service was given at St John's, Frome, on Monday, 26 February 1973, and six people from Holy Trinity attended. In March the PCC meeting was preceded by a Eucharist according to the *Series 3* rite. Although no vote was taken that evening regarding permanent usage, it was decided to use the service from time to time so that people could come to a decision. In fact it was not adopted during the Revd Byles' incumbency.

Deaconess J J Turner preached at both services at the Harvest Festival in 1973, possibly the first time a woman had preached at Holy Trinity. She was the deaconess at Chingford parish church where the Revd Byles had previously served. The following year the Revd Sidney Wood preached at Evensong at the Dedication Festival.

The church was not introspective despite all the financial concerns at this time. During this same period, Lent boxes had produced £10 for USPG, and almost £14 had been sent to Christian Aid. Also, support was given to the Somerset Churches Family Welfare Association, the Wells Archdeaconry Clerical Charity and the Church of England Pensions Board. Collections on Christmas Day were sent to the Helen Keller School for blind children in Jerusalem.

More gusts of the wind of change manifested themselves in November 1973 when "the vicar reported that the Diocesan Board of Finance asked for the co-operation of the PCC when the matter of the vicarage had to be dealt with. The DBF wished at a later stage, when there is a change of incumbency, to sell the present vicarage which they consider uneconomic, and build a new one in the grounds". Meanwhile, early in 1974, the death occurred of the Rector of Holcombe, the Revd Osmund Tunnell. The Revd Byles informed the Coleford PCC that this would probably mean that he would in due course become priest in charge of Holcombe, but that this would not affect Coleford. He was also very anxious to emphasise that it

---

Deaconesses The deaconess ministry was a lay ministry, i.e. not part of the three-fold order of ordained ministry of bishop, priest and deacon, and was introduced into the Church of England in 1862. In 1987 the General Synod passed a Measure permitting the ordination of women as deacons, and many former deaconesses were duly ordained. It was not until 1992 that the Synod passed the Measure allowing women to be ordained to the priesthood, and the first ordinations did not take place until 1994. The debate continues in the Church of England regarding the consecration of women as bishops, but other parts of the worldwide Anglican Communion, notably the USA, Canada and New Zealand, have already taken this step.

did *not* mean he would be paid a double stipend! (As recently as the 1970s, parishes were still accustomed to having their own vicar, and while a generation later it does not seem unusual for several parishes to be grouped under one incumbent, it was not normal at that time. Things were just about to change on a large scale throughout the Church of England.) Clergy salaries, known as stipends, were notoriously low at this time, and the Bishop of Bath and Wells sent out a Pastoral Letter to all parishes urging them to pay an extra 10% on their Parish Share so that the clergy stipends could be brought up to the minimum suggested by the Church of England's Central Board of Finance. The Coleford PCC, having considered the matter, agreed to pay the extra.

In May 1974 the Revd Byles told the PCC that "the Bishop had suspended presentation to Holcombe [i.e. had deferred appointing a new Rector], but there was no question at present of the parishes being linked. The vicar had been asked to be, for the present, priest in charge of Holcombe". But things moved fast and a month later he told the PCC that "the Bishop had postponed the date of his licensing to Holcombe but he would be acting as priest in charge for the present". This time of uncertainty was probably very stressful for both parishes and for the Revd Byles and his wife. By July 1974 the whole situation had changed once more, and at the beginning of the PCC meeting the vicar "announced his impending resignation which was to take place in September. He said that he and Mrs Byles were very happy in Coleford, but that the failing health of his wife and other recent happenings in respect of his family, had made him decide to retire at the age of 65 which he would reach in September. Mr Coles spoke for the Council in saying that it was regretted that the poor health of Mrs Byles should have made this decision necessary."

There was a special meeting of the PCC on 24 July 1974, and a discussion was held about the future incumbent. The Secretary (Miss Ackroyd) was directed to write to the Patron of the living (the Rector of Kilmersdon), making the following points: "that the new incumbent should be happy and willing to uphold the traditions of the church and its standard of worship. That he should have a concern for the young people, and be prepared to visit those who could not get to Church. It was also felt strongly that he should live at the present vicarage, and suggestions were made how this could be done. A letter from the Diocesan Board of Finance was also to be answered in these terms."

The PCC had a valid concern because at this time they had no direct influence in the appointment of a new incumbent. Traditionally, this was done by the Patron of the living in consultation with the Bishop. It was not until 1986 that a new Pastoral Measure of the General Synod, the Patronage (Benefices) Measure, enabled two parish representatives to interview applicants and strongly influence the choice of their new incumbent.

The Archdeacon of Bath, the Rural Dean and the Patron attended the PCC meeting in September 1974, and the Archdeacon outlined the reasons for suggesting the uniting of Coleford with Holcombe. His three main proposals were:

- The uniting of the two benefices, i.e. the two parishes
- The decision regarding the vicarage
- Agreement for suspension of presentation to the living of Coleford and the appointment of a priest in charge.

After a long discussion three resolutions were passed unanimously:

1. The PCC agreed to the proposed union of the benefices of Coleford and Holcombe;
2. The PCC considered it essential that the incumbent should reside in Coleford, and would welcome a consultation with the diocese concerning the present vicarage;
3. The PCC agreed to the suspension of presentation to the living, pending pastoral reorganisation. (Once the two parishes were united, the new incumbent would be instituted as Rector of the new united benefice.)

Meanwhile, the Revd Byles' final Sunday was 8 September, his 65th birthday, and a presentation was made to him after Evensong. He and Mrs Byles left the parish for their retirement in North Devon on 17 September.

A large and varied number of signatures in the Register indicates the variety of clergy and lay readers officiating at services during the interregnum. The year closed with a new set of crib figures, costing £45, given by the Sunday School. They were used for the first time at Christmas 1974.

In November 1974 a delegation from the Diocesan Board of Finance had inspected the vicarage and decided to retain it for a further five years. Essential repairs would be done and a financial contribution would be required from Holy Trinity. The PCC undertook to raise money by various means, including a jumble sale, and a coffee evening at the home of Fred and Rose Plummer. In February 1975 the appointment was announced of the **Revd Alan Coleman** to the united benefice of Coleford with Holcombe. Fr Coleman attended the February PCC together with Mrs Coleman and eight members of Holcombe PCC.

The **Revd Alan Coleman** was born in 1922, and he had been awarded the DFC in 1944 and Bar in 1945, giving him a lifelong interest both in the Forces and in the uniformed organisations that met in the village. He trained for ordination at Wells Theological College and was ordained deacon in 1966 and priest in 1967. He was curate of St John's, Bury, 1966–68; Vicar of Wilton-in-Cleveland 1969–73, together with Senior Chaplain, Missions to Seamen, Middlesborough, 1969–73; Vicar of Flamborough 1973–75. He became Rector of Coleford with Holcombe 1975–82. He then returned to the Missions to Seamen, 1982–83; Rector of Gunhouse with Burringham in Lincoln diocese 1983–87. He retired in 1987 and died in 1990.

The licensing of Fr Coleman as priest in charge of the joint benefice took place at Holy Trinity on Monday, 7 April 1975, in the presence of the Bishop of Bath and Wells (Bishop Edward Henderson), the Archdeacon of Bath (the Venerable John Burgess) and the Rural Dean (the Revd Roger Fookes). This was to be Bishop Henderson's last visit to Coleford before his retirement. He had proved to be a very popular bishop, and as a mark of gratitude he was presented with a book token by Jack Coles, and his wife was presented with a bouquet of flowers by Vivienne Plummer. There was a Service of Welcome for Fr Coleman at St Andrew's, Holcombe, on 10 April, and a coach was booked for the choir and congregation from Holy Trinity.

Once the legal proceedings were completed, Fr Coleman was instituted as the first Rector of the united benefice, by the Bishop in his chapel at the Palace in Wells. This took place on Thursday, 10 July 1975. The joint Service of Induction took place at St Andrew's, Holcombe, on Sunday, 7 September at 6.30 pm.

The PCC Minutes reveal a similar pattern to parish life as in former years, with the familiar struggle to make ends meet financially, the difficulty of maintaining an aging building which was also subject to vandalism, and there was the Church Hall to maintain too. The advent of a new vicar always boosts church attendance (at least for a time), and Fr Alan Coleman's arrival was no exception. After two aging incumbents who did not stay very long, his time in the parish brought a period of stability, while taking on board fresh challenges. Certainly the incumbency of Fr Alan Coleman is fondly remembered by parishioners a generation later.

The pattern of services continued in the same vein as before, with 8.00 am Holy Communion, 10.00 am Sung Eucharist, and 6.00 pm Evensong. Numbers increased at all Sunday services and remained healthy at around seven to ten at 8.00 am, and thirty-five to forty-five at 10.00 am. However, it became apparent that with two churches in the benefice there had to be some adjustment to the service times. From Easter 1977 the 8.00 am Holy Communion would be at Coleford on the 1st, 3rd and 5th Sundays and at Holcombe on the 2nd and 4th Sundays. The Parish Communion would be at 9.30 am at Coleford and 11.00 am at Holcombe. Evensong would be at 6.00 pm at Coleford, except on the first Sunday of the month when it would be at Holcombe. Weekday Communions were celebrated on various days, and on Saturday evening there was Compline (Night Prayer) and prayers for the sick.

The parish newsletter had struggled along in its stencil-duplicated form, but in January 1976 it was replaced by a new magazine to be called *On the Map*. The newsletter had been distributed free of charge, but the new magazine, which would be for both the church and the wider community of both villages, would be sold at 5 pence per copy, or 50 pence for the year. Decimalisation had arrived!

Records show that there was a lively social calendar at Holy Trinity with a Shrove Tuesday Social, and a Harvest Supper.

Some improvements to the church interior took place in 1976. The choir stalls and other furnishings in the chancel were stripped and polished, and cord carpet was laid in the aisles. There had been some vandalism to the church windows.

The Bishop of Bath and Wells had written a paper called *A Standard for Anglicans* in which he urged all Anglicans to give 5p in the pound of all remaining income after meeting domestic commitments. This money would be used for the work of the Church. After discussion the PCC decided not to implement "the standard" in the form suggested, but to encourage people to consider their commitment and their level of giving. Writing in *On the Map* in March 1977, Fr Coleman suggested an overall approach to Christian commitment. "I hope we can find ways and means of increasing the income of our two Parish Churches … But I would like to propose a different standard for Anglicans in Coleford and Holcombe. It concerns not just the raising of the giving but more importantly the raising of the spiritual standards, the quality of life and the quality of worship, and the regularity of worship by more and more Christian people here. If we raise our spiritual sights, I have faith enough that the financial needs will be met by natural and free means, rather than by enforced and detached methods … I urge all Christians, of whatever denomination to make a firm resolve to turn to Christ … to use Lent to get back into the regular habit of church-going." Although the numbers attending Holy Trinity were good when compared with numbers in the early 21st century, the conflict of loyalties between Sunday worship versus secular interests was already under way. Affordable motor cars and the increase in secular Sunday activities were beginning to plot the downward trend in church attendance which would accelerate in the coming years.

1977 marked the Silver Jubilee of Queen Elizabeth II, and on 5 June (Trinity Sunday) at 3.15 pm there was a Thanksgiving Service at Holy Trinity. Numbers were not recorded but over £30 was sent to the Prince of Wales' Jubilee Fund.

In March 1977 Fr Coleman informed the PCC that advance notice had been given that plans would shortly be made for the building of a new vicarage within the grounds of the then vicarage. But by the September meeting the diocesan architect had recommended that the vicarage be retained and that repairs and improvements should be made to it. Fr Coleman recommended that the PCC should send a letter to the Diocesan Board of Finance outlining the required work. By October there was confusion all round. The Diocesan Surveyor had sent Fr Coleman a schedule of work to be done on the vicarage, but this had been followed by a telephone call and a letter from the Archdeacon of Bath saying that the decision had been made to build a new vicarage at a cost of £35,000–£40,000. A meeting was arranged between the Archdeacon, members of the Houses and Glebe Committee of the diocese, the vicar, and the Churchwardens of both parishes. By February 1978 the Diocesan Board of Finance had decided (subject to planning permission) to sell the vicarage and to build a new one within the grounds. The issue was to continue throughout 1978, causing increasing frustration both to the PCC, who felt they were being deprived of an important and integral part of the parish structure, and to the incumbent, whose living space and garden were to be seriously disrupted. The year ended with a diocesan decision not to build the new house for three to five years.

As the 1970s gave way to a new decade, thoughts were turning towards July 1981—

the 150th anniversary of the dedication of Holy Trinity. In November 1979 a group from the PCC, to be known as the '81 Committee, was convened, consisting of Malcolm Plummer (chairman), Ann Crawford, Marion Connock, Liz Bull and Roy Thurkettle. Their task would be to raise funds to put the church and the hall into good order, and as a start there would be a children's disco on 20 November 1979 from 7.30 pm until 9.30 pm. Other events included mince pies with bring and buy on 10 December at the home of Fred and Rose Plummer, a cheese and wine party at the vicarage in January, and a local crafts exhibition in the Church Hall in February. In addition there were car treasure hunts, musical evenings, and a "talent" scheme where people were given a "talent" of £1 and invited to increase it by a given date. (The "talent" scheme was inspired by Jesus' parable of the talents in St Matthew 25:14–30 and parable of the pounds in St Luke 19:11–27.) And there were sponsored events such as "knit-ins" and "bake-ins". Fundraising activities continued in a similar way throughout 1980 and up to the 150th anniversary. The target figure was £5,000, which seemed a colossal amount in the early 1980s.

Nor did Holy Trinity forget the needs of the wider world at this time. Christian Aid, the Church Army, Missions to Seamen, diocesan clergy charities, and the United Society for the Propagation of the Gospel all benefited from special church collections at this time.

The coming of the new decade was to be the swansong for the vicarage and its extensive grounds. During 1980, the Rector and Churchwardens had been informed by the Archdeacon that plans to sell the vicarage and build a new one in the grounds would now proceed as a matter of urgency. It was hoped that the work would be finished by the autumn of 1981. Following the receipt of a letter from the Church Commissioners asking the views of the PCC, it was decided to frame a written objection to the Commissioners. But at a special joint meeting of both PCCs held in October 1980, the decision was made to withdraw the objections and to agree to the provision of a new vicarage. (Twenty years later the diocese decided to sell, as a building plot, half of the garden of the new rectory. The PCC were informed by the diocesan authorities that the decision was final. Nor did Holy Trinity benefit financially from the sale of the land, all the proceeds going to the diocese.)

1980 drew to a close with a number of special services in church in addition to the usual Advent and Christmas Services, including Midnight Mass. Bishop Henderson School came to church and presented the Christmas Story in their own special way, including an upbeat rendering of *The Holly and the Ivy*. Then on Advent 2 at 6.00 pm and the following Tuesday at 7.30 pm, the Coleford Theatre Group presented *Everyman*. While being reluctant to mention the cast by name, the vicar did mention Jeff Power in the title role, Roy Pannel as the Producer and the organist Norman Button. And on Advent 3 at 6.00 pm, the Paragon Singers came from Bath for an Advent Carol Service. The evening of Advent 4 saw the Festival of Nine Lessons and Carols led by the church choir.

1981—the 150th Jubilee year of the church—dawned with an enthusiastic report in

On the Map by the '81 Committee giving details of work to be done. Although a target of £5,000 had been set, only £1,607 had been raised, but this was sufficient to proceed with redecorating the main part of the church interior. The vestries and porch would be done by volunteers from the congregation. During the redecoration, services were held in the vicarage and the Church Hall. Also, the Committee planned new toilets for the Church Hall. The church clock, which had given much trouble, was now put in good working order once again, and had been lit up too. Fundraising for the church was also being undertaken by village organisations, and in January 1981 the Brownies donated £50, which they had raised themselves.

There was a parish confirmation on 10 March (Lent 3) at which ten candidates from Coleford and six from Holcombe were confirmed by the Bishop of Taunton. But the event was overshadowed by a burglary at Holy Trinity during the previous night. Amongst the items stolen were three pairs of altar candlesticks, the alms dish, the font ewer and the missal stand. These were later recovered or replaced.

A special souvenir edition of *On the Map* was produced to mark the 150th anniversary of the church, and it included a brief history from the parish records, researched and written by Barbara Ackroyd. It also included a sketch of the church interior in 1981. After many changes over the 150 years, the interior has not changed greatly since then. The 150th anniversary celebrations were spread over two weeks from 13–26 July and encompassed both social and religious events. The actual anniversary of dedication (19 July) fell on a Sunday. The 8.00 am Holy Communion was celebrated by Fr Leonard Baker, back in Coleford for the celebrations, and there were thirteen communicants. The Festival Eucharist at 9.30 am was attended by 192 people of whom 132 received Holy Communion. Bishop Edward Henderson, former Bishop of Bath and Wells, preached, and three former vicars were present—Fr Sutters, the Revd Leonard Baker and the Revd Ernest Byles. In the evening there was Festal Evensong at which the preacher was the Rt Revd John Bickersteth, Bishop of Bath and Wells, and there was a congregation of over 180 people. There was a Festal Evensong for the churches in the deanery on Tuesday 23 July at which the preacher was the Bishop of Gloucester. The Archdeacon of Bath (the Venerable John Burgess) was also present, as well as a congregation exceeding 200.

A photograph of the newly painted church interior shows it looking splendid. And the choir had their photograph taken with Fr Coleman. The anniversary celebrations also included an exhibition in the Church Hall of photographs of "old Coleford", a concert by the children of Bishop Henderson School, a musical evening by the choir and organist, a garden party at the vicarage, a concert by Frome Operatic Society, and a barbeque at the vicarage. All in all it was an anniversary to remember.

The '81 Committee, having discharged its duties, was wound up in September 1981, and its remaining funds were transferred to the church and hall accounts. £3,696 had been raised (plus interest, which would bring the total up to around £4,000). It was estimated that an outlay of approximately £1,500 had been saved by members of the congregation helping with the various restoration projects.

The newly painted church interior, 1981

D HULL (*CHOIRMASTER*), F PLUMMER, N BUTTON (*ORGANIST*), REV A COLEMAN (*RECTOR*), J TURNER (*SEXTON*), E COLES, W WITHERS
P EDWARDS, J POWER, B WITHERS, H HAMBLIN, J DONALD, G COLEMAN, R PLUMMER, A CRAWFORD, P COLES
S GOULD, G PLUMMER, A BULL, S PLUMMER, M VINE, M BULL, F GOULD, J FLOWER, J TILL, A TURNER

The Choir with Fr Coleman, 1981

After all the build-up to the 150th anniversary, the responsibility of pastoral care for two parishes single-handedly, and the ongoing saga of the future of the vicarage, it is hardly surprising that Fr Alan Coleman was struck down by sickness in September 1981. A whole series of signatures from local clergy appear in the Service Register from 24 September until 29 October when the rector returned. (One signature that appears during this time was that of Don Thompson, Lay Reader from St Andrew's, Holcombe.) Advent 3 was like a return to the frozen winters of many years before, with a note in the Service Register: "Coldest weather for 100 years. Minus 20 degrees Centigrade. Snow and ice. Blizzard in evening prevented Sung Evensong—said in vicarage." The bad weather did not prevent the children from Bishop Henderson School coming to church for their Carol Services in the afternoon and evening of 17 December, and the collections were given to Helen House Hospice for Children in Oxford. By the following Sunday, weather conditions were still poor: "Sub-zero temperature all week, but sunny. Snow & sleet, horrible this morning." And then on Christmas Eve, Fr Coleman collapsed again and was absent from his duties until the end of January 1982. By this time it became clear that he must resign due to his failing health, although it was not to be the end of his priestly ministry. Writing in *On the Map* in a letter dated 28 December 1981, Fr Coleman remarked, "I shall continue to pray for you all, and that a new parish priest will be found whom you can love as much as you seem to have loved me."

There was another sadness at Holy Trinity early in February 1982 when Norman Button collapsed and died at the organ just after receiving Holy Communion. He had been organist at Holy Trinity since the end of World War II and had contributed greatly to the strong musical and choral tradition. Fr Coleman was well enough to receive the coffin into church on Friday 19 February and to officiate at the funeral next day. £226 was collected in memory of Norman Button, and this was used to purchase a piano for use in the church.

> **Joyce Button** recalls that her husband Norman became organist early in 1946. His unexpected death came on 14 February when, having received Holy Communion, he returned to the organ and was playing "There is a green hill far away …" Although, as Phyllis Coles suggests, it was a terrible shock, Joyce felt that this was the way Norman would have chosen to die, and that has been a comfort to her over the years.

Also at this time, a pair of brass altar candlesticks was bought in memory of Jason Ilott, who had died tragically aged 15 years. These were bought to replace a pair stolen a year previously.

Fr Coleman's final Sunday as Rector of Coleford with Holcombe was on 28 February 1982 (Lent 1), although his signature appears in the Register until 14 March because he was not well enough to meet the demands of a Farewell Service and party. His final note in the Register said: "Thanks be to God for the joy of ministering in Coleford, and the love that has been shown to me and my wife over the past seven years, from all the dwellers here, and especially from those of the household of faith. And now abideth faith, hope, love; but the greatest of these is love." The Colemans moved to Shoreham on 15 March, after being presented with various gifts and cheques from both parish churches and the school. Fr Coleman was to be Missions to Seamen Chaplain at Shoreham harbour. He had exercised a fruitful ministry in Coleford and Holcombe and had encouraged the uniformed organisations and cultivated their attendance in church. He is remembered as one of the great incumbents of the parish.

The saga of the vicarage played on, and the July 1982 issue of *On the Map* reported that "the vicarage garden being in such a sorry mess due to the new building, Coleford Church Fete this year was held in and around the Hall. Not quite the same …" But by the next issue, as well as welcoming the new Rector, the **Revd Martin Percival**, the magazine editor was able to report that the new Rectory was ready for occupation.

But before looking at Fr Martin Percival's ministry, here are **Clarissa Cridland's** memories of the 1980s:

I moved to Coleford on Friday, 17 September 1982, two days after the licensing of Fr Martin Percival. I had put in an offer for 4 Rock Terrace in December 1981, but for various reasons it had taken over nine months for the house to become mine. In the meantime, I had been living in temporary accommodation in Peasedown St John, and on the previous Sunday, 12 September, Fr Peter Hazleton had announced that Coleford and Holcombe's new rector was to be instituted on Wednesday 15th, and urged as many people as possible from the congregation from St John's to attend. I decided that my first service in Coleford should be once I had actually moved, and so it was that I came to Holy Trinity shortly before 9.30 on Sunday 19 September—and found the spiritual home for which I had been looking.

I had come to Rock Terrace to collect my keys on the evening of Thursday 16th, and no sooner had the car been parked in the drive than Marge Smith, from number 2, was there to find out who I was. She asked me every question that she could think of, except how much I was earning, and then went to telephone people (she told me she was going to do this!). The question she didn't think of asking was whether I would be going to church.

On the Friday morning, I went and checked the service times on the church noticeboard, and met Mrs Habershon and Mrs Maddock. Mrs Habershon attended the 8.00 service, but when I arrived for the 9.30, Mrs Maddock ushered me into her pew. I was pleasantly surprised at how full the church was (having no idea that a new vicar attracts a large congregation!), and soon John Turner entered, carrying the cross, and the choir followed with Mike Turner, who was server, and Fr Martin behind. There seemed to be a lot of people in the choir, and I think Marge spotted me before I saw her. I am not sure whether she was more amazed at my being there, or annoyed that she had not found out beforehand.

After the service, there was coffee in the Church Hall, and Mrs Maddock took me there and proceeded to introduce me to a number of people. After about five minutes, Marge shot through the door and grabbed me from Mrs Maddock, hissing "she's my neighbour" as she took my arm and introduced me all over again. I cannot now remember exactly who I met, but certainly Joyce Button, Phyl and Eddie Coles, Jack Coles, and Eric and Eileen Whiffen. They were naturally all thrilled to learn that a 27-year-old had come to join the congregation!

Gradually I became more involved with the life of the church—I brought marrows to Harvest Festival that year; in November I started coming to Evensong, and I am sure I must have attended if not helped at the Christmas Bazaar. I was working for Purnells in Paulton at the time, and, following a talk I gave at Holcombe WI to which I brought some free books, Mrs Maddock asked me to help at the Summer Fete, and to bring some books there. There was a bit of resistance to the books from those who attended the fete—people did not want to spend 10p on a book, even if brand new. However, the free books became a feature of our Christmas and summer sales, and soon I was besieged by people asking what I had. This lasted until 1994 when I started work for myself, and I think the most we ever made on the book stall was over £90. I should say that the books were either officially given, or taken from the pile to be thrown out!

I had arranged to go away for Easter in 1983, being quite unprepared for the fact that there were special services during Holy Week. (After that, I made sure I was always here, although there were some years when I had to miss Palm Sunday and the first three days of Holy Week due to going away to the Bologna Book Fair, the dates of which fluctuated because of Easter. In the early 1990s, the Fair authorities proposed dates which would have meant I would have had to fly to Italy on Easter Day. I sent them a furious fax, and they changed their minds!)

Mrs Mercia Maddock and Miss Ackroyd at the church fete

In the summer of 1983, I joined the PCC, and began to learn more about how the church was run. In early 1984 I received a letter from Fr Martin to say that he would be leaving. I can remember Jack Coles saying that he hadn't thought he would stay very long, but he didn't think it would be this short! Soon after that, Mr Coles said that he would remain as Churchwarden to see the new vicar in, but that after that he needed to retire. At the same time, Miss Ackroyd indicated that she wanted to give up as PCC secretary. She was also on the Deanery Synod, and I was elected to take her place on that. When I gave my first report on the Synod to the PCC, I told of an evening of refreshments and wine, which rather shocked Miss Ackroyd, who said it had never been like that before.

It was Miss Ackroyd who made the arrangements for Fr Harry Franklin to take most of our services during the interregnum. He was a wonderful priest, and he used to come down the aisle blowing me kisses and calling me his darling girl!

Miss Ackroyd and Miss Jones shared a house between Coleford and Holcombe, and while Miss A was a member of Holy Trinity, Miss J was a member of Holcombe Methodist Church. Each supported the other's social and fundraising events, and we too found ourselves at Holcombe Methodist Church on more than one occasion. They had wonderful Strawberry Teas at Wheal Friendly, and if you were asked to help, you didn't say no. These carried on for several years, until Miss Ackroyd's health began to fail. Eventually she was in Frome Hospital, and I used to drive Miss Jones and Mercia Maddock there on a Sunday evening to visit.

Within a few months of my moving to Coleford, most people called me "Clarissa", but Miss Ackroyd and Miss Jones always refused, no matter how often I asked, insisting that they should call me Miss Cridland. It was probably at the Christmas Bazaar in 1984 that I heard Miss A say, "I'll just go and ask Clarissa ..." Then she came up to me. "Miss Cridland," she began ... After that, I was always Clarissa.

Fr David Watson (always Father Watson, or more usually simply Father, although since his retirement, David) and Beti arrived in the summer of 1984. They were both from New Zealand originally, but from different islands. They often used to have members of their family to stay, and I particularly remember Beti's niece, Rosemary, and David's daughter, Wendy, and her husband Keith. Their first child was christened in Holy Trinity in the late 1980s, and as soon as her grandfather took her in his arms, she screamed so much we couldn't hear the rest of the service! Soon afterwards, Beti asked me if I could look after the latest member of the family for a weekend. I was thrilled, though a little surprised when Beti asked me to come into the kitchen to see the latest member. Alas for my hopes! It was not the baby I was being asked to look after, but a budgie which Beti had acquired.

In the spring of 1985, Robert Maxwell, who owned Purnells, merged the publishing company for which I worked (run quite separately from the printing) with one of his other companies, Macdonald in London. I was one of the lucky ones not made redundant immediately, and I was given the choice of taking redundancy or working for Macdonald. It was a difficult choice but in the end I opted for the latter, but I didn't want to leave Coleford, and more importantly, Holy Trinity, and so I arranged to live in London during the week, and come home at weekends. At first this meant getting home late on Fridays, but in 1987 I joined Macmillan and was able to be in Basingstoke on Fridays, and home by 6.30. I would return to London on Monday morning, leaving shortly after 4.00 am. I did this weekly commute for nine years. During this time, I had to resign from the PCC and Deanery Synod, since I was unable to get to meetings, but I remained a Sidesman, and later became Sacristan. At one point Fr Watson asked me to lead the Sunday School he was forming, but I refused. He was very taken aback, but I had always hated Sunday School as a child, wanting to come to church instead (the vicar where I was living at the time would not have children in church except at Christmas and Easter). When I came home on Fridays, I would often find notes from members of the congregation, reminding me that there was a coffee morning, or, horror of horrors, that I was due to help with the flowers.

Joyce Button was in charge of the flowers, and very soon after I arrived in Coleford, she told me she was putting me on the flower rota, and took no notice when I said that I couldn't arrange flowers. Being on the flower rota simply meant doing the altar flowers as Joyce did the rest, and the first time my name was on the list, I met Joyce in church and she showed me how to arrange flowers. I think she was a bit taken aback by my hopelessness in this area, but she left me on the rota. The next time I quite forgot, and the congregation arrived on Sunday morning to find an empty pedestal, Joyce having taken out the flowers. The time after, Joyce didn't want to take the risk, and so she left the flowers in. I took one look, and decided that they looked better than anything I could do, and so I did nothing. This happened a few times, and then I suggested to Joyce that I should just give her some money and she could do my flowers. She was hugely relieved. A few years later, in the early 1990s, I was doing business with a Japanese man, and he sent flowers for the church at Easter. The first year the florist rang me, and I changed the order and asked for spring flowers to be delivered. Joyce was not pleased as I had messed up the colours she had chosen (yellow and white), and so the following year I was warned and asked for lilies instead. Yoshi Kohno continued to send flowers for several years, although sometimes they arrived after Easter, and even now he occasionally rings up and asks after the church.

Jack Coles remained an active member of Holy Trinity after his retirement, and several years later he took Evensong one evening, when no one turned up. He simply got up, and did what he had done so often before, singing everything so that it really was Even*song*.

John Kestin was the other Churchwarden when I arrived in Coleford, taking over from Charlie Lambert. John was at that time a widower, but one Sunday in the mid 1980s he appeared in church with Sylvia, whom he showed to a pew, while he went to sing in the choir as usual. John and Sylvia were married very soon after this, and Sylvia was just as much an asset to our church family as John was. They lived where the hairdressers is now, and opened their home and garden when we had "open gardens and teas" a couple of times. They moved when Preachers Vale was built, because that meant that they lost the view which they had treasured.

Two other couples who moved to Coleford in the 1980s were Bob and Bridget Stoughton-Harris and Irene and Bill Atkin. Bob was a Lay Reader, and he had a particularly good ministry with the youth organisations, being very involved in the monthly services they attended. He had been a housemaster at Radley College, and occasionally he would treat us as though we were the schoolboys he had looked after for so long! I was sharing a flat in London during the week with a chap who had been in Bob's house, and I heard what a wonderful housemaster he had been.

Irene and Bill Atkin lived in Farley Dell initially, but after a few years they moved to Douglas Yates Court. Irene did not enjoy good health, and was not always able to get to church. Eve Tucker used to go and sit with her, so that Bill could attend. Bill took over as server from Mike Turner, and found a real vocation in this ministry, becoming a member of the Guild of Servers. At one stage, he was going to train as a Lay Reader, but he had to give this up because of Irene's health. Towards the end of Irene's life, and particularly after she died, Bill used to go several times a year to stay with one of his sons in America, and he used to come back telling us what a terrific time he had had.

As well as having Mike Turner, who was then server and administered the chalice, Fr Watson was keen to have some young boys to assist. He found some small cassocks and cottas, and recruited a few boys, not all of whom found this ministry to their liking. But for a number of years we were served by Lee and Kevin, and we benefited very much from this.

In the late 1980s, Fr Watson asked me to go on a training day with Bill to learn about altar work. This was in Bath, and it was a wonderful day. We were shown all the robes and vestments worn by a priest, and how to wear them, and which colours were worn when, and also how to lay up for a Holy Communion service. Afterwards, Fr Watson asked me whether I would like to act as Sacristan. I was thrilled, and this became a very important ministry for me. I didn't do everything— Rona Bruniges was the weekday Sacristan, and I think it was Mercia Maddock who washed and ironed all the linen at first, and then it was taken over by Mary Plummer and Rona.

News of Fr Watson's retirement came quite unexpectedly to many of us, and we held a farewell party for the Watsons upstairs in the church hall. As was usual, Holcombe provided the drink and Coleford provided the food. We spent the day of the party decorating the hall, with Eric Whiffen organising me to stand on tables to arrange balloons as he was too small to do this (it was he who jokingly pointed this out, not anyone else!). During the party, David and Beti treated us to a New Zealand Maori dance. Although David had had his final official service in Holy Trinity, it was not his last. One snowy Sunday a few weeks after he had retired but before he had moved out of the rectory, Bob Stoughton Harris was preparing to take a Service of the Word since the priest who was coming was unable to get through the lanes. Just as he had gone to robe, David and Beti appeared. I was on the door, and promptly asked David to celebrate Communion. I think this was probably the first, and so far only, time that a priest had celebrated Communion here in collar and tie under a chasuble!

During the interregnum between Fr Watson and Fr Peter Down, Fr Peter Hazleton took most of our services since he had retired from Peasedown and Wellow. But sometimes we had other priests, and I can remember Fr Clarence Tester, who took most of the services at Holcombe during this time. He was a lovely man, but had a very quiet voice. The interregnum lasted a long time, and it was a great relief when Fr Peter arrived.

The licensing of the Revd Martin Percival by the Bishop of Bath and Wells, and induction by the Archdeacon of Bath, took place in Holy Trinity on Wednesday, 15 September 1982 at 7.00 pm. Pastoral reorganisation was in the air once more, and in his sermon the Bishop had alluded to the parishes of Leigh-on-Mendip, Stoke St Michael and Downhead. This came as no surprise to Coleford PCC members because they had already discussed and agreed to proposals by the Deanery Pastoral Committee that Coleford, Kilmersdon, Holcombe, Stoke St Michael and Leigh-on-Mendip should be grouped together. Writing in the October 1982 issue of *On the Map*, Fr Percival explained that he had been appointed on the understanding that the parishes of Leigh, Stoke and Downhead would eventually join up with Coleford and Holcombe. The diocesan authorities were looking for a suitable house in Leigh, and an assistant curate would be licensed to Fr Percival, who would be responsible for the three parishes. The next stage would be for all five parishes to work more closely together.

The **Revd Martin Percival** was born in 1945. He was a graduate of London University and Linacre College, Oxford. After training at Wycliffe Hall, Oxford, he was ordained deacon in 1970 and priest in 1971. He held curacies and posts as Team Vicar in several dioceses before coming to Coleford with Holcombe in 1982. He then became Chaplain to Rossall School, Fleetwood, 1984–88; and Chaplain to Woodbridge School, Suffolk, 1988–2002; after this he returned to parish ministry in Chelmsford diocese from 2002 onwards.

The Revd Martin Percival with bride Michaela Perry and her father, John Perry

The Archdeacon of Bath attended a joint PCC meeting in December 1982 and informed those present that the proposals for reorganising the parishes were to be abandoned. A second scheme was aired, namely that Kilmersdon and Babington should be linked with Radstock, but members were told that Kilmersdon and Babington had asked to be joined with Coleford and Holcombe. After a lengthy discussion, it was proposed by Jack Coles (Coleford) and seconded by David Preston Bell (Holcombe) that, in view of the growth of the two villages, no further additions should be made to the united benefice of Coleford with Holcombe. This was agreed unanimously.

Financial problems were rife in 1982, not simply in Coleford but throughout the diocese, and the parishes were warned of a 25% increase in the Parish Share payable to the diocese. This would mean an increase of £500 at Holy Trinity by 1983, or £10 per week, before normal running costs such as heating, lighting and insurance had been considered. Therefore the PCC decided on a two-pronged attack. Firstly, the introduction of a system of planned giving through weekly envelopes. There had been a planned giving scheme previously, but it seems to have been on a less organised basis. Secondly, to encourage covenanted giving for those who paid income tax.

In 1980 the *Alternative Service Book* had been authorised by the Church of England for use until 1990 (this was later extended to 2000). It was meant to provide *alternative* services to those in the *Book of Common Prayer* but not to supplant it entirely. The experimental forms of Holy Communion known as *Series 2* and *Series 3* now became *Rite B* and *Rite A* respectively. The PCC had already adopted *Rite B* for the 9.30 am service towards the end of 1981, and in October 1982 Fr Percival announced the PCC's agreement to the extended use of the *ASB*. In addition to using *Rite B* for Holy Communion, the *ASB* Collects and Lectionary were to be adopted in place of those in the Prayer Book. The congregation were encouraged to buy their own copies of the new books although there would be some copies placed in church.

There was an "interim meeting" of the PCC after the service on 31 July 1983, at which it was proposed by Jack Coles and seconded by John Kestin that Clarissa Cridland should be co-opted to the PCC. The decision was unanimous.

The ministry of Martin Percival at Coleford and Holcombe was distinguished by its brevity, amounting to merely eighteen months. On 31 March 1984 he resigned from the benefice in order to take up the appointment as Chaplain and Head of the Religious Education Department at Rossall School, Fleetwood, in Lancashire. Although the April 1984 issue of *On the Map* is missing from the file, there was no mention of his impending departure in any of the earlier issues for that year. At a PCC meeting on 7 March 1984, the Rector was thanked by the Churchwarden (John Kestin) for his ministry and "particularly for his initiative in setting our finances on a sound footing".

A fairly short interregnum followed during which time most of the services were taken by Prebendary Harry Franklin, Sub Dean of Wells, and other services by local clergy and lay readers. On 13 July 1984 the **Revd John Davidson Watson** (known as Fr David Watson) was licensed and inducted as Rector of the benefice by the Bishop of Taunton and the Archdeacon of Bath.

On 20 September 1984 Fr Watson celebrated the Silver Jubilee of his ordination with a High Mass. The special preacher was Fr Peter Vokes-Dudgeon, Prebendary of Exeter Cathedral, and there were fifty-three communicants.

The Church Hall was still in need of repair, and during 1984–5 the roof was renewed at considerable expense. Coffee mornings, all-day sales and similar events were held to bring in the funds to do the work.

The church was still subject to vandalism, and in the course of the latest onslaught the green Eucharistic vestments were despoiled. Some generous donations allowed a new set to be bought, and these were dedicated on Sunday, 28 October 1984 at the Sung Eucharist at which Prebendary Harry Franklin preached.

As Christmas drew near, Holy Trinity's choir toured the village singing carols, all proceeds going to the Ethiopian Famine Appeal. While the average number of

The **Revd David Watson** was born in New Zealand in 1925, and after training at Kelham Theological College, he was ordained deacon in 1958 and priest in 1959. He served as curate of St Marychurch 1958–62; Brixham 1962–70; Vicar Treverbyn 1970–73; Vicar St Jude's South Shields 1973–78; Vicar Rekendyke 1978–84; Rector Coleford with Holcombe 1984–91. He retired in 1991 and lived in France for several years before returning to residential care in England.

Fr David Watson with bride Karen Jones and her father, Haydn Jones

communicants on ordinary Sundays was thirty-five to forty-nine, there were many more for special occasions. For instance, on Remembrance Sunday 1984 there were sixty-nine communicants and probably many others who did not receive Communion. And on Christmas Eve there were eighty-nine communicants for the Blessing of the Crib and Midnight Mass (which was all one service at this time). Unfortunately, Fr Watson only recorded communicant numbers in the Service Register and ignored the neighbouring column for attendance numbers.

In February 1984 Jack Coles, long-time Churchwarden of Holy Trinity, had celebrated his 80th birthday. Now in June 1985 he had decided at the age of 81 to retire from his parochial duties. A presentation was made at the 9.30 Eucharist on Advent Sunday, 1 December 1985. Jack Coles might have retired from his official church duties, but he would remain a faithful member of Holy Trinity until his death in 1993.

On 15 September 1985 *Rite A* from *The Alternative Service Book* was introduced for Holy Communion. This was the modern language version of the Service. Fr Watson had suggested its introduction for the Dedication Festival in July, but the PCC had decided it would be inappropriate to introduce a new service that day. Following its use during September and extended experimental use until the following Easter, the decision was made to retain *Rite A* for the Sung Eucharist.

There was a new venture in Advent 1985—the presentation of a Nativity pageant by Holy Trinity Choir and Coleford Theatre Group, produced by Ann Crawford. It took place on 19 and 21 December, and £156 was raised, of which one third was given to St Andrew's, Holcombe (this was their centenary year and they were raising money for their new meeting room at the back of the church). The remainder of the money raised was given to the Church Hall roof fund.

The end of 1985 and early part of 1986 saw a Pastoral Review of Church Buildings by the Diocesan Pastoral Committee. This was an attempt by the diocese to review the provision of church buildings by asking if all such buildings were needed and whether the high cost of upkeep could be justified. A questionnaire was sent to each parish and there were two main questions: firstly, is it pastorally essential to have a church building in this place in the foreseeable future? And secondly, is the existing building suitable

---

Jack Coles had been PCC Treasurer from 1934–80; Sacristan from 1937–85; Lay Reader from 1940–70; and Vicar's Warden from 1947–85. In all he had served officially for fifty-one years, though as a member of the Church for a lifetime. His years of service spanned nine incumbents, starting with the Revd Harry Ralph-Bowman. As well as serving the church, Jack Coles had served on the civil Parish Council for thirty-seven years, having been first elected in 1946 when Coleford was still part of the civil parish of Kilmersdon. Coleford became a separate civil parish in 1949, and Jack Coles was its first Chairman. In 1959 he became a Justice of the Peace, retiring in 1974.

for present and expected future pastoral needs? In order to answer these, further questions were posed, and the answers give an indication of the role of Holy Trinity in the life of the village in the 1980s.

Thus we learn that there were 2,410 residents in the village, and that there were 134 people on the Church Electoral Roll. Transport to neighbouring village churches would be a major problem for people if there were no church in the village. There had been some post-War building, and about twelve new houses were planned for the village by the end of 1987. Over the previous five years there was an annual average of fifteen baptisms, six weddings and seven funerals. There was one mid-week Holy Communion attracting about fourteen people, and a choir practice with about eighteen people. Numbers at the mid-week Holy Communion had increased since the service time had changed from 8.00 am to 10.00 am. The usual Sunday total attendance was eighty-five, but this was increased at special times. The average attendance over four years at Easter was 118, Harvest 152, Christmas 170, and Remembrance Sunday 146. In addition to services, the church was used for Nativity plays, Flower Festivals, choral and orchestral concerts. During the past five years, Holy Trinity's PCC had paid its Diocesan Quota and clergy expenses of office in full, and 12.3% of income had been given to the Church overseas and to charities. But this had also meant that not all the necessary repairs to the church had yet been carried out. Sadly, over the past thirty years, the congregation had declined in numbers, but there was a strong sense of commitment and fellowship. With regard to the wider community, the congregation had formed the Church Playgroup and the Women's Fellowship, both of which had been running for twenty years. Also, church members served as School Governors, Parish Councillors, and as officers of the uniformed organisations and of the Royal British Legion.

In May 1986 Barbara Ackroyd resigned as PCC Secretary after serving for twenty years. She had also been Secretary of Midsomer Norton Deanery Synod for some years, and a Diocesan Synod member. As with Jack Coles, this did not mean the end of her service to Holy Trinity. The position of Secretary was taken by Mr Bob Stoughton-Harris, who was also a Lay Reader in the benefice.

The Dedication Festival for 1986 was to incorporate a Flower Festival with a "Royalty" theme. This took place from 18–20 July and was masterminded by Joyce Button. Individuals and village organisations, and some contributions from Holcombe too, made the festival an unforgettable occasion. In Fr Watson's opinion it even outdid the Royal Wedding (Prince Andrew and Sarah Ferguson) on 23 July! He wrote in the August 1986 issue of *On the Map*, "Joyce and her helpers worked extraordinarily long hours, both before and during the Festival, to achieve the resulting tableau. Westminster Abbey on 23 July was indeed a lovely sight, but nothing can detract from the splendour of Holy Trinity as seen by a host of visitors that weekend. Well done, Joyce, and thank you."

Parish outings were not entirely a thing of the past, for in September 1986 there was a parish visit to Wells Cathedral. A fifty-three-seater coach was booked, and everyone took a picnic to eat on arrival. This was followed by a guided tour of the cathedral followed by Evensong when both parishes in the benefice were prayed for. This was so successful that the following year a similar visit was organised to Sherborne Abbey and School.

Two young people brought pride to the benefice in 1987. Richard Harrison was chosen to attend the World Scout Jamboree in Australia; and Elizabeth (Nalda) Johns of Holcombe was to join "Operation Raleigh". No doubt the experience would stay with both these young people for years to come.

On Sunday, 19 July 1987 (Dedication Festival), Eddie Coles (husband of Phyl) celebrated sixty years as an active member of the church choir. Fr Watson wrote in the August issue of *On the Map*, "We tender him our prayers and gratitude for these many years of devotion and service, a splendid example to us all."

In June 1988 the Coleford Parish Plan was launched in order to consider the role of the Church within the life of the village. Much preparation had gone into this, beginning with a visit to the PCC by the Diocesan Resources Advisor in February 1987, and several follow-up meetings took place. The first stage was aimed at members of the church Electoral Roll, parents of children brought for baptism, the newly confirmed, and those concerned for the future of the church in Coleford. These people were visited, their opinions sought and help requested. The Archdeacon of Bath (the Venerable John Burgess) preached at the Dedication Festival, but there was no vast increase in the congregation despite the Parish Plan. However, during the autumn some action was taken on points raised during the visits earlier in the year. Over thirty people had expressed a wish to meet with others to discuss their faith. So—various meetings were

Right: *The Women's Fellowship outing, 1993. From front: Eve Tucker, Stuart Wadley, Eileen Smith, Enid Wadley*

Below: *The Women's Fellowship outing to London, 1988. Left to right: Betty Turner, Winifred Allen, Nancy Parfitt*

arranged. Firstly, a fortnightly Monday evening discussion group similar to that held a few years previously; but when it was held no new members joined. Another suggestion had been meetings with speakers; one was held at the Rectory and only three people came. The third suggestion was a revival of the Mothers' Union, and by 1989 the membership had increased to twenty-one. Apart from this one positive result, Fr Watson was disappointed with such a poor response after all the time and preparation that had gone into the Parish Plan.

1988 was the year of the Lambeth Conference, when Anglican Bishops from all over the world gather together in England at the invitation of the Archbishop of Canterbury to pray and discuss spiritual matters. Fr Watson announced in the July issue of *On the Map* that Bishop Robert Okine from the diocese of Koforidua in Ghana would be staying at Coleford Rectory for a few days following the conference. The Bishop preached at a Deanery Evensong at Holy Trinity on 14 August and presided at the confirmation of Betty Cobb in her home the next day. The Bishop enjoyed his short stay in Coleford before the long journey home. He was given some Bibles for use in his diocese and the sum of £125.

Towards the end of 1988, it was announced that on the 1st and 3rd Sunday evenings of the month, the congregation would join with the Methodists for a joint service. This followed an earlier joint service which had been very well received by all who had attended it. Towards the end of 1990, these arrangements were extended so that there would be joint services in the church on the 1st and 3rd Sundays and in the chapel on the 2nd and 4th Sundays.

1988 ended with a pat on the back for *On the Map*, edited by Jennie Gregor, which was awarded a commendation in the Village Ventures Competition.

During the 1980s, the General Synod (the Church of England's governing body) had produced a number of reports which were passed down through the diocesan structures to the parishes for discussion. These included the Tiller Report on clergy numbers; reports dealing with Christian unity schemes; the admission of children to Communion before confirmation; the controversial report *Faith in the City*; and *Children in the Way*, which dealt with the church's response to children. Holy Trinity's PCC spent considerable time studying and discussing these reports which gave them a perspective on the wider church, even if the recommendations contained in the reports were not always relevant to a rural parish.

On Saturday, 18 March 1989, the four Gospels were read in their entirety by members of the congregations of Holy Trinity and St Andrew's. This took place in Holy Trinity, beginning at 9.00 am, and took thirteen and a half hours. The readers were Beti Watson, Clarissa Cridland, Sylvia and John Kestin, Ann Crawford, Bridget and Bob Stoughton-Harris, Ian Butterworth, David Preston Bell, Don Thompson, Colin Turner, Gordon Fry, Bill Atkin, David Baker and Michael Turner.

Fr Watson announced that as from June 1989 there would be a Family Service on the 3rd Sunday of each month, beginning on 18 June. This was in addition to the Sunday School and would take the form of a Eucharist oriented towards families and children. There were only thirty-eight communicants on 18 June, but as the Register does not indicate the total numbers attending, it is impossible to know whether there was a large congregation of non-communicants. Also, a crèche was begun in the Church Hall for small children. These initiatives were partly based on responses to the Parish Plan and ideas expressed to PCC members during visits to members of the wider parish.

In 1989 Fr Watson attempted to introduce some family-oriented services for Advent and Christmas. On Sunday 10 December there was a Christingle Service at Holy Trinity, followed by a party in the Church Hall to celebrate twenty-one years since the Children's Society had organised the first Christingle Service in Britain. A large number of families attended; and as the Christingle candles were distributed and lit, a large circle of light was formed all round the darkened church. (In fact Fr Watson had introduced Christingle to Coleford three years earlier in 1986, and this popular service has continued as part of Holy Trinity's tradition ever since.) On the 4th Sunday of Advent, which in 1989 fell on Christmas Eve, Fr Watson introduced another service which would become popular over the years. This was the Blessing of the Crib, and it took place at 5.30 pm. In former years, the Christmas Crib had been blessed before the Midnight Mass, but by making it the focus of an individual service, it gave an immediate appeal to children and families. And thirdly, on 7 January the uniformed organisations led a service of readings, prayers and hymns connected with journeys, thinking in particular about the journeys of Mary and Joseph, and of the Wise Men. With the completion of the cycle of Christmas and Epiphany Services, thus passed another year and another decade in the life of Holy Trinity.

A key couple at Holy Trinity moved away in June 1990—John and Sylvia Kestin had undertaken various ministries within Holy Trinity. John Kestin had served as a Churchwarden and had been instrumental in the publication of *On the Map*. Those duties connected with the parish magazine were now to be undertaken by three people—Joanna Fricker as the typist, Bill Atkin as treasurer and Nancy Parfitt to organise collation and distribution. Sylvia Kestin had been responsible for running the Sunday School since it restarted in 1985, and so appeals were made for someone to take over this important work.

The new Bishop of Bath and Wells, the Rt Revd George Carey, was endeavouring to get to know his diocese, and to this end he was planning a Teaching Mission to the Midsomer Norton Deanery from Wednesday 18 to Sunday 21 July 1990. Much planning had gone into the visit, so much so that the Deanery Synod representatives (Bill Atkin and Bob Stoughton-Harris) felt that too many people were involved and that too many meetings were being called. They feared boredom would be the end result! All the parishes in the deanery were to participate, and so it was decided to observe the Dedication Festival at Holy Trinity a month early, on Sunday 17 June. The Mission itself was well publicised, and transport was provided for people without cars so that all could get to the evening meetings. In addition, the Bishop came to Coleford for Evensong at 5.00 pm on Friday 20 July. Later in the year came the news that Bishop Carey was to become the next Archbishop of Canterbury.

1990 also brought news of two former incumbents. On 19 May Fr John Sutters celebrated fifty years in the priesthood. He was by this time living in Oxford, having retired in 1980, and he celebrated his Jubilee Eucharist at St Thomas', Oxford, the church where he had celebrated his first Eucharist in 1940. And then on 8 July came news of the death of Fr Alan Coleman, who had died in hospital following surgery a few days previously. He had been in ill health for some years. Ann Crawford, who had kept in touch with Fr and Mrs Coleman, attended the Service of Thanksgiving at Christ Church, Thornton Cleveleys, near Blackpool. On 11 July there was a Requiem at Holy Trinity for Fr Coleman at which there were eleven communicants.

1990 ended on a gloomy note. There was likely to be a deficit of about £1,400 by the end of the year, making it impossible to pay the Parish Share in full. It was estimated that it cost about £10,000 to keep the church running in 1990, excluding the cost of repairs. The weekly income amounted to about £7,000 per year. Extra fundraising events such a Gift Day and the Garden Fete helped to close the gap, but it still left a large deficit. An appeal was made in *On the Map* for people to increase their giving and for those tax payers who had not covenanted their giving to do so.

The December 1990/January 1991 issue of *On the Map* did not mention Fr Watson's impending retirement. However, at the PCC meeting on 5 December 1990 Fr Watson confirmed that his retirement date was 31 January 1991, but, with leave due to him, beginning on 1 January. Writing in the February 1991 issue, he said, "Beti and I have been very moved by your response to the news of my retirement and our departure from the parish … The decision came quickly in the end, but I believe that this is the right time for both the parish and ourselves … For the Parishes and Churches it is a wonderful time to be making a truly new start. The Decade of Evangelism is just beginning and I pray that you will be fired with enthusiasm, under a new Rector, for all that the future has to offer …" Fr Watson's last official Service at Holy Trinity was a Eucharist on 31 December 1990 at which there were eight communicants.

The new incumbent would be appointed according to the terms of the new Patronage (Benefices) Measure 1986, which came into force on 1 January 1989 and under which new procedures for appointing an incumbent were laid down. The Measure made provision for two lay representatives from each parish in the benefice to meet the candidates and participate in the selection process. Gone were the days of incumbents exchanging parishes with each other and with no consultation with the people. So too under the Measure, the power of appointment previously vested in the Patron was very much curtailed. A Parish Profile prepared by the PCC was now required, giving information about the benefice to prospective candidates. However, the benefice would have a lengthy vacancy because any appointment to be made must still be ratified by the Bishop, and there was now an impending episcopal vacancy created by Bishop Carey's move to Canterbury. Therefore after 27 March, the right of presentation to the benefice would devolve to the Crown, and all future consultation would be at the Crown's discretion.

On 16 January 1991 a joint PCC meeting was held at the Church Hall to discuss the new appointment procedure, to choose the parish lay representatives, and to discuss the Parish Profiles prepared by each PCC. The two lay representatives were: Colin Turner and Bill Atkin for Coleford and Ian Butterworth and Gordon Fry for Holcombe. The decision was made to retain the two separate Parish Profiles, rather than merge them into one.

Holy Trinity's Parish Profile paints a portrait of a changing village community, with some constants such as a number of core families who had lived in the village for generations. But it was a village standing also on the cusp of change, with new housing developments such as Mendip Vale, Farley Dell and Preacher's Vale bringing new families into the community. The statistics for church attendance show a marked drop in numbers in just a few years when compared with the figures given in the 1986 Diocesan Pastoral Review of Church Buildings. Now, at the beginning of 1991, the Church Electoral Roll stood at ninety-two; the average total Sunday attendance was forty-five; during the previous twelve months there had been nine baptisms, one person confirmed, four marriages and twelve funerals. The average age of the congregation was high, and the average number per Sunday morning service was twenty-five to thirty. On the quarterly Parade Sundays the church would be 80% full, and at Midnight Mass the church would be 100% full. There were good connections with Bishop Henderson Primary School, with the Rector taking a weekly assembly and the children attending Holy Trinity as a school three times a year. A good relationship was enjoyed with the Methodists, with shared Sunday evening worship. Once a month the Rector had held a Communion Service at Douglas Yates Court.

In February 1991, Bill Atkin and Colin Turner, Churchwardens at Holy Trinity, made the following announcement in *On the Map*: "On Sunday 17 February we are beginning a series of Family Services on the 3rd Sunday of each month. These services will consist of hymns, prayers, readings and address and will replace the usual 9.30 am Parish Communion. We hope that many families will wish to come to these services and share in our worship." The services would last about half an hour and would be led by Bob Stoughton-Harris, Holy Trinity's Lay Reader. However, by the end of the year the PCC were informed that these services were poorly attended, with even smaller congregations than for the Parish Communion.

Many of the Eucharists during the interregnum were celebrated by the Revd Peter Hazelton. The 1991 Christingle Service was attended by 170 people, but the Blessing of the Crib on Christmas Eve attracted only forty people.

Following the advertisement of the post of Rector of the benefice, four candidates were shown round the two villages and interviewed on Wednesday, 28 August 1991, and one of the candidates was offered the post. However, this was subject to the Bishop of Taunton's approval and that of the Crown Appointment's Commission, so an announcement could not be made immediately. Meanwhile, church life continued with the usual struggle to make financial ends meet and to maintain both the church building and the hall.

Holy Trinity has always been a church where several generations of the same family have worshipped, and this has been reflected in earlier chapters. Here in pictorial form are five generations of Colin Turner's family.

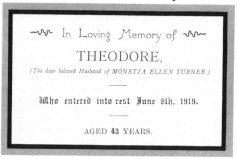

Above: *In Memoriam card for Theodore Turner, 8 June 1919, aged 43 years*

Left: *His son, Leonard Turner, Baptism card 1912*

Right: *Leonard's son, Colin Turner, First Communion 1954*

Below left: *Colin's daughter, Sarah Turner, Baptism 1970*

Below right: *Sarah's daughter, Zoe Ilott, Baptism by Fr Peter Down 2001*

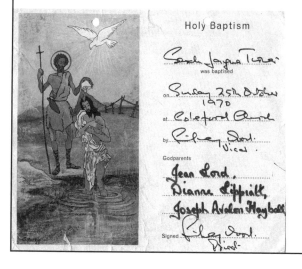

The **Fr Peter Down** was born in Bristol in 1954. After graduating from King's College, London, he trained for the priesthood at the College of the Resurrection, Mirfield and was ordained deacon in 1979 and priest in 1980. He served as curate of Christ Church, Swindon, 1979–82; Southmead 1982–84; Team Vicar of Cannock 1984–92. He was Vicar of Coleford with Holcombe 1992–2001 and resigned on health grounds. He is, at the time of writing, a non-stipendiary priest at St Mary's, Frome, and also has a teaching post in Frome.

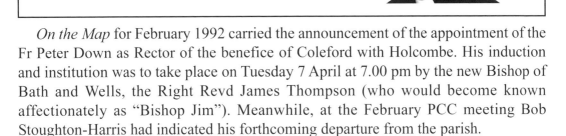

Fr Peter Down

On the Map for February 1992 carried the announcement of the appointment of the Fr Peter Down as Rector of the benefice of Coleford with Holcombe. His induction and institution was to take place on Tuesday 7 April at 7.00 pm by the new Bishop of Bath and Wells, the Right Revd James Thompson (who would become known affectionately as "Bishop Jim"). Meanwhile, at the February PCC meeting Bob Stoughton-Harris had indicated his forthcoming departure from the parish.

Writing in the February 1992 *On the Map*, Fr Peter observed: "Coleford and Holcombe will be a great change for me, as so far, all my ministry has been with colleagues, so working on my own will be very different, and I look forward to the new challenges posed by this new ministry. The Church faces many challenges in this final decade of the century in the face of growing secularism and indifference to the Gospel. I hope that together we can make good use of a Decade of Evangelism and rise to the challenges facing us locally."

Soon after his arrival, Fr Peter, with PCC approval, moved the altar forward so that he could face the people instead of having his back to them at Holy Communion. This was not an innovation but was a return to the practice of the early Christian Church and was undergoing a revival. This has been the arrangement in the sanctuary ever since. Also under discussion by the PCC in Fr Peter's early ministry was the question of the marriage in church of those whose former marriages had ended in divorce. The decision was made to allow Fr Peter to use his discretion depending on individual circumstances. (The Church of

The Decade of Evangelism was an initiative from all the mainstream churches to use the last ten years of the 20th century to evangelise the nation, in the hope of turning round the increasing indifference to the Christian faith, and to try new ways of reaching people in the hope of winning them back to church, and of attracting people who had never been regular church attenders.

England General Synod would later produce specific guidelines but this lay a decade away.)

At the request of St Andrew's PCC, a working party of three members from each PCC was formed to discuss the pattern of Sunday worship in the two churches. Following their deliberations, it was proposed by Bill Atkin, seconded by David Baker and voted upon unanimously to try a new pattern for six months beginning on the first Sunday in October. Writing in the October 1992 *On the Map*, Fr Peter explained that the time of the Sung Eucharist would alternate between 9.30 am and 11.15 am at both churches every other Sunday. Looking through the Service Register, there appear to be fewer in the congregation when the service at Holy Trinity was at 11.15 am; and after the end of the trial period, both PCCs agreed to revert to the previous service times of 9.30 am at Holy Trinity and 11.00 am at St Andrew's.

There were, however, some successes in 1992. A monthly Parade Service for the uniformed organisations had succeeded (with an average attendance of seventy), where the Family Service in the interregnum had failed. Of the Advent and Christmas Services, the Christingle was well attended with 138 people, but Fr Peter was disappointed with the turnout for the Midnight Mass with only fifty-eight present and thirty-seven receiving Holy Communion. The Blessing of the Crib on Christmas Eve was continued, and in 1992 there were just twenty-five people present, but this was a service that would increase in popularity over the coming years.

Julie Dexter recalls the Blessing of the Crib Service: To begin with, only a handful of people attended, braving the elements and an often chilly church on Christmas Eve for a special children's service. Since then, the service has grown in popularity and become a part of many people's Christmas worship. Callum, Rhiannon and Fintan Pritchard, all baptised at Holy Trinity, now live in Belgium but follow the tradition of many village families who return to Holy Trinity for special events.

Callum, Rhiannon and Fintan recall: Every year we come back to England and stay in Coleford for Christmas. On Christmas Eve we go down to the Church for the Blessing of the Crib, and Mum makes us wrap up warm because it's always cold. Something funny usually happens. When Callum was little he asked, "Why is that man [Fr Peter Down] wearing a dress?" Once Mum thought she left her purse behind, and one year the head fell off the shepherd. It's fun because you can take part. Auntie Robyn [Dexter] always used to put the Angel Gabriel in the crib. The youngest person always puts baby Jesus in the crib, and once that was Fintan. The vicar usually lets us three do the wise men round the church because they have travelled a long way like us. Then we all go and get money from people [i.e. take the collection] and I always get chosen for the collection. And we sing songs for Jesus. And right at the end of the service, we get sweets from a big tin of chocolates.

1993 saw Fr Peter endeavouring to make improvements to the 9.30 Service. These included: serving coffee in the Church Hall after the service; having a non-Eucharistic service on the first Sunday in the month (the Eucharist would then be at 6.00 pm); producing simple cards for the order of service; using a family-oriented hymn book; and exchanging the Peace. This latter was a practice from the early Christian Church which had been lost sight of, and was now being revived. There was some opposition from PCC members to this. Fr Peter also expressed his concern to the PCC about the majority of the congregation sitting at the back of the church. Sometimes new things take time to succeed, and after a slow start the Family Service began to bring in good numbers. A new hymn book was obtained called *Hymns Old & New*, and by early 1994 the attendance was between seventy-five and eighty-five.

Miss Ackroyd's grave

The 1993 Vestry and Annual Parochial Church Meeting had seen the resignation of Bill Atkin as Churchwarden and the election of David Baker in his place. Colin Turner continued as Churchwarden as well as Treasurer. Bill Atkin had also signified his desire to resign as Deanery and Diocesan Synod representative and as a member of the Bishop's Council, but he continued to serve at the altar until his death.

An era ended in December 1993 with the death of Jack Coles. His wife Dorothy had died in 1979. And now he was laid to rest with her in the churchyard just beyond the east end of the church. His funeral took place on 7 December and ninety-seven people were present. A chalice and ciborium (a vessel used for holding the Communion wafers) were given in memory of Jack and Dorothy Coles and are in regular use at the time of writing. The inscription on the chalice reads:

In memory of Dorothy Coles, 1909–1979.

And the ciborium is inscribed:

In loving memory of John Coles, faithful servant, 1904–1993.

Another loss was sustained by Holy Trinity in the death of Barbara Ackroyd on 12 January 1994. She had been an active member of Holy Trinity since her arrival in 1956. For many years she was PCC secretary, and with her friend, Miss Jones, had held regular fundraising events at their home "Wheal Friendly". Her body was received

147

into Holy Trinity at 5.00 pm on 19 January 1994 and the funeral took place the next day, though the numbers at the service were not recorded. Her grave is in the churchyard near the front boundary wall.

Barbara Ackroyd was born in Bradford on 19 October 1908, the second of the four daughters of Alfred and Jessie Ackroyd. Her family were committed Christians in the Anglo Catholic tradition of the Church of England. At the beginning of the 20th century, a Commission of the Diocese of Ripon decided to build a new church in Bradford (in addition to the existing ones), and a portion of land was given by the Ackroyd family as a site for a church, vicarage and schoolroom. The new church of St Chad's, Bradford, was consecrated on 27 September 1913 and is still a parish church, situated in a now largely Muslim district but serving an incoming congregation from a wide area.

In October 1932, on her twenty-fourth birthday, Barbara Ackroyd joined a Religious Community at Rusholme, Manchester, and was clothed as a Novice in March 1933. In August 1935 she took temporary vows (these would be for three years prior to taking lifelong vows). In 1938 she was helping at a home for unmarried mothers run by the Community, but she left during that year. The Community later moved to Horbury and became part of the Community of St Peter, and in later years Barbara Ackroyd maintained contact with the Community by becoming an Associate. After leaving the Community, she decided to train as a social worker and moved to Bristol where, in 1939, she met Marion Jones. This was the beginning of a lifelong friendship. Marion Jones was born near Cardiff and was five years older than Barbara Ackroyd. She was a committed Methodist and remained so all her life.

In 1944 Barbara Ackroyd became Matron of Rosemundy Home in St Agnes, Cornwall, under the direction of the Cornwall Social and Moral Welfare Association, and in her first year over forty unmarried mothers and their babies were cared for at the home. In 1948 Marion Jones came to work at the home and at the same time studied to become a Methodist Local Preacher, being accredited in June 1951. In 1956 both Miss Ackroyd and Miss Jones left St Agnes and came to live at Ham, between Holcombe and Coleford, in a bungalow which they named "Wheal Friendly" after a tin mine near St Agnes. It was conveniently situated so that Miss Jones was able to become a member of Holcombe Methodist Chapel, and Miss Ackroyd settled very well at Holy Trinity, Coleford, where the vicar at that time was Fr John Sutters, an Anglo Catholic after her own heart. Barbara Ackroyd became the Organising Secretary of the Somerset Churches Family Welfare Association, a post she held until her retirement in 1970, and during this time it gained the support of Holy Trinity. As well as being PCC Secretary she was also a member of the Deanery and Diocesan Synods for several years and, together with Miss Jones, was a tireless fundraiser for both Holy Trinity and Holcombe Chapel as well as many other good causes. The late 1980s saw a gradual decline in Miss Ackroyd's health, but it was not until 1993 that she became seriously incapacitated. Following Barbara Ackroyd's death in January 1994, Marion Jones found life difficult at "Wheal Friendly", and after a few months she moved to Wells to be near to Mrs Maddock, a former member of Holy Trinity whom she had known for many years. Marion Jones died on 20 February 2005 aged 101, and her ashes were interred in Barbara Ackroyd's grave in Coleford churchyard.

Rosemundy Home in St Agnes became a hotel soon after Miss Ackroyd and Miss Jones left in 1956. During their time there, an attempt was made to transform a natural amphitheatre in the grounds into an open air theatre similar to that not far away at Minack. It was formally opened in 1954 by the Bishop of Truro and the Methodist Superintendent Minister, but the project never really got off the ground. Inscribed on stones set into the retaining wall of the stage were the names of Barbara Ackroyd as Matron and Margaret Smith, who had turned Rosemundy House into a Mother and Baby Home. Signs of the theatre may still be traced in the hotel grounds, including the carved stones. **Liz Smith**, daughter of Dennis and Sybil Hodges, remembers visiting the hotel some years ago and finding the stone tribute to Miss Ackroyd bearing the inscription **"The gentle mind by gentle deeds is known"**. That same inscription is in Holy Trinity and also on the plain wooden cross that now marks her grave.

Barbara Ackroyd in her 80s

Writing in the March 1994 issue of *On the Map*, Colin Turner paid tribute to "three of Holy Trinity's most respected members, Alice Alford, Barbara Ackroyd and Jack Coles. They all strove endlessly towards ensuring that the Church had an important role to play in the lives of the people of Coleford. Even in the twilight of their days they requested that in the event of their death mourners were to donate monies, in lieu of flowers, for the benefit of Holy Trinity Church." Over £1,400 had been received and this would be used for restoration purposes.

Following the departure of Bob Staughton-Harris, the editing of *On the Map* was taken on for a time by Julie Dexter, followed by Mike Turner for several years. In the years since, *On the Map* has gone from strength to strength and is read widely, even finding its way to Australia.

Meanwhile, other familiar names such as Dennis and Sybil Hodges continued to support Holy Trinity, and also other charitable causes, with fundraising events. Dennis Hodges was a builder and helped with many maintenance projects, as did Brian Perry. Sybil Hodges, as well as being a PCC member, was also committed to Scouting and was a stalwart member of the Huckyduck Carnival Club. At the time of writing Sybil is in residential care near Swindon. Harold Crossley was also a PCC member, whose knowledge as a civil engineer was of great value. At the time of writing, Harold remains a regular member, indeed at ninety-seven the oldest member, of Holy Trinity. Another faithful stalwart was Joyce Button, in the mid-1990s still a PCC member, and organiser of many fundraising events not only for Holy Trinity but also for the Women's Section of the Royal British Legion. Joyce also organised the church cleaning and flowers. At the time of writing Joyce lives in residential care in Frome and is still under the pastoral care of the Coleford clergy, from whom she regularly receives Holy Communion. Molly Bull, another faithful member of Holy Trinity, died in June 2009, aged 95. Mercia Maddock, PCC member and stalwart of the Mothers' Union, left Coleford after twenty-two years at the end of 1994. The PCC presented her with a photograph of the interior of Holy Trinity as a leaving present. She moved to Wells, from whence she kept in touch with Coleford friends until her death in 2003. Her funeral was at St Cuthbert's, Wells and was attended by several people from Coleford.

The once numerous choir at Holy Trinity was diminishing. Older members had died and young members had left to go to college or had married and moved away. Perhaps for the first time ever, the choir was losing more members than it was gaining and numbered only nine on a good day by the mid-1990s. An appeal was made by Ann Crawford for new members, but numbers never returned to those of former generations.

The finances at Holy Trinity continued to be a problem as faithful members died or moved away and were not replaced. Colin Turner informed the PCC at its meeting in September 1994 that the Parish Share payable to the diocese amounted to £11,158 and that only £2,000 had been paid. By the end of the year only £6,000 had been paid. The next year the figure payable would rise to £12,377.

On 28 August and 30 October 1994 Fr Peter was absent from the parish, and Matins and Evensong were taken by Clarissa Cridland. The following year Fr Peter was on sick leave for a month after Easter, during which time the services were taken by Clarissa Cridland, who was by now a Churchwarden, and by local clergy.

Miss Jones had offered a donation in memory of Miss Ackroyd to pay for the repair of the clock light. In 1995 the PCC decided to erect a glass plaque in the church to commemorate the late Barbara Ackroyd and to acknowledge the illumination of the church clock as her memorial. The wording was "In memory of Miss B Ackroyd for the kind bequest providing the funds for the illumination of the church clock December 1994". Churchwarden Dave Baker was deputed to show it Miss Jones. The PCC Minutes take up the story: "Glass plaque—Miss Jones is not happy with the wording. Another plaque is to be made with different wording." The November Minutes noted, "Glass plaque is well in hand [and] the finished result was shown to PCC members and will be taken to Miss Jones for approval." The January 1996 Minutes record the happy outcome: "Miss Ackroyd's plaque is now erected in the church and Miss Jones is happy with the result." The original plaque was placed in the Church Hall and the new one had the following inscription:

The illumination of the Church Clock is in memory of Barbara Ackroyd
19th October 1908–12th January 1994.
The Gentle Mind By Gentle Deeds Is Known.

On Friday, 27 October 1995, the funeral of John Turner took place in Holy Trinity.

He was sixty-nine years old and had been a life-long member of Holy Trinity, having been in the choir for sixty years. He was an altar server, a PCC member, and, among his many other works for the church, had cut the grass in the churchyard and ensured that all looked clean and tidy. His care for others extended into the wider community, and many people appreciated his Bingo evenings. His family were also members of Holy Trinity, and while at the time of writing some have left the village, his widow Ann is still a member of Holy Trinity and other family members attend from time to time.

Holy Trinity sustained another loss early in 1996 with the death of Eddie Coles (husband of Phyllis) following a lingering illness. His funeral took place in church on Friday 16 February, and a former choirman and workmate, Les Gilson, paid the following tribute to him in the March issue of *On the Map*. "We joined the Church Choir at approximately

John Turner

the same time, singing treble. After a while I carried the cross and had to wear a red cassock. However, being stockily built, the red cassock wouldn't fit me, but it did fit Eddie, so he became the worthy cross bearer. We were both Sunday School teachers and remained as choristers, singing tenor and sitting next to each other for many years. I had to leave after 13 years because of other commitments, but Eddie remained until his illness—a lifelong devotee. At work he never swore, didn't partake of alcohol, and as far as I know, didn't smoke. Work colleagues used to argue about sport, sometimes getting a little out of order and excited, but Eddie always remained placid. He was a good footballer, playing hard but always fair. He had one girlfriend, Phyllis. They started seeing each other when they were young and remained true and faithful to each other for many years before finally getting married. They both attended Church as choristers, regardless of weather. I respected Eddie for the … way he led his life, a perfect example to us all." Mr Gilson also recalled how Eddie saved his life one day at work: "I held a live electric wire and I couldn't let go. I fell to the floor with electric [*sic*] surging through my body. Then suddenly it stopped—Eddie had run to the power house and switched all the power off, thus saving my life." At its meeting in March 1996 the PCC expressed its sympathy to Phyllis Coles and noted Eddie's faithful service over many years. After Eddie's death Phyllis returned to the church choir (having been absent for the three years of his illness), and is a member at the time of writing.

In October 1996 there was a new fundraising venture—a Bridal and Fashion Show. This was organised by a Working Party (soon to be called the Support Group), consisting of Ann Mackie-Hunter, Rona Bruniges, Joyce Button, Ann Crawford, Clarissa Cridland, Margaret Crocker, Esme Harrison, Nancy Parfitt, Mary Plummer and Eileen Whiffen, and the event was held at the Royal British Legion Hall. Brides of former years dug out their finery and were escorted down the catwalk by 'proxy bridegrooms', one of whom was Colin Turner. In fact they walked up and down the 'aisle' fourteen times! Wedding dresses were on display, music was provided by Rex Parfitt, and the evening raised £225 for church funds.

During Fr Peter's incumbency a number of the present congregation were confirmed. These included Shirley Newton, confirmed at St George's Beckington on 11 April 1995; and Doris and Peter Russell, Tony and Diane Pratt, Nicola Tasker, Curtis Ilott, Michael Vecchio, Maryann Baker and Leslie Kite were all confirmed at Holy Trinity on 11 May 1997 by the Bishop of Bath and Wells. Robyn Dexter and Jean and Gerald Coles were amongst those confirmed at Holy Trinity on 13 October 1999.

Fr Peter was building a strong relationship with Bishop Henderson School under the recently appointed head teacher, David Hayward. The school choir came to the Carol Service on 15 December and the church was filled to overflowing. The Blessing of the Crib Service on Christmas Eve 1996 featured the judging of a Christmas card competition in which all the school had taken part. There was one category for each school year and the winning cards were exhibited in church from Christmas Eve until 6 January, the Feast of the Epiphany. There were a large number of entries, and this may have boosted the attendance at the Crib Service which in 1996 was attended by twenty-eight children and twenty-nine adults. Even so, numbers at this service had been increasing and they continue to do so.

Throughout 1997 the Support Group worked very hard organising fundraising events such as jumble sales, coffee mornings, refreshments after special services, and master-minding the annual Gift Day, Garden Party and other events. Also, from early in 1998 members of the Support Group, co-ordinated by Esme Harrison, took on the responsibility for the church flowers, Joyce Button having felt unable to continue after many years.

In April 1997 Steve Hodges, son of Dennis and Sybil, cycled all the way from Coleford and Holcombe to Coleford and Holcombe in Devon in aid of Church funds. He raised £95.50 for Holy Trinity.

On 31 August 1997 the nation was shocked by the death in a car accident in Paris of Diana, Princess of Wales. On Friday 5 September a Memorial Service was held in Holy Trinity attended by 142 people. £235.61 was raised in the collection for the Memorial Fund.

At Christmas 1997 there was a Nativity tableau at the Carol Service. The Junior Drama Group was largely responsible for this under the guidance of Ann Crawford and Esme Harrison, both of whom made the costumes. This was one of the more successful Christmas Services that year, bringing in a congregation of eighty-two adults and forty-four children. Less successfully, Fr Peter announced that the First Mass of Christmas would be held at 9.00 pm on Christmas Eve rather than at 11.30 pm. This was not a success, the congregation numbering only fifty adults and three children. The following year the service reverted to the usual time. Also, by way of an experiment, in addition to the rather poorly attended Christmas morning Holy Communion, a Family Service was held at 10.30 am. Fr Peter had to be at St Andrew's at this time, so the Family Service was taken by Clarissa Cridland, but it was attended by only seven adults and one child. It was not repeated in 1998.

Holy Trinity acquired a new look early in 1998 with the removal of the hangings which provided a backdrop behind the altar, thus exposing the stone reredos (the stone screen with carved lettering behind the altar). The cloth hangings were changed according to the season of the church year, and it was heavy work due to the weight of the material and the fact that they required ironing each time before being hung behind the altar. The hangings were removed for the two months before Easter and people's opinions were sought. On 6 May the PCC decided to permanently remove the cloth hangings and to restore the stonework. This work was done by Geoffrey Plummer, who spent long hours cleaning the stone and carefully highlighting the lettering in black and gold paint. The work was sponsored by Rona Bruniges in memory of her husband, Martin, whose funeral had taken place at Holy Trinity on 27 April 1998.

In February 1998 the death occurred of Richard John Marchant Jones, son of William Marchant Jones. Fr Peter presided at the burial of his ashes.

Many years previously, in 1963, under a Faculty for various works on the church interior, provision had been made for a children's area. Nothing had been done at the time to bring this about, but in 1998 at long last the PCC decided to make the church more "child friendly" by providing an area for young children to call their own. An appeal was made for appropriate books and other materials. Even so, the children's area was not completed until 19 September 1999, when it was blessed for use. The note in the October issue of *On the Map* gave a special word of thanks to Ann and Richard Usher for all their time and effort. There were thirty-six adults and twelve children at the Sung Eucharist that day.

Two more members of the congregation died towards the end of Fr Peter's ministry at Coleford. Marge Smith died in August 1998. Her funeral at Haycombe Crematorium on 24 August was followed by a Memorial Service in church on 10 September at which her friends were present. On 1 June 1999 the funeral of Ruby Brewer took place in Holy Trinity. She had been a life-long member of Holy Trinity and a supporter of the Mothers' Union. In his tribute at her funeral, Colin Turner said that Ruby had started life as an only child and had been the mother of eight children, had twenty-one grandchildren and twenty-two great-grandchildren.

The stone reredos behind the altar

The new millennium was greeted with a Songs of Praise Service and Party on Sunday 2 January. This was a joint venture with St Andrew's Holcombe and with the Methodists from both villages. Twenty-nine adults and one child attended. There were big plans afoot for a Coleford Village Day to celebrate the Millennium, and this went ahead on Saturday 1 July. The day had been in the planning process for a long time, and many people were involved, including a good number of church members. In addition to carnival processions and a fete with numerous stalls and sideshows, there were the fruits of more lasting projects. The Methodist Chapel provided the venue for the Millennium tapestries telling the history of the village, and these tapestries, sponsored by various individuals and groups, are still a feature of the Chapel at the time of writing. Also, two books were published. *Coleford as 'twere* was produced by the Oral History Group and consisted of memories of Colefordians relating to the first half of the 20th century, and illustrated with many photographs. *A Short History of Highbury and Coleford* was produced by Julie Dexter and Les Kite, and gave an insight into the history of mining in the village. The millennium yew tree was planted in the churchyard on 13 August 2000 at a Children's Service at which thirty-four adults and eight children were present.

There was a change of editorship of *On the Map* in August 2000, Mike Turner having indicated his wish to give up after several years. The new editorship was job-shared by Clarissa Cridland and Ann Mackie-Hunter.

But this was not the only change at Holy Trinity in the year 2000. On Shrove Tuesday, the day before the beginning of Lent, Fr Peter went on what was to be a period of long-term sick leave eventually resulting in his resignation from the parish in 2001. The Churchwardens, Dave Baker and Clarissa Cridland, together with the Churchwardens from Holcombe (Michael Fleming and Christine Fulton), were left with the responsibility of providing services and pastoral care for the benefice.

During this time many of the services were taken by the Revd David Barge, curate of Westfield; the Revd David MacGeoch, curate of Midsomer Norton; the Revd Geoffrey Thomas; Canon Boyce and the Revd Brian Sutton, two retired priests living in the deanery. Every effort was made by the Churchwardens to maintain the usual pattern of worship. When it was not possible to provide a service of Holy Communion, an alternative was provided, either a prayer service, or (on the second Sunday of the month at Coleford) a Children's Service. Clarissa Cridland was instrumental in introducing the Children's Services and they were very successful.

On 13 December 2000 Bill Atkin died suddenly and was laid to rest by Fr Peter Down on 29 December. He had been fully involved in the life of Holy Trinity since moving to Coleford in 1984. He had served as Churchwarden alongside Colin Turner and had played a leading role in the interregnum before Fr Peter's appointment. He had served at the altar and administered the chalice at Holy Communion. Also, Bill Atkin had helped in many practical ways and had been generous at times of financial hardship for the church. On the evening of 13 December he had attended the Friendly Club Christmas Dinner at which he had said the grace, and had enjoyed both the meal and the entertainment. Then on returning home he had collapsed and died—a great shock and loss to all who knew him.

The year 2000 was marked in the Church of England by the introduction of *Common Worship* which replaced the *Alternative Service Book* which had been introduced in 1980. The *ASB* was authorised initially for ten years, followed by a further ten, and was meant to be an interim scheme in preparation for a completely new set of services. The *Book of Common Prayer* was to remain in use alongside the new services. The Churchwardens now began the introduction of the new services with different illustrated service booklets produced by Clarissa Cridland.

On the Map for March 2001 contained news of Fr Peter Down's resignation. In a letter to the parishes he explained that he had been suffering from depression for the past year, and possibly longer, and that he had decided to give up full-time ministry. He had decided to train as a primary school teacher and to become a non-stipendiary priest on a part-time basis. Fr Peter's farewell party was hosted by Michael and Vanessa Fleming at Flint House, Holcombe on 10 May 2001. Meanwhile a Parish Profile was produced for prospective candidates. Work was also done to clean the church. Rex Parfitt and Geoffrey Plummer did some painting in the vestry, and the outside doors. Advertisements were placed in the *Church Times* on 8 and 15 June with a view to interviewing candidates early in September.

A Village Weekend was held in Coleford and a special service was held at Holy Trinity on Sunday 1 July. Over 100 people attended, and the collection, amounting to £132, was donated to those affected by the foot and mouth epidemic.

Two deaths shocked the congregation of Holy Trinity in July 2001. Dennis Hodges died on 16 July after a long illness and his funeral was held in the church on 20 July. He had been a member of Holy Trinity for almost fifty years, and as well as attending regularly had done a huge amount of maintenance work. Shortly before his death he restored a lectern which now holds the Book of the Gospels. (This may have been the lectern which was given by the vicar and congregation of Buckland Dinham in 1939, as noted in chapter 10.) Fr Brian Sutton took the funeral service and Clarissa Cridland gave the address to a packed church.

Dennis Hodges

Four days later, on 24 July, the funeral of Les Kite took place in Holy Trinity. Les had regularly attended Holy Trinity since he and Shirley moved to Coleford in 1989 and he had been confirmed there in 1997. As well as being a member of the PCC he had become very involved in village matters. He became Footpath Warden, a member of the Wildlife Group and of the Millennium Group. Together with Julie Dexter he produced *Coleford and Highbury: a short history*, which was published for the Millennium Village Day.

Les Kite

Clarissa takes up the story of the interregnum After the Holy Trinity PCC meeting on 1st March 2000, Fr Peter asked his two Churchwardens, Dave Baker and myself, to stay behind. He explained that he would be seeing the doctor the following Monday, and that it was likely that she would sign him off sick. After Evensong on Sunday 5th Peter and I discussed this further, and I asked him to ring me when he had spoken to the doctor. He duly did so in the evening, and he said that he would leave me some instructions in the vestry about what to do.

Peter's going on sick leave was in many ways a relief since he had clearly been struggling for some time with his ministry, and he needed to have a real break. In some ways the timing was good too—because the Monday he was signed off sick was two days before Ash Wednesday, and the beginning of Lent.

I had been in a pit since November 1993. In November 1992, just after the General Synod had agreed to accept the ordination of women, I had spoken to Peter about being ordained. All the lights were green, and I went to a selection conference (the final hurdle before training) in November 1993, and was turned down flat. I went immediately into a pit. I had still been working and living in London during the week but was made redundant (at my insistence) in March 1994, and worked from home, thus enabling me to be more involved with the work of Holy Trinity on a day to day basis. Indeed I found myself back on the PCC and Deanery Synod, and in 1995 I became Churchwarden, taking over from Bill Atkin. But I could not get myself out of the pit.

It was on Shrove Tuesday 2000 that God lifted me out of the pit I had been in, and told me to lead his people. It was an amazing moment, one minute I was in despair, the next moment I felt enabled. But I could not have done this on my own, and Holy Trinity moved forward with the help of Dave Baker and all the PCC, as well as the Churchwardens at Holcombe and the St Andrew's PCC.

I had taken my first service in 1993, and the PCC were happy for me to lead Evensong when necessary, and also services on Sunday mornings when we could not find a priest to celebrate the Eucharist. We had a number of wonderful priests to help out, and in particular I must mention Canon Brian Boyce, and Father Brian Sutton. Father Brian became an especially good friend and helper in so many ways.

Peter was initially signed off for two weeks, but it was clear that this sick leave would continue for quite some time, and so we planned as though we were in an interregnum. The first few weeks were a little touch and go, but after about four weeks we four Churchwardens went to see the Archdeacon of Bath, Bob Evens, who was extremely helpful. He was, I think, pleased with the way in which we were moving forward, and he agreed that it would be sensible for us Wardens to be licensed to administer Communion, both in church and to people at home. At this time, Bill Atkin was our Server, and administered the chalice each Sunday, but there were times when he was away, and it was obvious that it would be helpful for Dave and myself to take it in turns to do this. Also it was essential that people at home continued to receive their Communions, and we could not always afford to pay a retired priest to come and do this. Once the Bishop's licence had come though, Canon Boyce came over and taught Dave and I how to serve. The Canon had a medical condition which meant that his hand shook, so rather than have him pour wine and water into the chalice, we did this—and for all other priests as well. They all took this without complaint! The other thing which was unique to Canon Boyce was that, after Communion, it is now normal to wash the chalice out with water, which is drunk by the priest. But Canon Boyce had served most of his ministry in Africa, and so he used wine instead—and a lot of it! (Wine did use to be used, but because of priests dashing from one church to the other in a car as opposed to on a horse, clearly that became a bit much, and water took over.)

Over the next months, we grew much more together as a PCC and congregation. In March or April 2000 we had an extra PCC meeting, attended also by one or two others. I remember that the meeting was in the church, as I had completely forgotten that the Theatre Group would be using the hall, and it was rather cold! We agreed then on a number of things that we would do, the most important being mid-week worship, and the school. At that stage, it was completely unclear as to whether we would be able to be helped financially by the diocese (in the end, we were), or not, or whether we ourselves would have to pay the retired priests who came, and so it was suggested by Mary Plummer that we should only have a priest to celebrate Communion on Wednesdays once a month, and that on other Wednesdays Mary would lead a prayer service. I should say that it was Mary, Rona Bruniges and Jill Smith who really kept the Wednesday service going until Valerie's arrival. Sometimes the priest would take out Communion to those at home, but at other times I did this. The Wednesday priests were Father Brian Sutton and Revd Geoffrey Thomas, and they were very encouraging both to the congregation and to the home communicants, and also to me. I was doing a lot on my own, and they always took time to help me, and give me training.

Peter Down had done a huge amount of ministry in the school, and so I had met with David Haywood and Mike Darville (Chair of Governors) on that fateful Shrove Tuesday. It was clear that we would need someone to be a Governor, and equally clear that neither Dave nor I could manage this. At that extra PCC meeting, we talked round this, and Ann Usher suddenly volunteered. I am sure that God called her to do so because Ann has done a huge amount for the school, and indeed managed to do so all through times of bad health. She still serves as a Foundation Governor, and still spends a huge amount of time with the school, as indeed does her husband, Richard.

Once we had received our licenses from the Bishop, I began to take Communion to the sick, using the sacrament reserved each time the Eucharist was celebrated on Sunday. I rang Mary Plummer, and asked her to ask Clare Tresidder if Clare would be happy for me to do this. I was both a woman, and also not a priest, and I was not sure if Clare would be happy; she was and she and the other main people—Joyce Button, Hilda Hamblin and Gwen Jones—helped me enormously. At the time of writing, I am still taking Communion to both Joyce and Gwen, in their care homes.

A Churchwarden is not able to take funerals in church, baptisms or weddings and so I needed help with these. Very quickly I found particular help from the local funeral directors, and they nearly always let me know when someone in Coleford had died and usually asked Father Brian Sutton to take the funeral service, whether this was in church or at the crematorium. Sometimes it would be Revd Geoffrey Thomas. When I could, I would visit the bereaved, and I began to feel real unhappiness that I was not ordained and could not do the funeral. There was one exception. When Shirley Chambers died in mid 2000, her husband and son Vic and David insisted that the funeral be at the crematorium, and that I should take it. I tried to talk them out of this, and consulted various people, but to no avail, and I did end up doing it. I had huge support from Chris Adlam, and Vic and David were pleased, but I still think that someone ordained would have done a much better job—I had never taken a funeral before, and had not then been to very many.

During the interregnum we lost three members of the congregation. In December 2000, Bill Atkin died. Although he had not been well this was a tremendous shock. As I came down from his flat in Douglas Yates Court, I met Fr Peter, and told him, and, although he was still on sick leave, I asked whether he would like to take the funeral. I then rang Canon Brian Boyce and Fr Brian Sutton and told them: both of them expressed an interest in taking the funeral, and I think this sums up what a wonderful person Bill was, and how much he meant to all of us. In July 2001 Les Kite and Dennis Hodges died, within twelve hours of each other. Dennis had been ill for a while, but only recently Les had been in church with us. Arranging their funerals was not easy, because it was important that one did not overshadow the other. In the end we had Dennis' funeral on Friday, then the Fete and Dedication Sunday, and then Les' funeral early the following week, and this worked well. I was privileged to give the address at both funerals, Father Brian officiated, and Curtis Ilott was the Funeral Director—his first two funerals in the village since he had left Adlams.

When Peter went on sick leave, there were already a couple of weddings in the pipeline, and so I went to see the Rural Dean, Jim Balliston-Thicke, and he was very helpful. We had several more weddings the next year, and for these I did much in the way of preparation, using the *Common Worship* service for the first time. I think Father Brian took all the 2001 weddings.

Again, there were some baptisms in the pipeline, and over the next year or so a good number of babies and children, and one adult, were christened at Holy Trinity—sometimes during the morning service, and sometimes in the afternoon. I learnt a huge amount through preparing parents and children for these.

Common Worship: I had heard that there would be a change in the Church of England worship, but I knew very little about it. In April 2000, there was a day at Wells, and clergy and others interested were asked to go. I went with two people from Holcombe, and found the presentation absolutely wonderful. It was clear that the new *Common Worship* services could be so much better than the *Alternative Service Book* we were using at the time, but that they could also be very confusing to use, if not given to people in an easy format. I came back knowing that I had the ability to produce the booklets we would need on the computer, and at a joint PCC meeting I gave a presentation myself. This was completely unscheduled, but both PCCs were very helpful. At that time, we did not know if Father Peter would be returning to us, or if we would be having a new vicar, but it was obvious to me that we should not wait—we did not want a vicar spending all his or her time doing this—and the PCCs agreed. Over the next few months I downloaded the Communion worship (something which was then very complicated to do!) and produced two sample booklets, which I first of all discussed with my fellow Wardens in Coleford and Holcombe, and then presented to the two PCCs (separately). They were both incredibly supportive about what I had done, and it was agreed that we would use the new booklets from January 2001. When Valerie arrived in January 2002, it was clear that our feelings about a new vicar not spending her time doing this were absolutely right, and she wanted very few changes made. Since then, we have updated the booklets, as we have had new material (now finalised) from the C of E, and also as my computer has improved! I have discovered a great joy in providing the booklets, and it has led to an interest in the liturgy (not just the words of a service, but all the movement as well) which I had never expected.

But the first service booklet I produced was not for a Eucharist—it was for Mothering Sunday in 2000. Dave and I both agreed that I should lead this, and I knew what I wanted to do. The trouble was that I had never produced a service booklet before, and didn't have a clue what to do. I asked a friend, and she roughed something out, and talked me through all the changes I needed to make. Looking back, there were things I missed out from the service, but at the time that didn't matter. We had a full church, and as people left they said how much they had enjoyed it (and several asked me when I would be ordained!). This was hugely encouraging, and at the next PCC meeting we agreed that we would hold a Children's Service on the second Sunday each month at 9.30, instead of our Eucharist. I would work out a theme for each, and produce a booklet. The services worked really well, and some people who had brought their children for baptism remembered their promises to God, and brought their children to these services. And we had children and grandchildren of members of the congregation.

One problem I had is that I had no theological training at all, and also at this time in 2000 I was struggling to find work, and thus was not able to buy books. I did buy some for the children's services, which the PCC paid for, but that was that. So when I was due to preach, I had no learning, and few resources. But somehow I managed, and the congregations were incredibly helpful, commenting on my sermons for good and for bad. The Evensong congregation were especially good here, and it was usually the Methodists who asked me what I meant by something, or who said that I would improve, but who were so supportive in how they said it, and so helpful with their comments.

In 2000, we had to take the decision to move our fetes from the Church Hall or Rectory garden to the top of the village. Quite a few people were very unhappy with this, but allowed me to push this through. Our first summer fete was in the grounds of Bishop Henderson School, and was a real success—it was attended by loads of people, and people brought a pony to be ridden, and there were animals to look at as well. We had loads of clergy too—Canon Bryan Boyce, Fr Jim Balliston-Thicke, Fr Brian Sutton and Revd Geoffrey Thomas, and possibly Fr David Barge. The weather was glorious, but in 2001 it was pouring and we had to be inside, which was rather squashed. We had had our 2000 Christmas Fete in the Royal British Legion, and that had been hugely successful, so after the summer of 2001, we decided to have all our fetes, and our jumble sales, at the RBL. We are still there, and it is a wonderful place in which to hold them.

Towards the end of 2000, we Churchwardens met with the Rural Dean and Archdeacon who told us that Peter would be resigning, but that he would be coming back while he bought a house. In January 2001, the Archdeacon met with both PCCs and gave them this news. We began to welcome Peter back, and also to prepare for a new vicar coming. Peter's return was initially going to be very short, and so it was agreed that he would take one service each Sunday morning, alternating each parish week by week, and also Evensong, and that he would take the mid-week services, and we would agree anything else as necessary. We did not want to rock the boat of everything we had set up. In fact, he was back for about three months, but during this time the PCC had voted for Dave and myself to be their representatives in the process of appointing the new vicar, and we began to draw up a new Parish Profile, which had to be joint with Holcombe. I drafted this out, and we four Wardens then discussed it, and then went through it word by word with our PCCs. We actually managed this incredibly easily, and as I have since heard how difficult this can be, I am hugely grateful for all the support we gave each other.

The advertisement went in the *Church Times* in June, and we had quite a lot of applications. These didn't come to us as Churchwardens, but went to the Bishop, who, with the Archdeacon of Bath and other members of his team, chose some candidates to come for interview. The interviews were held in September. The two candidates were to be shown round on Tuesday 4th September and the interview was to be on the Wednesday. We decided that it would be a good idea to have a joint parish party in the church hall (Holy Trinity to provide the food, and St Andrew's the drink as usual!). When I mentioned this to Archdeacon Bob, he said OK, but only PCC members. Bob is well aware that we quite disregarded this, and we asked all members of the congregations of Holy Trinity and St Andrew's who wanted to come. Many people did come, and on the previous Sunday morning I told the congregation that they must let us know how they felt that night. We would be appointing, or not appointing, on the Wednesday morning, and it was no good if someone had strong views about one candidate but hadn't told us before we interviewed. So the congregation talked to the candidates, and to each other, and every so often I was taken outside and told that Valerie was the candidate who seemed to be the right priest to be our vicar.

The interview itself was quite formal, and after the two candidates had gone, we went round the garden and sat round the table and debated. Then the three clergy left (Archdeacon Bob, Rural Dean Jim and Revd Colin Turner, who as vicar of Kilmersdon was Patron of Coleford), and we Wardens discussed. Without the clergy we could say more, and it became absolutely clear that we wanted Valerie as our Priest. We had planned to have a joint PCC that night and announce it, but (fortunately or unfortunately?) I mentioned this, and was shot down by Bob who pointed out that the Bishop still had to officially make the appointment, and so we would not be able to say anything until he told us. There were one or two explosions at the Coleford PCC that evening, but Dave and I were very firm. And on Sunday morning we were able to make the announcement.

Clergy are on three months' notice, and they have to move, and a Bishop has to find space in his diary to licence, and so it would not be until mid-January that we would actually have our new vicar. I remember that last four months as being incredibly hectic, with a few difficulties. One problem was that I could not find a Priest to celebrate Midnight Mass. Fr Brian Sutton would come as early in the morning as we wanted, but he could not do midnight, it was just too late. Valerie would be living in the Rectory by that time, but not licensed so she was unable to take the service. So, I took a Midnight Service, and was incredibly touched that so many people came to this. I had always wanted to preach about (Just) William's Truthful Christmas, and so I did, with the Holy Spirit putting the ending into my mouth, as so often happened then, but almost never seems to now!

I must end this writing about the interregnum with a big thank you—first of all to all the congregation who were so helpful, and perhaps especially so when they disagreed with me, and to all the PCC who kept things under control. But especially to my fellow Warden, Dave, who was, and indeed still is, such a wonderful encouragement and help.

I have mentioned ordination, but having been turned down so flat in 1993, I needed to make sure. In January 2001, I went to talk to Revd Colin Turner, and he was incredibly helpful. But sometimes these things move very slowly, and for me they did. By the end of 2001, I was half way through a reading course, working with the Revd Nigel Done, then Curate at Croscombe and almost immediately afterwards appointed Vicar of Norton St Philip (he had been particularly interested in my descriptions of how we had appointed Valerie!). And so, while I had started this process during the interregnum, I was not to go to a Selection Conference until June 2003, when they said Yes, please! It was Valerie, whom I had been one of the people instrumental in appointing, who was so encouraging and so helpful, and without whom I never would have managed that very long time. So, thank you, Valerie.

Meanwhile, one of those advertisements in the *Church Times* for the post of Priest in Charge of Coleford with Holcombe was spotted by the Revd Valerie Bonham.

Revd Valerie recalls: I was coming towards the end of my time as curate at Cookham on Thames in the diocese of Oxford, but I was not thinking of leaving the diocese. I remember saying to my Bishop that I hoped to stay in Oxford Diocese, preferably in a small town and part of a Team Ministry. I had extended my stay at Cookham to see the parish through an interregnum and was enjoying working with the new vicar, Fr Michael Smith, whom I had known for many years. I had decided to wait until after the summer holidays before seriously thinking about moving on. But I always glanced through the job advertisements in *The Church Times* just out of curiosity. And on that particular Friday there it was—a priest needed for two parishes in Somerset, and there was something about that advertisement that told me "this is it". A bit like falling in love at first sight! So I sent for the Parish Profile and liked what I read. I applied and then spent several anxious weeks until the Archdeacon of Bath (Bob Evens) wrote to say I had been short-listed for interview.

Fred and I thoroughly enjoyed the twenty-four hours we spent looking round the parishes, the social evening meeting the people, the hospitality of Tony and Diane Pratt, and I even enjoyed the interview at Flint House. Archdeacon Bob had assured me that he would telephone at 5.00 pm to say whether I was to be offered the post. We hastened home and got back well before 5.00. No 'phone call … 5.00 became 6.00 and still nothing. I went off to my evening meeting feeling disheartened, going over all the questions and wondering which one I had got wrong! When I returned home the 'phone still hadn't rung. Next morning I went to church for the early service and then at 9.00 am at last the telephone rang. It was the Archdeacon, and he was offering me the post. But it was conditional upon the Bishop of Bath and Wells (Jim Thompson) officially making the offer, so we had to go all the way back to Wells the next day. It's a long way from Cookham to Wells, but the post was duly offered and accepted, and the announcement made in both parishes on the following Sunday. Meanwhile, back in Coleford (so I was told later), there had been a PCC meeting on the night of the interview, but the Churchwardens were unable to announce the appointment because the Bishop needed to see the successful candidate. Little did the Churchwardens know that the successful candidate had not received her 'phone call. All's well that ends well, and we moved to Coleford on 18 December 2001 with a month to get settled in before my Licensing on 16 January 2002.

It will be for future generations to assess the ministry of the Revd Valerie Bonham, but some of the highlights of the time from 2002 until May 2009 will be found in chapter 14, Holy Trinity in the 21st century.

INTERLUDE

DEDICATION FESTIVALS THROUGH THE YEARS

HOLY TRINITY has celebrated the anniversary of its Dedication in many ways over the years. Here are some highlights:

1832—A simple fete at the "Manse" was how the Revd Joseph Wade, quoting from the Church logbook of 1832, described it in the August 1906 parish magazine.

1833—A dinner for the most regular church goers.

1835—The Dedication anniversary was celebrated with Holy Communion.

1836—"Anniversary a pelting wet day. The Revd R Hamilton preached a long powerful sermon at an afternoon service. Mr Paget Present."

1837—The Revd George Newnham noted in the church logbook, "Self at Laugharne."

1838—"A very well conducted dinner to 30 morning church goers—an evening service attended by friends from Chilcompton, Leigh and tumultuous tea party to a school of starving children."

1839—"A cruelly wet day kept away all friends but the preacher the Reverend Daniel, but by a better arrangement 120 children had tea of 27 cakes—the teachers then sat down to theirs while books and readings were distributed."

19 July 1906—"We celebrated this day the 75th anniversary of the consecration of the church. A thanksgiving service … at 4 pm." The Bishop of Bath and Wells was absent through illness, but Bishop Stirling, Canon of Wells, preached, and the collection was taken for the Pan Anglican Thank Offering. Afterwards there was a garden party in the vicarage garden, when 150 sat down to tea. The services continued on 23 July, when the Revd Price of Wells Theological College preached. A parish mission from the Church Army Van was held to coincide with the 75th anniversary of the church's dedication. The Revd Wade wrote in the parish magazine that "the crowning glory of our festivities was, of course our birthday party and the festival … Thanks to the fine weather and the cordial co-operation of everybody, it was a downright triumph". The collection at the evening service was for the "Chancel Fund", the Revd Wade having decided that "if ever the Church should require enlargement, the extension would have to be made by the erection of a chancel".

1907—The Revd Dwight was the preacher at the Dedication festival and was also a guest at the garden party.

19 July 1908—The church was "prettily decorated and there were fairly good congregations". Three days later came the annual garden party: "For some time past the ladies attending the sewing class had been busily preparing for the event, and the success of their efforts was seen in the capital display of useful ornament and fancy articles arranged on the principal stall …" Stalls included: Sweets and Books— Mesdames J Hamblin, F Candy, G Turner, J Spiller and F Clarke; Cut flowers and pot plants—Misses E Turner, L Craddock, C Harding; refreshments—Misses Robbins and Bryant, Mesdames T Ellison and G Hamblin. "A good deal of fun was caused by 'Aunt Sally' which was in charge of Mr O Plummer. The East Mendip Band, under the direction of Mr Walter Seymour, played charming selections during the afternoon and evening. Later, dancing was very popular … In the church room a museum was on exhibition …" The various activities raised a total of £21 10s.

1931—Centenary celebrations included games, dancing, and maypole dancing for the garden fete, and the Midsomer Norton Town Band was hired at a cost of £3 15s.

1933—The PCC considered whether to hire a band or a "melody van" for the garden fete to entertain at the anniversary, but didn't record which they chose.

1936—Rain forced the garden party celebrations indoors; efforts were made to hold a smaller outdoor event in September.

1947—Celebrations included a confirmation at Holy Trinity by the Bishop of Bath and Wells (the Rt Revd H William Bradfield). Twenty-three candidates were confirmed: N A Button, Jeffrey Webb, John Webb, Brian Arthur Price, Walter? Dudley Perkins, Royston Ian Moore, Oliver John Chivers, Graham Herbert Plummer, Geoffrey Roland Plummer, Anthony Hamblin, Derrick Glynne Price, Edwin William Phillips, Michael George Wells: Vera Joan Mascord, Elizabeth Wells, Lilian Joyce Hamblin, Marina Heather? Price, ?Mary Simkins, Shirley Flora Chamberlain, Mary Gwendoline Chamberlain, Martha Myrtle Maureen Robbins, Jean Whale. They received their first Communion on the following Sunday at 8.00 am when there were forty-nine communicants.

1956—In the 1950s, Gift Day was often combined with the Dedication Festival. In 1956, the 125th anniversary of Dedication, Gift Day on Saturday 21 July brought in £48 15s 0d, several pounds more than in 1955. The 125th anniversary was kept on the actual day (19 July), beginning on the eve with a procession at Evening Prayer at which the Bishop of Taunton preached and blessed the new aumbry for reserving the Sacrament of Communion for the sick. Incense was used for the first time.

1959—On Saturday 18 July there was First Evensong of the Festival at 7.00 pm with a special preacher, Bishop Fabian Jackson. Also, the Bath branch of the Church Union attended. The same day was Gift Day, with envelopes being received in church from 8.00 am until Evensong, when they were offered at the altar. Sunday services were as usual with a festive flavour. The Canon Moore prizes for Children's Church attendance were to be deferred until Christmas when they would be presented at the Christmas Party.

1967—There was a Flower Festival combined with Gift Day.

1981—150th celebrations included the return of a number of former incumbents. See chapter 9 for further details.

1985—The usual Garden Party was held in the Rectory grounds on Saturday 20 July with stalls, teas and the Holcombe Majorettes.

1986—There was a Flower Festival, organised by Joyce Button, portraying aspects of Royalty. Representatives of organisations in both villages contributed arrangements.

2006—In conjunction with the 175th anniversary celebrations, a Flower Festival was held in the church over two days, organised by Ann Mackie-Hunter, with over sixty arrangements from a large number of contributors.

Part 2

BRICKS, MORTAR,
GOOD LIME
AND
COAL ASH

10

SOLID JOYS AND LASTING TREASURE—THE UPKEEP OF THE CHURCH BUILDING

FOR many people, the most obvious face of Holy Trinity is the church itself. **Esme Harrison** remembers the church as it used to be in her childhood:

My first memories of the church were hanging oil lamps; in the centre of the church was a large ring with several oil lamps on it. Large stands with many candles stood in the chancel.

Men and boys sat in the choir stalls, and lady choir members sat in the front seats of the congregation. The organ was at the front of the church, with a curtained cubicle for the person pumping the organ.

On both sides of the altar were stone tablets with the Ten Commandments written on them, later they were replaced by blue trellis-like windows, much to the annoyance of some of the congregation.

Harvest was quite an occasion with garden produce filling the church, and corn from the fields, and coal from the local mines. The church would be crowded with people, and extra chairs put down the aisles. The choir sang an anthem, and the one that stands out in my mind was "The valley stands so thick with corn".

George Phillips Manners was a well known Bath architect who, in the 1830s, boasted the title of "City Architect" and designed a number of buildings including St Mark's Lyncombe, St Michael with St Paul Broad Street, the Bath Union Workhouse, and restoration work of part of the Roman baths. In addition, from 1833–4 he was responsible for the first major restoration of Bath Abbey, a project that proved to be controversial.

But how has Holy Trinity changed over the years? In fact there is a certain amount of confusion regarding the design and building of Holy Trinity. It is listed in *Pevsner's Buildings of England* as the work of G P Manners of Bath.

It is more likely that Manners did not personally supervise the building of the church, even though the contract (D/P/Coleford 8/3/2) of 3 February 1830 states that "George P Manners of the City of Bath Architect hath prepared and furnished the necessary plans and drawings …" It is more likely that his design was executed by John Sperring, a surveyor from Frome. The contract goes on to state that the work would be "under the inspection and direction of such Surveyor or Clerk of the Works … as shall be appointed …" Sperring is sometimes attributed as the architect because his name appears on the ICBS plan for the seating and the gallery. This plan is very sketchy and not to scale and was not a building plan but merely to indicate which pews were rented and which were free. Mr Parfitt the builder would have been under Sperring's supervision.

For a long time it was thought that there were no other plans, but the file of correspondence at Lambeth Palace Library (ICBS 1109, see chapter 2), between the Coleford Church Building Committee and the Incorporated Church Building Society, refers to other plans. The Articles of Enquiry dated 31 July 1829, submitted to the ICBS by the Church Building Committee, bear the note "a bundle of 7 Plans and drawings herewith". A letter to the ICBS from the Secretary of the Committee dated 5 December 1829 informed them: "The Solicitor employed to draw up the Contract with the Builder … having applied for the Plans in order to attach them to the Contract, I am desired by the Committee to request they may be returned." Although the contract has survived, the plans seem to have disappeared without trace. This is hardly surprising, as the plans may have been used on site and have become wet, muddy and damaged, and deemed not worth keeping when the job was done.

Advertisements inviting tenders for the new church specified building particulars which included: 400 free sittings at 2ft 4 ins by 1ft 6 ins each, a pew for the clergyman, reading desk, pulpit, altar, baptismal font, clerk's seat and vestry room; a gallery with sufficient pews for sixty plus singing gallery with open staircase leading thereto; a tower to be built at the west end with one bell and one clock. They went on to describe the materials to be used, including: roof of best red deal covered with concrete slates; gallery and open sittings floors of red deal; aisle and altar floors of free stone. The altar was to be "3ft above [the] floor of the church body" and visible from all parts of the church, with the reading desk on the north side. Rough stone for the building was to be taken from the quarry near the aqueduct, owned by Mr Fussell, and door cases, windows and other dressing of Freestone.

The contract of February 1830 gives more detail about the building of the church and in particular the materials to be used. "All the windows of the Church, Chancel and robing room" [i.e. vestry] "to be glazed with second Newcastle Glass, well and securely leaded in lozenges, and the same to be left whole and perfect when the works are completed. One iron frame casement to be fixed and hung in each window … for ventilation." This Newcastle glass was largely replaced when stained or painted glass windows were added later. However, some of it may have survived in the form of the greenish opaque glass surrounding some of the later stained glass.

The gallery was to be supported by two cast iron columns. Much care was taken with painting the furnishings of the church. "The front of the Gallery, Pulpit and Reading Desk to be painted—also the fronts of all the pews, handrails and banister to staircases, outside and inside doors and jambs [with] four coats grained in imitation of oak and varnished with Copal Varnish. All iron bars to windows and straps to the roof to be painted three coats, the inside of the Pews, top and middle rail and ends of the free seats to be painted three coats and left plain when finished. The whole of the above work to be well knotted and stopped and left perfect and free from blemishes when the works are completed."

The contract gives further information on the materials used for furnishing the church. "The Pulpit and Reading Desk to be of 1¼ inch Gothic moulded framing with square backs, [and] inch wrought deal flooring … A neat oak handrail to the Communion [table] and Gothic cast iron balusters properly secured to the floor with a gate in the centre and latch fastenings … All the Baltic Timber Deals and Oak to be the best … and no American Timber whatsoever to be used in the building."

Even though people's homes were very cold by 21st century standards, and they did not therefore expect a warm church, the building must have been very cold indeed. The only heating referred to in the contract was: "a smoke flue and parget for the same to be carried up in the walls of the Church for a hot air stove, and also for a Fireplace in the robing room with a sham stone Freestone chimney piece and slab for the same." This smoke flue is still visible from outside the church to the right of the porch, although the hot air stove (situated where the font now stands) has long gone.

As referred to in chapter 6, Ron Brewer remembers his grandmother (born in 1892) talking about an old round iron stove situated where the font is now. This was the only heating in the church at the time and was replaced in 1924 by a solid fuel boiler and hot water pipes. As noted in chapter 6, Ron remembers his grandmother talking about an old font, which had previously been at the back of the church, lying broken up in the churchyard. Presumably it was replaced by the present font. When the great storm of May 1906 resulted in water cascading through the tower trapdoor, the Revd Wade had reported that the baptistery was flooded, and therefore this must have been at the back of the church under the tower.

No mention is made in the contract of whether the interior walls were to be lime-washed. Certainly the interior was covered in lime plaster with scored lines to imitate stone, presumably to save money. During the restoration of 2007, when several coats of paint going back at least a century were removed, the handprint of the plasterer was revealed. As noted above, dressed stone was used for the door cases and windows, and the contract specifies: "the whole of the Freestone to be from the Doulting quarries and of the best quality and to be well cleaned down and left in a perfect state when the works are completed. The Mortar for the said works to be composed of good lime and coal ashes and road Dirt in the proportion 1/3 of lime and 2/3 of coal ashes/road dirt. The best brown lime to be used for setting all the Freestone." The church Minute book (D/P/Coleford 8/3/1) records the itemised expenditure by Mr Parfitt the builder: contract for the church £1,169; boundary wall £49 13s; raising the walls and tower £25; and the elliptic ceiling £32. The vestry room (or robing room) was not built at first as the proximity to the parsonage was felt to make it unnecessary, thus saving money; and the clock was dropped from early plans as a further measure of economy.

But what would the church have *looked* like? The early 19th century was not an era distinguished for its church building, and those churches such as Holy Trinity which were built at this time were very basic—plain preaching halls with plastered ceilings to aid acoustics, plenty of seats, usually box pews, including a gallery if possible, so that the congregation could hear the sermon, which was regarded as the most important aspect of the service. The sermon would have been long by today's standards, lasting up to an hour or even longer. The small altar, set back into what was really little more than a recess, reflected the lack of emphasis on the sacraments at this time. By 1851, the first year in which Coleford answered the Articles of Enquiry for the Bishop's Visitation, the Holy Communion was celebrated ten times a year. But in the earliest years it may have been less frequent. If Holy Trinity had been built thirty years later, it would probably have reflected the style of the Victorian Gothic Revival—a far more ornate interior with pillars and aisles; more developed window tracery; an open timber roof rather than a plastered ceiling; and a far larger chancel and a more prominent altar. The Victorian Church builders were influenced by the Oxford or Tractarian Movement, with its renewed emphasis on sacramental worship as well as the sermon. (See the box in chapter 3.)

A photograph of the interior of Holy Trinity taken in the early 20th century shows this influence, such as the text painted over the Chancel arch; an embroidered altar frontal; and the crucifix behind the pulpit. It also shows the oil lamps and the old stove where the present day font stands. Thus it is possible to date the photograph to sometime between 1905 (when the text over the chancel arch was painted), and 1924 when the stove was removed.

Church interior following the 1905 renovation: note altar rails, location of organ at the east end, the pulpit canopy, oil lamps, stove where the font now stands, and text above the chancel arch

However, Holy Trinity looked much different when it opened in 1831. Alas, there are no pictorial records of the church interior in 1831 except for a rough sketch of the seating plan, showing which of the box pews were free and which were rented to the local gentry. The new church included 408 free seats, and the remainder were rented: 48 at 10s and 40 at 5s.

If all the seats had been let, they would have provided a regular income of £34, but

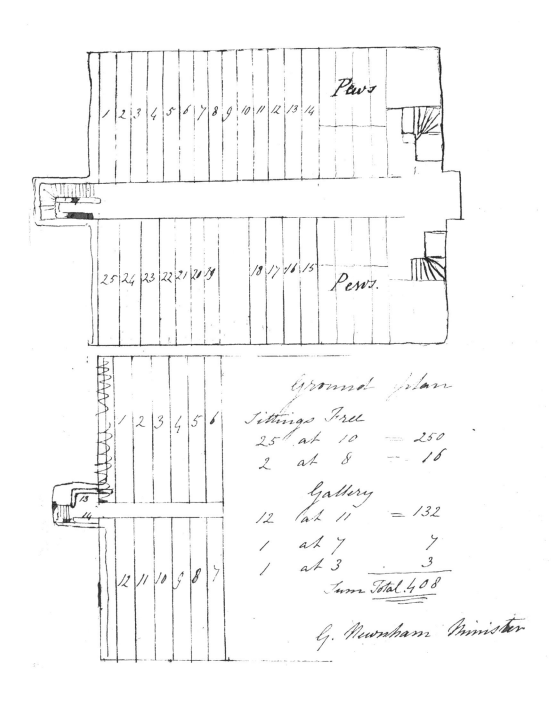

Seating plan of the church, 1831

in practice they raised about £17. The parish clerk was paid 2s 6d for collecting the pew rents at Christmas and midsummer. A list of early pew renters identifies:

Name	Pew No.	Seats	Amount
Col. Jolliffe	1	8	£4
Mr Paget, Newberry	2	6	£3
Mr Craddock, Lypeat	3	4	£2
Mr Hobbs–Mr Tucker	4&5	(1+1) 2	10s
G Brice, J Button	6	(2+2) 4	£1
Mr Jeffries	7	2	10s
Executors The Revd G Gregory	8	6	£3
Mr Thomas Brice	9	1	10s
M H Brice & Harding	10+13	(2+2)	£1 10s
Mr James Brice	15	3	15s
Mr Knatchbull	16	4	£2
Mr R Green & servants	17+14	(6+2) 8	£3+10s

The pew rents, together with fees from burials and marriages, and funding from other sources including Queen Anne's Bounty (see box in chapter 2), made up the income of the "living", i.e. what the vicar could expect to be paid. Pew rents continued to be paid, although in dwindling numbers, until 1900, after which time all seats were legally declared free. At Holy Trinity, as a concession to those who rented pews, it was agreed that they could continue to do so until they voluntarily gave them up. The last pew rents were paid in late 1906. The loss of income that resulted had a direct impact on the living, which was augmented by additional funds from the Ecclesiastical Commissioners, so that in 1911 the living was £206 per annum.

The Revd Thomas Yewens

Although the clock was dropped from the early plans in order to save money, there was certainly one by 1870, as the Churchwarden's Accounts (D/P/Coleford 4/1/1) note that H Webb was paid £1 5s 0d for repairing it, and this seems to have been an annual fee for its upkeep. During the Revd Yewens' time as Vicar the interior of the church took on its present day appearance. The *East Somerset*

Pew rents Wealthy parishioners paid a fixed rent to reserve a pew, or number of pews, and no one else would be permitted to use them, even in the absence of the person renting. This often meant there were very few "free" seats, and often "daughter churches" were opened with free seating to serve the poor. During the 19th century there was a growing movement to abolish pew rents. The Church Building Society, founded in 1818 (Incorporated Church Building Society from 1828), made grants towards building or restoring churches on condition that seating (or the majority of it) should be free and unappropriated.

Telegraph of 10 January 1885 gave notice of the impending closure of Holy Trinity and some of the anticipated changes. "The Church being now under repair in the shape of colouring and re-pewing the inside will be closed for some time, and the service held in the Infant schoolroom at the usual hours. The present unsightly pews are to be replaced with some of more modern construction, both free and appropriated sittings being similar in appearance; the gallery is to be taken away, and the organ placed at the East end of the church. The pulpit will be lowered and the present vestry be open throwing a good light into the church from the west window under the tower. Messrs Willcox, Wilson and Ames of Bath are the architects, and Mr Joseph James, Lipyeat [*sic*] is the contractor … The cost of the alterations will, it is expected, be about £200."

There was more information in the issue of 18 April, once the work had been completed. "The alterations … consisted of a complete renovation of the interior, by substituting open pine seats for the old fashioned boxes, so common in churches throughout the country. Instead of the poor parishioners being compelled to sit in the rear, the arrangements now are on a far more liberal scale, and the humble attendant is placed on an equal footing with the other members of the congregation. The sittings are now so arranged that on each side of the church from the east to the west comfortable seats to hold three persons are free. There are now three aisles instead of one, and in the centre of the church are the appropriated seats. The old gallery has been entirely removed, the organ which has been thoroughly overhauled placed at the east end of the church. A new reading desk of modern design replaces the old one and the pulpit has been considerably lowered. The vestry has been done away with and the west window thrown open giving the church a light and open appearance. The walls and ceiling are coloured, the doors repainted and varnished, and as a whole the church has a light and airy appearance … We are happy to say the work reflects great credit on the contractor for the excellent manner in which it is carried out. The church during Tuesday was thrown open to the public, and during the afternoon there were a large number of visitors."

A modern picture of the pulpit installed in 1885

Although the newspaper report does not specifically state that a new pulpit had been installed, stating rather that the pulpit had been "considerably lowered," it is likely that the present stone pulpit was placed in the church at this time. It is certainly not contemporary with the rest of the church as built in 1831, the tracery of the pulpit being in a much later Victorian Gothic style which resonates with the 1880s. The original pulpit would have been much higher so that the preacher could see the congregation in the box pews. The replacement of these with open seating meant that the pulpit could be lower. The internal arrangement of St Andrew's Old Church in Holcombe gives a good idea of a pre-Victorian church interior complete with box pews, a three decker pulpit and large hat pegs for the men's hats. The contract (D/P/Coleford 8/3/2) specified a wooden reading desk to be on the north (left) side of the sanctuary, but the seating plan of 1831 appears to show the reading desk on the south (right) side, and a wooden pulpit on the north side where the present pulpit stands. But as the seating plan was only a rough sketch designed to show the pew sittings it cannot be relied upon as accurate evidence. As noted above, the reading desk was replaced in the 1885 restoration but was later again replaced. The Churchwarden's Accounts for 1885 (D/P/Coleford 4/1/1) note that £9 10s was paid to Sweetland for the organ. This would be for the cost of moving the organ to its new position, which may have involved taking it apart and rebuilding it. At the time of the 1885 restoration the west window (i.e. the window in the tower) was not filled with stained glass, so the removal of the organ and the gallery would have allowed the daylight to flood in at the west end.

The Revd Joseph Wade

A new organ was installed in 1901 replacing the original Sweetland organ, and changes to the altar were effected in 1902. At Easter, new Doulting stone panels were placed at the base of the east window to provide a background for altar candles, "the old stone re-table was made into a sill for the window and a new oak re-table placed thereon to receive the ornaments". (A re-table is a wooden or stone shelf or ledge behind the altar upon which candlesticks may be placed.) The altar itself was repaired and raised upon a wooden platform of one step, the work being paid for by the Revd Wade. The following October, the Revd Wade also paid for a pulpit canopy, "for the permanent adornment of the church", and with the hope that it would make his voice more audible. Two new pitch pine seats were also purchased at a cost of £1 7s 6d, for use in the sanctuary (but while one is still in existence it is no longer in use).

Structural changes to the church building were also made under the Revd Wade. In June 1903 Badman and Sons of Holcombe erected a new vestry between the south wall of the tower and the west wall of the nave. The new building cost £56, half of which was raised by public subscription and half by fundraising events including special collections, organ recitals, concerts, entertainments, garden party, jumble sale, tea party, church offerings and sale of photographs. At Easter 1904, a cast iron cross was also fixed at the apex of the chancel roof at a cost of £6 15s 6d. In September 1904 there were further additions to the church building, with a building for coal, funeral requisites and other odds and ends completed on the north side of the tower, corresponding to the vestry on the south side. This is now the clergy vestry. Built by

Holy Trinity from the west, showing both vestries at the base of the tower

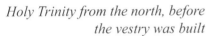

Holy Trinity from the north, before the vestry was built

Holy Trinity, from the parish magazine, 1905

Messrs J & U Wilcox of Leigh-on-Mendip, at a cost of £41 11s 6d, the exterior wall was faced with cement, rather than Freestone.

Changes to the interior continued in 1904. On 15 April a cast iron rail was fixed at the front edge of the choir platform to form a "kind of low chancel screen". Supplied and fitted by Charles Hamblin, the rail was an Easter gift from the Revd Wade. Writing in the parish magazine for April 1904 he commented, "We are again under the necessity of sounding a trumpet as a call to alms. The condition of the interior of the church demands immediate attention. The very stones cry out for want of a little colour. The whitewash falls in a continuous shower from the ceiling like snowflakes; and the ochre on the walls runs away on the arm of every passing acquaintance … If the nave is to be coloured afresh, it should be well done. It is no use, as the sailors say, spoiling the ship (and our clothes) for a ha'porth of tar."

People evidently rallied to the call and the church was closed between 14 and 28 May 1905 for renovation, during which time the services were held in the schoolrooms. The Parish Magazine for April 1905 tells us that the church would be decorated light green. The Revd Wade commented wryly: "Dr Jones endorses the selection for medical reasons. It is the best colour for the eyesight; though there would be very little risk of the people of Coleford damaging their eyes, from the amount of time they spend in Church. Perhaps they are already suffering from housemaid's knee through excessive kneeling. However, we do not desire to furnish them with an additional excuse for absenting themselves from public worship, so green the colour shall be." (Traces of the green paint could still be found a century later when the church was being prepared for the 2007 restoration.)

Some people had asked for texts to be painted around the windows. This would add to the cost so the Revd Wade asked that they might "express their desires in the shape of a small contribution". The texts had been chosen to reflect Our Lord's titles. That over the chancel arch read: "Jesus Christ, the same yesterday, and to-day, and forever." Those over the windows were to have read: "The Word of God", "The Light of the World", "The Lamb of God", "The Bread of Life", "The True Vine", "The Good Shepherd" and "The Resurrection and the Life". Later photographs show the text over the chancel arch but not over the windows. Later restorations showed no evidence of the texts over the windows, but during the 2007 restoration pale traces of the chancel arch text were discernable, very faded and in poor condition.

The church reopened on Ascension Day, with a service lead by the Revd Boyd, the Rector of Bath, as the Revd Wade was suffering from pneumonia. He had been taken ill when he was "a couple of hundred miles from home" and was off duty for several months. The cost of the restoration work included: colouring the walls £16 10s 0d, woodwork, repairs to windows 18s, repairs to fabric £1 10s 8d, painting gates 7s, painting the stove pipe 5s, painting texts £12, and the cleaning of the altar 8s.

In October 1909 the old method of heating the church, through a stove passing hot air through a series of exposed pipes passing up the wall and through the centre of the roof, had outlived its purpose. Agreed to be unsightly, it was also deemed unsafe. The pipes were removed and replaced by an external stone chimney (built by Badman and Sons from Holcombe), the loss of heat from which was compensated for by the installation of a larger stove—a No. 7 Tortoise Stove bought from C Bailey and Co in Bristol at a total cost of £25 8s 3d. Evidently not everyone was in favour of the project. Writing in the *Coleford Parish Magazine* for November 1909, the Revd Wade remarked, "Many of the fears which were expressed when we embarked on our new enterprise, have already proved groundless. So far from the new chimney being an eyesore which some anticipated, we may almost claim the new chimney as a picturesque addition to the church. The appearance of the interior is at any rate considerably enhanced by the removal of the ugly iron pipes. But the proof of the pudding is in the heating … Some people are already beginning to express the fear that … for the future they may be baked instead of frozen … We may flatter ourselves at least that the church is now fairly secure from danger of fire …" The old stove pipes were sold for 6 shillings.

On 16 June 1912 at Evensong, "A stained glass window inserted at the East end of the Chancel in a memorial of the reign of Edward VII and in commemoration of the Coronation of George V was dedicated by the Lord Bishop of the diocese (Dr. Kennion) in the presence of an overflowing congregation." Designed by Jones and Willis of London, the window cost £63 7s 6d and was paid for by public subscription (including £28 11s collected by Miss Robbins) and the usual fundraising events. Photographs of the proposed window, taken by William Marchant Jones, were sold for 2d each and raised £1 3s towards the total cost. The window depicts Christ the King in the centre, flanked by King David and King Solomon. The Revd Wade noted in the July 1912

Magazine that "the symbolism is intended to suggest that the sovereignty of Christ is an everlasting kingdom and a reign of peace …" In fact the faces of Christ, David and Solomon are identical in order to emphasise that Jesus was born from the "house and line of David".

Following the success of the east window, the Revd Wade expressed a hope for the church which became a reality very quickly. "Personally we like it so much that it has excited in us the hope of one day being able to fill the West window with stained glass also. We should not like to have all the windows coloured, for the light and cheerful aspect of the Church is one of its most attractive features, but to paint the belfry window would add very

The 1912 commemorative window at the east end of the church

much to the appearance of the building and would do little to darken it. We cannot suggest a more suitable subject … than the incident immortalised by the Nunc Dimittis …" (Luke 2: 25–35)

The west window was in fact in the belfry under the tower and would have been visible to the congregation because at that time the organ was at the front of the nave, having been moved there in 1885. The organ was not moved to its present position at the west end of the church until 1950. A west window by the same designers as the east window would make sense aesthetically, and would catch the rays of the setting sun. It seems there was some money in hand from the east window project which could go towards the next one and the new project was embraced with gusto. The cost of the new window was £40 10s 2d, and the congregation struggled to raise the last £2 10s. However, the Revd John E W Honneywill, Vicar of Leigh-on-Mendip, sent a cheque for the outstanding amount. The vicar himself, together with Mrs Wade, had contributed £5 0s 0d towards the project, having already made two similar donations towards the east window. The decision was made to dedicate the window in memory of the first four incumbents of Coleford. Jones and Willis were again chosen to design the window and the Faculty was granted in July 1914. The subject was the Presentation of the infant Christ in the Temple and showed the small child being taken into the arms of Simeon, with Mary looking on. Simeon is about to utter his "Nunc Dimittis"—"Lord, now lettest thou thy servant depart in peace, according to thy

The window commemorating the first four incumbents, originally placed at the west end in the tower, and now situated near the font

In grateful recollection of the labours of the first four Incumbents of this Church who have now entered into their rest. G Newnham 1831–1840. J West 1840–1846. C [*sic*] H Whiteway 1846–1864. T D L Yewens 1864–1895.

word." The window was later moved to its present position to the right of the church door, near the font, though it has not been possible to find the date of the removal.

Although the Revd Joseph Wade had instigated the project, he did not benefit from it, as he left the parish just as the window was about to be installed. On Sunday,

1 October 1914, the new window was unveiled at Evensong in the presence of the Revd J H Lewis, Vicar of Christ Church, Frome; the Revd Cecil G Norton, Vicar of Kilmersdon and the Revd John Honneywill, Vicar of Leigh-on-Mendip. The new Vicar of Holy Trinity, the Revd J H Evans, had objected to the new window project and had tried to prevent its installation. But plans had gone too far and the window had been paid for. People were looking forward to seeing the fruits of their investment, particularly as it was to commemorate the first four incumbents. So the Revd Evans was foiled in his efforts to thwart the scheme but he registered his contempt for it by his absence from Evensong on 1 October.

Other changes followed: in 1913 the church clock was given a thorough clean by W H Thick of Catherine Street, Frome. The dial was also taken down and re-gilded by Mr Grant Jnr, also of Frome. The total cost was £10.

The Revd H F Ralph-Bowman

In May 1929, the PCC agreed to purchase kneeler pads, to replace the wooden kneelers that had been used since the Revd Dwight's day, and more stained glass was soon to follow.

For many years there has been an oral tradition that some of the windows at Holy Trinity came from Mells and consist of 17th century Flemish glass, but there seemed to be no documentary evidence to support this story. However, more information has come to light during the preparation of this book, and much of the story can now be substantiated.

On 26 July 1929 the Revd Ralph-Bowman reported that he had been given the offer of a stained glass window for the church, which was gratefully accepted. The gift would have required a Faculty from the diocese, and evidently nothing was done for some considerable time because the Petition for the Faculty was dated 28 April 1931. This was submitted by the Incumbent and the Churchwardens (Ernest Steeds and Edwin Spear). The Diocesan Chancellor wrote to the incumbent asking for further information in a letter (which has not survived) dated 25 July 1931. The Revd Ralph-Bowman replied on 27 July:

> The stained glass we now intend to use was given me for the purpose by Lady Horner of Mells. It was originally in the chapel of the Manor House but was removed some years ago by Sir John when the chapel was included in the library.
>
> Lady Horner, who is something of an authority on the subject says that this glass is really good in design, colour and drawing. It is Flemish and XVII Century.
>
> There are two lights in the proposed Window and the aforesaid is in four panels of four of the Holy Apostles. There would be two panels to each light.
>
> You will understand in the circumstances that I cannot send a design. If

the window were going to be made by some modern maker he would of course supply the design, in which case it would give me pleasure to forward [it] to you. But this is an exceptional case and I am sure will be so treated by your Board. I cannot afford to employ an artist to make [a] design. I find that to convey one panel to Bath to be properly photographed would cost about two guineas.

The work of putting the panels in does not involve touching the design or interfering with the figures in any way as they fit very well into the window.

The opinion has been expressed that these are really too good for our building which is dated 1831 and is more like a mission room than a church, unfortunately.

It has been a hard struggle to get the money to fix this memorial and to pay the Faculty fee. To employ an artist to make a design is beyond our financial power …

PS This is a very poor parish composed mainly of unemployed miners.

Lady (Frances) Horner (1858–1940) was a knowledgeable and discerning patron of the arts, and a close friend for many years of the artist Edward Burne-Jones. The fact that she had vouched for the origin, quality and dating of the window may be taken as an authoritative opinion. The chapel in the Manor House relates to the short-lived St Andrew's College (1848–58) established by the Rector, Prebendary Horner, for the education of young men as missionaries or teachers, and who would not have had the opportunity for a university education.

The Chancellor must have viewed the Revd Ralph-Bowman's plea sympathetically because the Faculty was granted on 5 August 1931: "To place Stained Glass in a Window in the Parish Church of Coleford, the said Window having been presented to the Vicar and Churchwardens." But the mystery deepens once more, because a handwritten note on the Faculty states: "the window was recently the East Window of the Church of Norton St Philip, Somerset and has been presented by the rector to the Church of Holy Trinity, Coleford." The present east window at Norton St Philip is a 20th century window by the renowned stained glass artist, Christopher Webb, which may have replaced an earlier Flemish window from Mells, now given by the Rector of Norton St Philip to Coleford.

This window was dedicated in memory of Mary Ann Turner on 6 January 1932 at Evensong, which was held at 3.00 pm due to bad weather. Even so, sixty people attended the service. The Revd John Charles Forrester, Vicar of Kilmersdon and Rector of Babington, was present as well as the Revd Ralph-Bowman. This window is at the west end of the north aisle (see page 184).

The Service Register notes that on 29 June 1932 (Feast of St Peter), more windows were dedicated at Evensong by the Revd Ralph-Bowman and the Revd Forrester. The Service Register does not record the number of people who attended, but the sum of

£2 4s in the collection indicates a large number in the congregation. These windows were dedicated in memory of two former Parish Clerks, Benjamin Martin (1831–61) and Philip Perkins (1885–1915). Benjamin Martin's window is in the north aisle, second from the west end, and Philip Perkins' is in the south aisle at the west end (see overleaf).

The saga of the windows continued when more stained glass was installed on the north side of the church. This was the memorial window to Hugh and Louisa Robbins and their daughter, Clara. It is in the north aisle, third from the west end. The window was dedicated at Evensong on Sunday, 20 September 1933. A number of visiting clergy signed the Register: J O Hannay, Rector of Mells, L R Hancock, Rector of Whately and S W Rowlands, Vicar of Kilmersdon.

The following undated press cutting gives a résumé of the four windows: "A coalminer [Philip Perkins], the first parish clerk [Benjamin Martin 1831–61], the mother of seven daughters [Elizabeth Mary Ann Turner], and a postmaster [Hugh and Louisa Robbins and Clara their daughter], are commemorated by four stained glass windows at the parish church of Coleford, near Radstock. The windows are composed of 17th century Flemish glass which was originally in the Chapel of Mells Manor, Somerset. Canon Hannay, Rector of Mells, who is better known as George A Birmingham, the humorous novelist, dedicated the windows." (D/P/Coleford 9/1/2, press cutting "Fourth Window Dedicated") As with many press reports, this is inaccurate in that Canon Hannay only dedicated the Robbins window, not all four.

> **The four 17th century Flemish windows**: see overleaf. The south aisle is the first as one enters the church from the porch, and the north aisle is the one furthest away. The west end of the church is that nearest the tower, and the east end is that nearest the altar.

The name of the contractor who installed the windows is not recorded, but they were installed in the wrong order! Each apostle has a phrase from the Apostles' Creed in Latin over his head, and traditionally St Peter is always first, but he does not appear first in the sequence, a pitfall no doubt of installing the windows piecemeal. Therefore the words of the Creed appear in the wrong order. Also, two extra lights were made to make up the set—these are St Dunstan, former monk of Glastonbury and Archbishop of Canterbury, and King Alfred of Wessex.

1935 brought other significant changes for the church, with the decision to install electric lighting which had originally been discussed in 1932. As a result, a £5 reduction in the Sexton's wages was agreed, as he no longer had to maintain the oil lamps. The Service Register notes that at Evensong on 27 October 1935 the electric lighting was dedicated, although the Faculty permitting the installation of "an electric lighting system in the said Church in accordance with the plan and specification filed with the petition and the regulations for electric lighting issued by the Bath and Wells Diocesan Advisory Committee for the Protection of Churches" was not formally granted until 20 November 1935.

Window in memory of Philip Perkins

South aisle, west end

St Matthew (with axe), An apostle (with sword), St James the Less (with club or pole), St Philip (with long staff with cross)

This window was dedicated to the Glory of God and the loved and honoured memory of Philip Perkins, Clerk of this Parish 1885–1915, who died September 18th 1930, and of Mary Jane his wife, August 7th 1941.
"Lord we have loved the habitation of thy house."

Window in memory of Mary Ann Turner

North aisle, west end

St John (with poisoned chalice), The Blessed Virgin Mary, St Paul (with sword), St Peter (with keys)

This window is dedicated to the Glory of God and the loving memory of Mary Ann Turner January 6th 1932.

Window in memory of Benjamin Martin

North aisle, second from the west end

St Bartholomew (with flailing knife), St Andrew (with X-shaped Cross), St Thomas (with lance), St Thaddeus

This memorial is dedicated to the Glory of God and the memory of Benjamin Martin First Parish Clerk of Coleford 1831–61

Window in memory of the Robbins family

North aisle, third from the west end

King Alfred (modern), Saint with a knife and book, St Dunstan (modern), St James the Great (with pilgrim staff)

The above window is dedicated to the Glory of God and to the memory of Hugh and Louisa Robbins and Clara their daughter Sept 1933

1938 brought more changes for Holy Trinity. On 8 February 1938 the PCC agreed to improvements and enlargement of the altar. The new altar, made by the Warham Guild, was installed in the summer of 1938 and formally dedicated by the Bishop of Bath and Wells, the Right Revd Dr Francis Underhill. (The Warham Guild was established between the two World Wars by a group of church artists and craftsmen in order to raise standards in the provision of church furnishings, altar requisites and art.) The new altar had been donated by Leonard Law in memory of his late wife Edith, née Perkins. Her father, Philip, was Parish Clerk for forty years, and her sister Celia Perkins continued the family tradition of dedicated service to Holy Trinity. (D/P/Coleford 9/1/2, Vestry and Annual Meetings, Press Cutting 1939) The press report of the dedication service, on Thursday, 15 June 1939, noted that "Coleford church is modern. It was built at a period when architecture and sculpture were not the most pronounced gifts of the builders. You may not see a museum of styles of building practised at different times, but you will find evidence of efforts to enhance the dignity of an edifice which suffered loss of architectural beauty. Much of the improvement has taken place during the incumbency of the present vicar [the Revd Ralph-Bowman]".

In his address, the Bishop noted, "Your Church is comparatively modern, there are larger churches and churches more magnificent, but this is the church you love because it is your church." He appealed to the 120-strong congregation to remember that they were members of a great spiritual body: "Therefore make the members of your congregation your friends, and be loyal to your parish priest and to your church." Again the Faculty authorising the work, dated 1 March 1939, was not granted until after it had been completed.

The old altar and altar cross were donated to the Lady Chapel at Buckland Dinham, and in return the Revd Pugh and his congregation gave an oak lectern to the people of Holy Trinity. (The Revd William Dwight had gone from Coleford to Buckland Dinham in 1900, establishing a link between the two parishes that obviously continued for some time.) Meanwhile, the organ was examined by Mr Brock of Peasedown St John. Tenders were sought for the work, which was eventually undertaken by Mr Brock himself. (See *Five Arches*, Issue 43—'The Brocks of Peasedown and Carlingcott: a heritage of miners and Methodism', for details of the Brock family role in organ building.)

The Revd Bernard Adams

During the incumbency of the Revd Bernard Adams (1946–54), many improvements were made to the church building. In a handwritten report dated 1948 he set out an agenda for improvements, many of which had been achieved in the two years since his arrival. They included the redecoration of the church interior, the rebuilding and resiting of the organ, and the replacement of two stained glass windows which he stated were filled with "hideous and bad glass". This begs the question, which windows? It is more than likely that the offending windows were the easternmost on the north side of the nave near the pulpit, and the one (at that time) nearest the font on the south side of the nave. In September 1948 Revd Adams reported that stained glass had been relocated at a total cost of £22, but did not give any details. The eastern window on the north side of the nave nearest the pulpit is still in situ and depicts Saints Peter and Andrew, and although colourful and loved by some members of Holy Trinity, it is poor quality Victorian glass. The pane titled St Andrew is probably St Jude, because he is holding a large club as the instrument of his martyrdom, whereas St Andrew would be holding an X shaped cross on which he was crucified. It seems likely that at this time the west window, i.e. the window in the tower dedicated to the first four incumbents, was removed and placed in the nave on the south side near the font, where it remains today. The Victorian window near the font would then have been removed and became the west window under the tower. This window is clearly by the same artist as the one near the pulpit and depicts St Philip and Our Lord. Neither window bears any artist's mark or name, so we cannot be certain whose work they represent, but both are probably the work of the same artist. There is a possibility that they could be the work of the Horwood brothers of Mells, both of whom were educated at St Andrew's College, and who were taught the art of making stained glass by the Revd W W Blackwell while at the College. The brothers set up their own stained glass studio and were working from 1853 until at least 1889, latterly in Frome. Some of their work is in Mells church, and they were well known both locally and nationally. But whether they contributed two windows to Coleford is pure speculation, though not beyond the realms of possibility. By the time the Revd Adams had finished moving his "hideous and bad glass" there was only one remaining window with plain glass; this was the easternmost window on the south side which had been obscured by the organ and was later filled with modern glass by Keith New.

In 1946, an Organ Fund was set up, which had raised £165 by 1948. A strip light was also purchased for the organ and a vestry carpet purchased for £1 17s 6d. The Revd Adams noted: "On Monday 30 October [1950] and the following three days, the organ was dismantled and taken to Taunton for repair and restoration." This was part of work authorised by a Faculty granted on 15 September 1950, "to erect a Platform at the West end of the Parish Church of Coleford beneath the Tower … to be supported by steel girders and to carry the Organ leaving a space at the back to be used as a Clergy Vestry. Access to the platform to be by way of a small staircase beneath the Tower."

In fact, access to the organ is by a staircase at the west end of the nave. Work also included the installation of an electric organ blower. By 1951 the balance in the organ fund had dropped to just £3 0s 9d, indicating that the work had now been completed. The removal of the organ must have made the church seem much more spacious in the choir area, although soon a new window would provoke strong reactions.

In February 1949 the church was closed for two weeks, during which time the services were held in the Miners' Welfare Institute. The Revd Adams noted in the Service Register: "The Church was reopened for Divine Service after being shut for two weeks for repairs to the Exterior, to repainting of gutters and woodwork and to a complete redecoration of the Interior. This was done at a cost of £372 9s 0d."

Village contractors undertook much of the routine maintenance of the church. In 1951 Mr E Osment was paid £14 2s 9d for electric wiring to the relocated organ, repairs to the boiler, moving a radiator and fixing bell ropes. In 1953, a Faculty authorised the installation of a portion of brass altar rail (formerly in Wells Cathedral) to replace the existing rail which was "very worm eaten", the work eventually being completed at a cost of £5 17s 7d. Work was also done on repairing the church roof, decorating the vestry, fitting a new step and a new ladder to the church tower. Repairs to the tower roof followed in 1953, yet more in a series of piecemeal repairs to the church roof and tower throughout this period, reflecting the cost of maintaining a building already over 120 years old.

The organ in its present position at the west end of the nave

Fr John Sutters

The first Quinquennial Inspection was made on 11 March 1955 by Mr Geoffrey Beech, the Diocesan Surveyor, under the Inspection of Churches Measure 1955. His report declared the main church structure to be sound, but the churchyard wall needed rebuilding and would cost about £200. The repairs to the wall were largely made possible through the generosity of William Marchant Jones (see chapter 11).

Other work over the next few years would include redecorating the church interior again. The Parochial Church Council decided to set up a Restoration Fund and money was raised from the sale of Christmas cards, a sale of woollens, coffee mornings, whist drives and tea parties, as well as the garden fete, a school concert, a Nativity play, gift day and boxes sold at the harvest supper. The money raised was used to fund repairs to the churchyard wall and the lightning conductor and pinnacle on the church tower during 1956.

But more extensive work followed shortly afterwards when a note in the Service Register of 1957 states that "between 3 and 19 June extensive cleaning and disinfestation of the roof timbers and inside of the roof were carried out by Messrs Dawson of Clutton, under the direction of Mr Beech, Diocesan Architect". Apparently, over the years a large amount of rubble and old timber had accumulated in the space between the plastered ceiling and the roof! This had encouraged damp as well as providing a habitat for furniture beetle (wood worm) and death-watch beetle. The work carried out in 1957 was done in the nick of time. Further major roof repairs were undertaken in 1959—the surveyor's fees cost £55 13s 6d, while the bill for the work done by A Hamblin was £536 15s 6d.

The Quinquennial Inspection Before 1955 church maintenance was left very much to the individual clergy and Churchwardens, but in that year the Inspection of Churches Measure came into being. Under the terms of the Measure each Church had to be inspected every five years by an architect approved by the Diocese. A report would be drawn up by the architect detailing the condition of the building and recommending the work to be undertaken within the coming five years. While this ensured a regular programme of maintenance, it caused many a headache regarding the fundraising.

Such routine work was likely to meet with little opposition. Other areas of work could provoke strong feelings, as was the case with the new window, installed in 1958. Commissioned by William Marchant Jones, it is on the eastern side of the south wall of the nave and depicts David and King Saul. This was intended as a gift to the church, but after William Marchant Jones' death in 1967 a memorial plaque was placed below it, leading people to subsequently think of it as a memorial window. The artist was Keith New, born in 1926, who was a pupil of Richard Marchant Jones. His studio was in Wimbledon, and among his other work may be mentioned commissions for Coventry, Bristol and Lincoln Cathedrals, All Hallows by the Tower and St Nicholas Cole Abbey in London. The nave windows in the rebuilt Coventry Cathedral are amongst Keith New's best known work.

A letter dated Monday 13 May, omitting the year but probably 1957, from William Marchant Jones' son Richard to Fr John Sutters gives more detail about the window.

Dear Mr Sutters,

My apologies for not writing before this but I am again in the middle of a school practice period. Thank you very much for your kind remarks and I understand the recipient was duly impressed and pleased.

Keith New and I were sorry to miss you as it would have been valuable to discuss with you the proposed window, which I understand is proceeding. It is difficult to write about and I only hope Keith will be allowed freedom of expression by his patron. Buying an aesthetic product may have its problems.

As you are aware the assignment is a challenge which I know Keith can cope with and perhaps on another visit we may have the opportunity of talking to you. W M J has specified his subject, Saul and David and as far as I know, that is it, we both had visions of St Cecilia and another figure appropriate to his work. Other than that Keith's problem is effecting the compromise with XVII Century Flemish, sober anecdotal Victorianism and the opposite window in a more violent Victorianism. Had I the means

I would gladly donate a second window to replace it as for me, it has always been a disturbing eyeful.

This is awfully impertinent of me and finally I risk confessing a mutual dislike for chocolate and cream but I felt you did suggest in your letter the outspoken impression.

We do not have the rest of the correspondence, although we do have the window! The Faculty was granted on 23 April 1958. One member of the congregation recalls that it "just appeared". The window was dedicated at Evensong at 3.00 pm on Saturday, 29 November 1958, by Bishop Fabian Jackson, Assistant Bishop in the Diocese of Bath and Wells.

Writing in the *Coleford Parish Paper* in October 1958, Fr John Sutters endeavoured to steer a tricky course. "By now everyone will have had an opportunity to see the new south-east window, Mr W M Jones' most magnificent gift to our Church … For most of us in Coleford this window is a completely new experience, to which time will be needed to adjust ourselves. To begin with, it is stained, not just painted, as are our other windows, and so the colours are deeper and heavier. In the second place … the artist has not been content simply to copy the stock ideas … to which we have grown used, but has expressed what the story of Saul and David means to … a young artist of 1958. But I think that the greatest shock for most of us … is to realise that the Bible story … has to face the hideous wickedness of which human beings are capable … People often want to find comfort and soothing in Church … but the religion of the Bible and the Church, the religion of our Lord Jesus Christ, has to face and deal with ugliness and wickedness, not to ignore it and pretend it doesn't exist." Grasping the nettle, he continued, "This window hits us. It is ugly; and its excellence is in its ugliness. It speaks of jealousy, hatred, spite and cruelty, and they did not die with Saul. I have seen them in Coleford: there have been times when I have been tempted to them in my own heart. This window stands to remind us of the devilish force of evil in our own lives … but over against it is God's power to deal with it … we have only to turn our eyes to the Crucifix on the Altar and the light by the Aumbry which speaks of our Lord's Presence to know where we may find forgiveness, peace and goodness."

In the same issue the artist, Keith New, explained the symbolism in the window. "In the left-hand light Saul is shewn with his javelin raised ready to strike at David. He is robed in royal purple and wears a crown upon his head … Dark clouds suggest the evil spirit afflicting Saul. The right-hand light shews David kneeling with a harp looking up at Saul … He is robed in blue, signifying sincerity and godliness. Above him, coming from between the clouds, is the Hand of God, holding a white dove from which stream golden rays. This symbolises God's special care for David … The main tracery light is filled with a pattern of three angels, sweeping down playing trumpets."

By May 1960 the church boiler was on the verge of giving up the ghost. Many a Sexton had risen from his slumbers in the dead of night to tend the boiler so that the

*Window by Keith New, presented by
W M Jones, 1957*

The brass plaque underneath the window was added after W M Jones' death. It reads:

In memory of William Marchant Jones, chorister & choirmaster, 1884 to 1967— Also of his wife Mabel Mary 1882 to 1935. "Lord I have loved the habitation of thy house."

Sunday congregation would be warm (or at least not frozen). But now it seemed as though it would not last into the following winter, having given trouble for some time past. Various forms of heating were discussed by the PCC, the cost being a major factor. Finally, it was decided to install overhead electric radiant heaters. The estimated cost was £199 and the Restoration Fund stood at £160. By April 1961 the new heaters were installed and working well.

The Revd Leonard Baker

Following the consecration of Coventry Cathedral in May 1962, William Marchant Jones took a group from Holy Trinity to see the new cathedral.

In 1963, during the Revd Baker's incumbency, more work was undertaken, making the most of the space made available by the relocation of the organ in 1950. The work permitted by the Faculty granted in July 1963 included a new altar in plain light oak, the enlargement of the Sanctuary, the existing floor level being extended by two feet into the Chancel, and the enlargement of the Chancel and Choir floor level by two feet into the Nave. The new altar replaced the one installed in 1938 given in memory of Edith Law, daughter of Philip Perkins. (No mention was made of what happened to the altar which was removed.) There were also new altar rails given in memory of Celia Ann Perkins, 1877–1963, daughter of Philip Perkins. These were dedicated by the Bishop of Bath and Wells on 17 July 1963 and are still in situ. Other work proposed at this time included the removal of the front centre pews, together with three pews against the south wall from the east end to the font, and the font floor level was to be built up in concrete. The space created on the south wall was to be set aside to create a children's corner (although this was not done until many years later). The work was to include the redecoration of the interior, the placement of a coloured link-cord to close off the

191

entry to the Chancel, and carpeting of the Sanctuary, Chancel and Nave. Electric storage heaters to support the existing heating system were to be installed, and a Sanctuary Lamp was given by the Mothers' Union. (It is not clear how much of this work was done at this time, or whether some of it was held back and was included in proposals made to the PCC by the next incumbent, the Revd Sidney Wood in 1971.) 1964 saw work on the vicarage, repairs to church guttering and new notice boards, while the following year saw major work to the tower as part of the maintenance work in response to the Quinquennial Inspection.

The Coventry Cathedral trip
Revd Leonard Baker, left;
W M Jones, second left

The Revd Sidney Wood

By the early 1970s the church interior was once more showing signs of dilapidation, but the PCC decided that redecoration could not be considered at that time. In 1971 new lighting was installed. The overhead electric heaters were deemed expensive and not very efficient, but lack of funds prevented any changes.

In June 1971 the Revd Wood proposed rearrangements in the sanctuary, and a special meeting of the PCC was held in the church to discuss them. It was decided that the following work should be undertaken immediately: the removal of the Ten Commandment tablets, the setting back of the choir stalls, the removal of the choir railing and the sanding of the chancel floor.

The Revd Ernest Byles

By 1973 the condition of the church interior was becoming more urgent, in particular the inadequate heating and the need for redecoration. Following the Quinquennial Inspection, this became even more urgent. Estimates had been sought for the redecorating, and the amounts varied from £140 to £500. Mr Mines of Holcombe had quoted a sum of £400 for the decorating and this was accepted, the work being completed by the end of the year at a final cost of £390.

The Revd Alan Coleman

As noted in chapter 9, 1981 saw the 150th anniversary of the church's dedication, and through the fundraising efforts of the '81 Committee, work was able to proceed on redecorating the church interior. The work was undertaken partly by professional decorators and partly by volunteers from the congregation.

Fr David Watson

The "great storm" of October 1987 wrought havoc throughout southern England from west to east. Holy Trinity had escaped fairly lightly although the north western finial on the church roof had fallen onto the clergy vestry roof. (A finial is an ornamental carved pinnacle placed on top of a roof at the base and/or the apex of a gable.) The damage was quickly repaired, costing £400, but other work soon became urgent. The tower was giving cause for concern, but work could not proceed before 1989, by which time a diocesan loan for re-roofing the Church Hall would be repaid.

By 1989 the PCC was able to consider the repairs to the tower, which constituted the main work still outstanding following the 1984 Quinquennial Inspection. There now followed a difficult time of non-communication and misunderstanding between the PCC and the church architect. So serious did the situation become that the Archdeacon of Bath (the Venerable John Burgess) was called in to mediate. Meanwhile a quotation for the work—repairs to the tower pinnacles, parapets and walls; nave pinnacles; lightning conductor; and repairs to the bell-frame—came to a staggering £15,000 and soon rose to £20,000. The PCC decided to do the most urgent work up to

---

The Church Bell There is a story that the church bell at Holy Trinity came from **Fonthill Abbey** in Wiltshire, but it cannot be proved. Fonthill Abbey had been built by an eccentric named William Beckford. It was not an abbey or monastery, despite its name, but was a rather extravagant mansion with an extremely tall tower. Building began in 1796, but when Beckford's money ran out he moved to Bath. The tower came crashing down in 1825, its foundations being completely unstable. All trace of the building has disappeared, although a new mansion was built half a mile away from the ruin in 1859. It is possible that artefacts were salvaged from the ruins and that some enterprising architect or builder claimed the bell for use at a future date, but whether this bell ended up at Coleford seems unlikely.

For many years Holy Trinity had two bells, and at some stage the second became redundant and was kept in the vestry. Inevitably it got in the way, and in March 1980 the possible disposal of the bell was raised at the PCC meeting. Nothing was done about this, but the situation became urgent in 1983 when the space was needed for a safe. Negotiations were held with the Diocesan Association of Bellringers and a Faculty for its removal was sought. The Faculty was granted in 1983, and the bell was removed to St John's Frome, the Trustees of St John's Bell Fund making a donation of £60 to Holy Trinity's Restoration Fund. The disposal of the bell was begun during the ministry of the Revd Alan Coleman and was concluded towards the end of the ministry of the Revd Martin Percival.

Bell engineer Matthew Higby of Holcombe states that the second bell at Holy Trinity was the treble of the ring of six bells at Aller on the Somerset levels.

---

a cost of £11,000 (there being £5,000 in the Restoration Fund and the possibility of a further loan of £6,000 from the diocese). The strife between architect and PCC continued, and it was decided to proceed with the repairs to the tower parapets and walls and the lightning conductor, and to leave the rest for the time being. This would cost in the region of £8,500. It was also resolved to make the tower pinnacles safe, and to defer work on the bell-frame until a later date. This work was completed by the summer of 1990.

Meanwhile, the Church clock was in need of repair. A separate Faculty was applied for after the Faculty had been granted for the tower repairs. Both the clock mechanism and the clock face needed urgent work and an appeal was made in *On the Map* for donations. By September 1990 the fund stood at £1,315 and work began. This was completed by October.

The architect at this time had proved to be unsympathetic to small village churches, and at a later date the PCC changed to the present (2009) architect George Chedburn of Chedburn Dudley Building Design and Conservation. A good relationship now exists between architect, PCC and clergy.

Fr Peter Down

During the period 1992–3 an induction loop system was installed for hearing-aid users with some microphones and amplification.

By 1994 the church interior was showing signs of dampness once more. Estimates were sought, but the daunting figure of £4,000 was quoted as a possible cost. No action was taken and the church interior continued to deteriorate until the restoration of 2007.

As noted in chapter 9, the church clock was illuminated in memory of Barbara Ackroyd, and this was completed in 1994/5.

The Revd Valerie Bonham

For details of work on the church building from 2002 until 2009 see chapter 14.

Part 3

THE CHURCH ENVIRONS

11

THE CHURCHYARD

THE history of the churchyard receives less detailed attention in parish records, but still enables us to glimpse the changes that have been made over the years. Before Holy Trinity was built, funerals for members of the Church of England took place at the parish church in Kilmersdon. Coffins had to be carried from Coleford to Kilmersdon, and as the quickest route was across the fields, a pathway (which became known as "the Coffin Path") was soon beaten by the feet of mourners. The terrain was not easy and one wonders how many coffins were dropped en route. One of the Millennium tapestries housed at the Methodist Chapel depicts a group of people taking a coffin on the parish bier across the fields for burial in Kilmersdon. And even though Holy Trinity had been the church for Coleford since 1831, and had become a separate parish in 1842, burials from Coleford were still carried out at Kilmersdon as late as the 1890s, presumably in family graves.

In 1879 the Westbury Iron Company provided gravel, probably for the church paths, from their Vobster quarry. On Tuesday, 1 September 1903 an extension to the burial ground was consecrated by Bishop Stirling, Canon of Wells. A fine day drew a good congregation for the service at 4.00 pm, and parochial tea, which followed at 5.30 pm in the schoolroom, after which the former vicar, the Revd William Dwight, preached at Evensong. Land for the extension was given by Lord Hylton at the west end of the churchyard, fenced by public subscription (at a cost of £32), the north wall of the churchyard was rebuilt at a cost of £9 10s, and the east wall re-pointed at a cost of £3 10s.

In September 1910 a truck load of gravel from J Wainwright and Co at Vobster quarry was donated for the re-gravelling of the paths. Things were

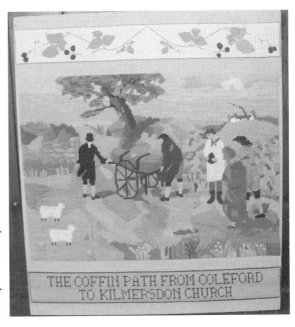

Millennium tapestry—Coffin Path panel

THE COFFIN PATH FROM COLEFORD TO KILMERSDON CHURCH

taken a stage further when, in May 1929, the PCC discussed a new development for the churchyard—the possibility of laying "mastic" paths to the church and vicarage. After a long discussion it was agreed to go ahead, using voluntary labour to dig the trenches to keep costs down.

Over time, maintenance of the churchyard became an increasingly troublesome issue. In July 1934 the PCC noted that "all parishioners have a perfect right to tend and help order the graves of relations if they wish to do so. That all graves not kept in order are liable to be cancelled [only] after due notice have been given to the parties concerned." (D/P/Coleford 9/3/1, PCC Minutes, 26.7.1934. It also noted that such decisions rested with the incumbent and the PCC.)

Nor was maintenance the only issue to tax the PCC. In July 1936, following letters to families of those whose graves were left unattended, a number of graves were levelled. Costs for digging graves also came under the review. In November 1934 they were set at 17s 6d for a single and £1 10s for a double grave. The following spring they were revised again, to 13s 6d to dig the grave, 4s for the clerk's fee, 2s 6d for the Sexton's fee (a total of £1 0s 0d for a single grave) with a 3s 6d surcharge for a double grave. (D/P/Coleford 9/3/1, PCC Minutes 27.2.1935. Mr Ashman was then Sexton.)

The maintenance of the churchyard generally fell to the Sexton and was, over the years, a cause for some considerable work and debate. In December 1950, forms were printed and distributed reminding relatives of the need for the upkeep of graves. The state of the pathways was another cause for much concern. In October 1952, the Notice Board Fund and Churchyard Pathway Fund were amalgamated to pay for the resurfacing of the pathways. The upkeep of graves related not only to keeping them tidy, but also to the type of memorial stone to be erected. By the 1950s the diocesan authorities had begun to tighten up on the rules governing the type of stone to be used (and even more importantly, what they deem may not be used). Over the previous generation some inappropriate materials, such as brightly coloured marble chippings and stone which was not natural to the area, had been used quite freely. Fr John Sutters had the difficult task of enforcing the new rules and this often met with protests, people mistakenly thinking that the new rules were his personally.

Writing in the first issue of the *Coleford Parish Paper* in July 1955, Fr Sutters reported that Mr Geoffrey Beech, the Diocesan Surveyor, had carried out the first Quinquennial Inspection under the Inspection of Churches Measure 1955. As noted in chapter 10, tasks requiring immediate attention included the rebuilding of the churchyard wall forming the boundary between the churchyard and the road. In addition to various fundraising events, volunteer collectors had toured the village to raise money for the wall and other urgent work in the church. G Alford & Sons had organised an evening coach trip to Stonehenge and had donated the proceeds to the appeal. In the December *Coleford Parish Paper* Fr Sutters reported that earlier in the year, a large piece of the churchyard wall had collapsed onto the road, and that Mr Gilson of Holcombe had agreed to repair it at the cost of £104, but for various reasons he had been unable to do the work. William Marchant Jones then took up the work, and, in addition, made a gift of the coping stones. As the work progressed it became necessary to rebuild the entire wall, the actual building work being done by Mr Berryman and his assistant. The work was finished by early 1956, and Fr Sutters reported that the cost of labour and materials had been £248 of which W M Jones had given £100, leaving £148 for the church to pay. The Appeal had raised £114 and the remaining £34 had been borrowed from the Restoration Fund, thus creating an internal debt which needed to be repaid.

In July 1961 the west wall of the churchyard (i.e. the wall furthest away from the road) was in great need of repair, and the PCC secretary was instructed to enquire about this with William Marchant Jones. But by the following January it was decided to leave the repairs until a future

Rex Parfitt and the rebuilt churchyard wall

date. Whether or not the wall was repaired in the 1960s, it was in a dire state by 2005 when it was completely rebuilt by Rex Parfitt over the next three years, at the cost of the materials only.

In 1961 £100 was left by Miss Much for the upkeep of the graves of William and Emily Bush. But the maintenance of older, untended graves was still a costly problem, and on 27 February 1963 a Faculty was granted, to "level all untended grave mounds in the Churchyard of the Parish of Coleford".

Many churchyards have amusing, sad or intriguing epitaphs on gravestones, but Holy Trinity being a relatively new churchyard has very little. Writing in 1910, Lord Hylton recorded the following epitaph, but now there is no trace of it:

> Danger stands thick through all the ground
> To hurry mortals home,
> And fierce diseases lurk around
> To push us to the tomb.

(Lord Hylton, *Some notes towards the History of Kilmersdon*, 1910)

We shall never know what sad story inspired that particular epitaph, because Lord Hylton omitted any name or date from his account, but there are other graves in the churchyard that tell their own sad stories. Mention has been made in chapter 6 of the Haskins children who died of measles in 1916. But there was an earlier tragic death, that of "Vincent WHELLER, died 5 August 1875, at Coleford Mills, in this parish, aged 42. And his third daughter, Florence, 'accidentally drowned at the above Mills' 29 Sept 1874, aged 5 years. Also his fourth daughter, Blanche, died 'of fever at Spargrove Mills, the residence of her uncle', 22 Oct 1875, aged 4 years." (*Memorial Inscriptions of Coleford Somerset*, Medlycott, 2006) Their grave is just opposite the church door and the stone is very worn. Jean Chivers (formerly Price) remembers reading the epitaph as a child (it is now undecipherable), but it read as follows:

> Children who die in infancy
> Are like a flower in bloom,
> For God who sent them
> Only lent them
> And takes what is his own.

This may seem macabre to the modern reader, but in an age where infant mortality was so common that it affected many families, it probably brought great comfort.

Coleford's mining history is brought to mind by the memorial to Frank Cullen (grandfather of Rex Parfitt), "who, in the performance of his duties as Under Manager at Mackintosh Pit, suddenly died 15 March 1913, aged 35." The stone was erected by his colleagues, workmen and friends at the Newbury Collieries. His wife, Lily, had a long widowhood, and died on 21 November 1967, aged 90. She was laid to rest in the same grave. (Medlycott, 2006)

The grave of the Wheller family

The grave of Frank Cullen

The grave of John Young

The graves of the Robbins family

Not far from Frank Cullen's grave is another mining casualty. John (Jack) Young died on 16 July 1925, aged 31, "from injuries received at Newbury colliery". His wife, Kate, lies in the same grave, and like Lily Cullen, she had a long widowhood. She died on 1 January 1973 aged 77 years.

As one approaches Holy Trinity along the main path, just before reaching the porch, there are three large and impressive gravestones. These are the graves of the Robbins family who were active members of the church in the early years. In chapter 4 Mrs Robbins and two of her daughters are mentioned as helpers at the celebratory tea after the reopening of the church in 1885. One of the Flemish windows from Mells was dedicated to Hugh and Louisa Robbins and their daughter, Clara. Their gravestones are inscribed:

Martha, eldest daughter of the late Alfred and Louisa ROBBINS of
Babington, died 11 May 1876, aged 27.
Hugh ROBBINS, died 25 March 1889, aged 69. And his wife, Louisa
Melena, died 6 July 1902, aged 80.
Clara, third daughter of the late Hugh and Louisa ROBBINS, died 8
May 1904, aged 38. And Albert Robbins, died 28 Jan 1920. Also Leila,
eldest daughter of Hugh Robbins, died 30 Oct 1946.

(Medlycott, 2006)

In the *Coleford Parish Magazine* of August 1902 the Revd Joseph Wade wrote, "We mourn the death of Mrs [Louisa] Robbins, so long associated with the Church and parish. We shall miss her familiar presence. Kind, cheerful, and consistent to the last, her memory will long be held in sincere respect." Her daughter Clara was also greatly missed, and the Revd Wade paid tribute to her in the parish magazine of June 1904: "Our congregation is again in mourning. We have now, alas, to record the loss of Miss Clara Robbins, who died on Sunday morning, May 8th. The sympathy of the whole parish went out to her in her heroic struggle with an incurable complaint, and very

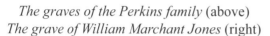

The graves of the Perkins family (above)
The grave of William Marchant Jones (right)

genuine was the grief with which the news of her death was received. Her brightness and geniality had endeared her to everyone, and the unfailing cheerfulness with which she bore her long and depressing illness was the admiration of us all. We shall sadly feel the removal from our midst of this bright and buoyant life."

Philip Perkins, parish clerk for forty years, lies on the north side of the church near the boundary. He is commemorated in another of the Flemish windows from Mells, having died on 18 September 1930, aged 81. His wife Mary J Perkins, who died on 8 August 1941 aged 91, lies in the same grave, as do their two children, Edith Alice who died 17 March 1883 aged 4 years, and George Elihu who died 10 August 1886 aged 5 years. Next to the Perkins' grave is that of their daughter, Edith Maud, wife of Leonard Law. She died on 2 December 1918 aged 33, and in 1938 her husband donated a new altar to Holy Trinity in her memory. Lying in the same grave is her sister, Celia Ann Perkins, who died on 4 February 1963, aged 85.

Not far away from the Perkins family is the grave of William Marchant Jones who died on 7 June 1967, and his wife, Mabel May, who died on 11 June 1935.

Immediately behind this is the grave of Benjamin Martin, who died on 30 August 1889 aged 59, and his wife, Mary Anne, who died on 17 September 1897, aged 65. However, this is not the same Benjamin Martin who was the first Parish Clerk from 1831–61, and to whom another of the windows from Mells was dedicated; but it could be the grave of his son. The grave of Benjamin Martin senior does not appear to be marked by a stone. Some of the older graves are very near to the hedge marking the churchyard boundary, and some of them might not have been marked by a stone, while others had cast iron crosses which have deteriorated, and other gravestones have weathered so badly that the names cannot be read. And some Coleford burials still took place at Kilmersdon as late as the 1890s.

Bob Swallow remembers his time as Sexton:

During the spring of 1960 I took over as the part-time Sexton of Coleford parish churchyard, the duties being gravedigger and caretaker (cutting of grass etc). Later on the grave digging was arranged by funeral undertakers. I remember during the winter of 1963 we had a large falling of snow and freezing conditions. The church drive was three and sometime four feet deep in places. This I had to clear for funerals and services. I was, at the time, working in Frome on twelve-hour shifts, so the work had to be fitted in as best I could. One week we had three funerals, which meant graves had to be dug. Jim Spear had previously dug graves so he gave me a hand. The only setback, apart from the snow and ice, was that we both had to work on our regular jobs by day that week. So, after consulting the Vicar, the Revd Baker, and members of the Parochial Church Council, permission was given to dig these graves at night, by floodlight (six-hundred watt bulbs) which we fitted ourselves. I think this was the first time this happened in Coleford and, as far as I know, the last. Also in the churchyard was a large vault with a lining of bricks. This was situated at the far end of the church drive, some eight or nine feet onto the grass. I can remember as a boy seeing the large four oblong slabs covering this. The Vicar asked me if I knew anything about this vault; my reply was I knew nothing at all. So it was decided he and Mr Jack Coles would do some searching. I take it this was through records etc. Unfortunately this was to no avail, so I was to open this, which I did. This was completely empty—only a few coins and bits of debris which had fallen through gaps in the covering slabs so it was decided to fill this in (I think the interest arising in this vault was because of safety—some slabs cracking and flaking).

Later in 1963 I was asked if I would take over the verger's vacant position in the church. At that time I also remember some well-attended services. Also, part of the verger's work was to wind the clock in the tower. During 1963 quite a large amount of work was being done in the tower. Two bells hung in there. There was one outside on the tower roof and the other inside, which was much larger. This was used for services etc, the smaller one outside striking the clock time. This was hung in a wooden cradle and owing to the deterioration of the wood it was decided that this would either have to be replaced or removed completely. Owing to the expense involved it was decided on the latter. The roof of the tower was also due for renewal, changing from wood and lead to concrete. The problem now was what could be done with regard to the striking of the clock time. Eventually, it was decided to fit another striker on the large bell situated inside the tower (the wooden wheel which once swung this bell is still attached but is no longer used and is secured for safety reasons). So, after much head scratching small wire cables and wheels made this possible. The village people would now be able to hear the church clock strike the hours as it had done for many past years. A lot of village people, such as quarrymen on early shifts, relied on that clock to get them to work on time. Several repairs were carried out on the clock by an ex-German POW, Gerhard Drescher (who married a local girl and lived in the village). Known to everyone as Gerald, all his work was done free of charge for the village people of Coleford.

I remember one particular time when I had the fright of my life. Owing to the shortening of the clock weight it had to be wound twice a week—on Wednesday and Saturday nights. On this particular Wednesday I had worked until 6 o'clock and had gone to the church but forgot to wind the clock. I remembered at about 11 o'clock and it was easier to go then than first thing in the morning, so I went. I had left the outer door into the church open. I came down from winding the clock and as I entered the vestry the draft made a surplice hanging from a hook flare up in front of me, and I thought it was a ghost! It scared me so much that I was still shaking when I got home.

Bob Swallow's work was noted by the PCC in April 1965. (D/P/Coleford 9/1/2, April 1965) "In the absence of Mr Swallow, who was unable to attend, the Secretary read his report. The churchyard plan has been brought up to date, bushes have been cut and reshaped and unattended graves have been levelled. The new mower was proving a great asset. The vicar commented on the greatly improved appearance of the churchyard, which had been remarked by many visitors, and spoke of his and the Council's appreciation of Mr Swallow's work."

Bob Swallow gave up his role in 1967. Following the lack of response to advertisements for a replacement, Bob resumed the work of Sexton a few months later, before finally giving it up in 1969. After living in Frome for some years, Bob Swallow and his wife, Shirley, returned to Coleford and once more worship at Holy Trinity.

In 1973 a further thirty-nine graves were levelled, with more still to do. A few more were levelled in 2003.

Over the years there have been a number of different people fulfilling the role of Sexton, only a few of whom have been named in this book. But mention must be made of Mike Harrison, another present-day member of the congregation whose past roles have included, amongst others, that of choirboy, and later Sexton. While his grave-digging skills are no longer

Sarah Ilott mowing the grass

employed, Mike is a gifted carpenter and joiner, and has made cabinets for the sound systems in Holy Trinity and St Andrew's churches. Today there is no Sexton; the graves are prepared by a gravedigger by arrangement with the funeral director. Upkeep of individual graves is in the hands of family members, and the mowing and strimming of the churchyard is presently undertaken by Sarah Ilott.

Anyone who walks through Coleford churchyard will see a virtual history of the village reflected in the surnames on the gravestones, such as: Collier, Hodges, Whitcombe, Witcombe, Chamberlain, Wines, Padfield, Moore, Chivers, Phillips, Cox, Hamblin, Steeds, Rossiter, Chambers, Vranch, Perkins, Paget, Ashman, Button, Plummer, Bull, Lambert, Thompson, Turner, Marchant Jones, Horler, Green, Tucker, James, Price, Coles, Edgell, Cosh, Reakes, Hobbs, Moon, Willis, Hancock, Parfitt, Trimby, Treasure, Sperring, Trussler, Cullen, Flower, Cradock and many more. (Medlycott, 2006)

12

THE CHURCH HALL

THE Miners' Welfare Fund

The building known since 1964 as the Church Hall began its life as the Miners' Welfare Institute. Under Section 20 of the Mining Industry Act 1920 a fund, to be known as the Miners' Welfare Fund, had been established with the intention of providing recreational facilities for coal miners. The money was raised by a levy of one penny per ton on all coal mined throughout the country, and the fund was invested in a body known as the Miners' Welfare Committee. A further Committee known as the Somerset District Committee, consisting of representatives of the mine owners and mine workers, was established to advise the Miners' Welfare Committee with regard to allocations of money from the Miners' Welfare Fund.

An argument in high places

The establishment of the Miners' Welfare Fund was controversial because of the great deprivation suffered by the miners in the aftermath of the Great War. Worse was yet to come, culminating in the General Strike of 1926. In a House of Lords debate on 21 June 1922, which focussed mainly on the plight of miners in Lancashire and Cheshire, the whole concept of the Fund was criticised on the grounds that starving miners needed material help rather than playing fields and village reading rooms. Responding to a facetious remark by Viscount Chelmsford that "the objective [of the Fund] was to bring sweetness and light into miners' lives", Lord Strachie angrily replied: "If the noble Viscount lived in the district where I live he would know that the poverty is enormous, that many men are only earning wages of about 20s a week, and that a large number of them have to go to the Poor Law guardians to ask for poor relief, a thing which they hate having to do … Instead of being told, 'You are going to have sweetness brought into your life by recreation grounds and by musical entertainments,' these men would much prefer to have some assistance given to them that would enable them to pay their rents … In the good time rents were very high, and now a man living in a colliery area in Somerset has to pay 6s., or 7s. or 8s., a week for his house, and he is only earning 20s. or 25s. a week … It is a most serious thing that a large number of men are compelled at the present time … to apply for outdoor relief … Therefore, anything that we can do to relieve the poverty of these men … we should do. The best thing that Parliament could do to bring sweetness into the lives of miners would be to get them some assistance from this Fund so as to obviate their having to ask for outdoor relief."

In reply Lord Somerleyton dismissed Lord Strachie's appeal: "This is not a question of choosing whether the men are to be supported out of this money, or are to have the various recreations … and improvements which have been suggested … This sum of money would not keep the men who are only partially employed, nor could it possibly raise their wages to a sum adequate to support their families properly … With regard to Somerset, I am not prepared to go into that question, because I was not aware that any application was to come in from Somerset … It was not the intention of Parliament, in instituting this Fund, that it should be used for the purpose of augmenting wages … the result of using it for this purpose would be to exhaust the entire sum available for the district in a comparatively short time, without having made any lasting contribution to the social well-being of the miners as a whole …" (House of Lords Debates, 21 June 1922, vol 50 cc1047–54)

In a further House of Lords debate on 2 August 1922, Lord Strachie asked, "What is the total sum paid into the [Miners'] Welfare Fund by Somerset district … and how much of that fund has been spent and how much allotted and for what purposes spent or allotted in each case." A lengthy reply was given by Lord Hylton: "The total sum paid into the Welfare Fund by the Somerset district is £5,206.18s.8d. In accordance with the Act, four-fifths of this total must be allocated for local purposes in the district … The total amount available … in the Somerset district is therefore £4,211.7s.9d … The total amount hitherto paid out … is £1,477. Payments are normally made by instalments as each scheme progresses … Six schemes in all have so far been sanctioned in the Somerset district; of these five are schemes involving the purchase and laying out of fields for recreational purposes, and one is a scheme for the building of a village hall and reading room for the workmen." (House of Lords Debates 2, August 1922, vol 51 c1046)

A hall for Coleford

The scheme for the building of a village hall and reading room was the one for Coleford. Accordingly, a sum of £1,150 was allocated from the Miners' Welfare Fund "for the purpose of erecting and equipping a Village Institute … for the use and benefit of workers in or about [the] coal mines at Coleford". (Trust Deed dated 2 November 1927) Under the Trust Deed dated 2 November 1927, the following Trustees were appointed to receive and administer the funding and to accept the Conveyance:

George Anthony Sellers of "Overdale", Park Road, Frome. Colliery Manager;
William James Vranch of Highbury, Coleford. Colliery Under Manager;
Frank Edward Chivers of Highbury, Coleford. Check Weighman;
Walter James Witcombe of Highbury, Coleford. Miner;
Herbert Frank Hobbs of "Ingledene", Coleford. Colliery Cashier;
Tom Ellison of Highbury, Coleford. Clerk;
John Button of Highbury, Coleford. Miner;
Charles Cullen, of Coleford. Examiner;
George Horler of Coleford. Miner; and
William Bagley Johnson of Highbury, Coleford. Surveyor.

"Not for any other purpose"

According to the terms of a Deed of Gift dated 31 December 1925, a parcel of land was conveyed to the Trustees for a Village Institute, "**and not for any other purpose**". This Deed of Gift was enacted between "Dora Estella Knatchbull of the first part, Frank Seymour Nilsson Isitt, The Honourable Arthur Edward Dalzell of the second part, Wyndham Persse Knatchbull of the third part, and the Trustees of the fourth part." Dora Knatchbull [of Babington House] reserved to herself and her successors all minerals under the parcel of land below a depth of three hundred feet from the surface. Furthermore, the Trustees had agreed that "no buildings should be erected upon the said plot of land save and except an Institute for the use of the village at Coleford neither should the said plot of land be used for any purpose other than for the erection thereon of the said Institute …" The sum of £945, as part of the sum allocated by the Miners' Welfare Fund, was paid to the Trustees for the building of the Institute, the balance to be paid when recommended by the Somerset District Committee.

The Trust Deed continued, "it is hereby declared as follows:

1. The Trustees shall stand possessed of the said property UPON TRUST to allow the same to be used for ever hereafter as a Village Institute for the benefit of workers in or about the coal mines at Coleford.

2. AND IT IS HEREBY DECLARED that it shall be lawful for the Trustees with the consent of the Charity Commissioners to execute a valid … Mortgage of the said property for any purpose necessary … for enabling the said property to be used as aforesaid. And further that it shall be lawful for the Trustees with the consent of the Charity Commissioners if and when they shall have notified … the Commissioners that in their opinion the aforesaid Village Institute … is no longer required or cannot be satisfactorily maintained or has increased to such an extent in value that it is desirable in the interests of the beneficiaries that the said property should be sold, to sell the … property either together or in lots and either by public auction or by private contract … and the Trustees shall apply the moneys arising from the sale … in paying off any debts owing … and shall apply the remainder … for such purposes connected with the social well being recreation and conditions of living of workers in or about coal mines as the Charity Commissioners may approve."

A further provision ruled that no application should be made to the Charity Commissioners for their consent to the sale of the property without first seeking approval in writing from the Somerset District Committee. A fourth provision declared that if any Trustee ceased to live in Coleford or within a ten mile radius for a period of twelve months, or if a Trustee became bankrupt or mentally incapable of fulfilling the role of Trustee, then that person should cease to be a Trustee. Furthermore, if the number of Trustees should be reduced to less than three, then the number should be made up to the original number. And finally, it was declared that the Trustees shall be the Managers of the Village Institute with power to make such Bye-laws as may be deemed necessary.

Mrs Knatchbull's good works

Mrs Knatchbull had initially reserved a parcel of land for a Village Institute and had organised a concert in Frome in order to fund the building. The *Coleford Parish Magazine* of August 1911 recounts a meeting called by Mrs Knatchbull on 30 June. "Her object in calling the meeting was to introduce herself to those whom she hopes to serve, and she carried out her object with characteristic thoroughness and spirit. She shook hands personally with everyone in the room … The projected building … is to be placed in Ashill, and it is to consist of a spacious club-room, divided into compartments for games, smoking and reading, and it is to be furnished with a library, caretaker's apartments, and a bowling green. The partitions … are removable … so that on special occasions the building can be converted into one large entertainment hall or concert room. Order … will be one of the fixed laws of the Knatchbull Institute, or Social Club … and there will have to be a fixed charge for membership, if the Institution is to be kept going. Mrs Knatchbull stated that the first step towards bringing the scheme into being will be a great public performance at Frome on Thursday and Friday August 10th and 11th, when several artistes who have never yet appeared outside the European Capitals have promised to give their services … The 'popular' performances at popular prices will be on the Friday, but there are to be cheap gallery tickets at the fashionable matinee on the afternoon of the Thursday, so we hope that those for whom the club is intended will turn up … in great numbers both to show their appreciation of Mrs Knatchbull's kindness, and to avail themselves of an opportunity that is never likely to occur again." So wrote the Revd Joseph Wade regarding Mrs Knatchbull's plans.

It is difficult to know exactly what the Revd Wade really thought about the "great public performance", except that his description in the *Coleford Parish Paper* of September 1911 was as overflowing with superlatives as the performance itself! It was, he wrote, a "performance of supreme excellence" with a piano duet between Mrs Knatchbull and her old tutor "one of the most perfect performances of the kind that we have ever listened to". The dances were a "whirling cloud of diaphanous drapery whisking across the stage and wreathed in every imaginable shape and form. It was a very lively exhibition of grace and agility, and in its way amazing". The Revd Wade was forced to admit that the "audience was not overflowing", but the biggest disappointment was that the programmes did not arrive on time, and they were to have been illustrated with an impression of what the club room would be like. He concluded, "We hope that the box office receipts … will fulfil Mrs Knatchbull's expectations, and will provide at any rate the foundation stone of the future Institute."

The concert was probably a little "highbrow" for its intended audience but it raised £100. However, further funds were not forthcoming, and the project went into abeyance for some years. So it was that after the foundation of the Miners' Welfare Fund, the

Miners' Welfare Committee was approached for financial help in building the Institute on the land given by Mrs Knatchbull. The project was deemed suitable, and in due course the Coleford Miners' Welfare Institute was built. Contrary to popular belief, the miners of Coleford did not pay for the building of the Institute themselves—this is a village myth that comes up time and time again, but is nevertheless untrue. The Institute was funded from the Miners' Welfare Fund, administered by the Miners' Welfare Committee via the Somerset District Committee. The Institute was opened on 14 June 1927 and proved to be a real boon to the village. At that time there was little in the way of recreational meeting rooms. The church had what was commonly known as "the Bug Hut" but this was in regular use, and so too was the Temperance Hall, the latter having strict rules. So there was a need for a meeting place for the miners that they could call their own. The new institute had two ground floor rooms and a large room upstairs. One of the ground floor rooms was equipped with two billiards tables, and the other room was reserved as a reading room. The upstairs room with its stage at one end was large enough for concerts. Many Coleford people remember the heyday of the Miners' Welfare Institute with affection.

Is there a future for the Miners' Hall?
The Miners' Welfare Institute thrived for about thirty years until the late 1950s, but during that time the village had changed. As well as the changes in society after World War II, the mines themselves were in decline. Some had closed in the 1920s, the men subsequently going to other mines that remained open, but after the War, more closed down. In 1947 the National Coal Board took over from the mine owners and the last pits closed in 1973. In the village, the Royal British Legion Memorial Hall was opened in 1956, providing a large hall and stage, a lounge area and a licensed club for members. The Miners' Institute was no match for these modern facilities, and gradually the membership fell away. By about 1957 the Institute had closed down and was showing increasing signs of dereliction.

Five years passed and no one showed any interest in the Welfare Institute, and its future seemed very uncertain. But then there were indications that it could once more be put to good use. The "Bug Hut" at the bottom of the vicarage garden was almost unusable by this time, and the Vicar, the Revd Leonard Baker, and the PCC thought the Welfare Institute would make an ideal Church Hall. Also, the Church School had expressed a hope that they might have the use of the Institute for assembly and PE. And thirdly, the National Youth Movement had established a number of youth clubs in neighbouring villages and had nowhere to meet in Coleford.

W M Jones to the rescue
By 1962 the Trustees of the Welfare Institute had referred the matter to the Miners' Welfare Section of the National Coal Board, and the decision was made to sell the hall by auction for building purposes, and they had advertised it in the local Press. The Coleford Parish Council called a special meeting in order to discuss the future of the

Colin Turner recalls being told off as a very small boy for putting his hand up over the top of the billiards table and touching the balls, thus ruining the game. He remembers the dances in the upstairs room, and Jack Steeds and his band providing the music. But most popular of all were the "Picture Nights" on Fridays, when films usually shown at the cinema would be projected onto a screen in the upper room. There would be large posters in the foyer advertising the forthcoming film, and seats would cost about 9d. The projector frequently went wrong, but no one seemed to mind. The room would be packed with people and Colin, Ron Brewer and others would bag the front row where they had full view of the screen. But one night *Great Expectations* was showing, and Colin didn't see very much of it because as soon as Magwitch appeared from behind the gravestones and grabbed hold of young Pip, young Colin (aged about 7 or 8) was so terrified that he ran out of the hall and down the stairs, crying his eyes out. He opened the door to run outside and there straight in front of him was the churchyard! So he kept on running until he got home. Weaker lads might never have darkened the doors of the hall or the church again; fortunately Colin was made of stronger stuff and continues to be a stalwart of Holy Trinity.

Ken Tucker recalls in *Coleford as 'twere*: "The Miners' Welfare Institute occasionally hosted a theatre company who perhaps would stay a week. One company was called The Lyceum Players, and another that came several times was known as 'Freddie Faye and His Frolics'. Mrs Faye had a number of Pekinese dogs and many of us had not seen that breed before."

Dennis Chambers recalls in *Coleford as 'twere*: "Jack Steeds' three-piece band started when we were still boys, before the War … We had a very good music teacher in the village, Mrs Myrtle Willis, and she often played piano for us. We played mostly at the Welfare Institute on Saturday nights …"

Jack Steeds and his band

(back row) Raymond Turner, Michael Perkins,
(front row) Jack Steeds, John Edgell, John Harris

Institute, but it was stated that the Parish Council [i.e. the civil parish] did not have the funds to buy the property. Other interested parties present were the local MP, the Chairman of Somerset Education Committee, the Clerk to Frome Rural District Council, the Revd Leonard Baker, Jack Coles, Tom Willis, Chairman of Coleford Parish Council, William Withers, Clerk to Coleford Parish Council, Mr Hyrons, Headmaster of Coleford Church School, and William Marchant Jones. After a long discussion, W M Jones said that if the village would otherwise lose the building, he would find the sum required by the Miners' Welfare Committee. At this stage £900 was being mentioned, but in later correspondence it had changed to £1,100. He hoped that the owners would reduce their asking price since the Hall would be used by the Parochial Church Council for the benefit of the village, thus continuing to fulfil its original purpose. This offer was supported by the Parish Council, and Mr Withers duly wrote to the Somerset and Bristol Group of the National Coal Board, the Ministry of Education and the County Education Officer.

The PCC met on 7 February 1962, and William Marchant Jones stated that he would be prepared to pay to the PCC an agreed sum if the PCC would make a bid for the premises. His offer was accepted unanimously, and on 8 February the Revd Baker and Mr Button, secretary of the PCC, wrote to the estate agents, Quartley, Sons and Wright, making a formal offer. They wrote, "We understand intending purchasers are required to make tentative bids and with the help of members of our Church we might eventually be able to offer a sum not exceeding £1100 if that be considered necessary. In view of the use for which the building would be devoted we beg the Miners' Welfare Fund Committee to consider the lowest figure they could accept. It will enable us to devote the Hall very much to its original purpose."

Muddy waters

The waters now began to get muddy, and it is difficult to ascertain exactly what happened, except that the negotiations became increasingly acrimonious. The Ministry of Education had become involved because of the possibility of the Institute's use by a youth club. It seems that all the "bidders" had been informed that their tenders had been refused, and they were now invited to resubmit them with an increased offer and that the Ministry of Education would make the final decision. Two other bids had been made for the premises, but upon finding that the church had expressed an interest these were withdrawn in favour of the church obtaining the Institute. Meanwhile, W M Jones wrote a strongly worded letter to the estate agents expressing "surprise and disappointment at the attitude of the Ministry of Education", and also informing them that the church had "no wish to participate in another competition with other bidders". This was followed on 1 March by a supportive letter to W M Jones from Mr J C Hughes, Clerk of Frome Rural District Council, saying, "It now seems clear that you have no competition in so far as the Tenderers are concerned; and therefore it is now a question of acquiring the premises as cheaply as possible, having regard to the origin of the building, the local purposes it will continue to serve, and the degree of use attached to the Mobile Youth Scheme organisation within the Frome Rural District … Having regard to these matters, I am writing to the Ministry of Education …" A copy of this letter dated 6 March 1962 was sent to W M Jones and to Somerset County Council.

"Protracted and unsatisfactory"

Mr Hughes then wrote to Mr J Harwood, Secretary of the Bristol and Somerset Group of the National Coal Board. In this letter, dated 10 April 1962, he set out the case for the PCC's acquisition of the Institute for the benefit of the church and wider village community. He also expressed his disappointment that negotiations through the NCB had become "protracted and unsatisfactory". He copied his letter to the Ministry of Education, the Chief Education Officer of Somerset County Council, Coleford Parish Council, Coleford Parochial Church Council, the estate agents, W M Jones, and the Chairman of Frome RDC Mobile Youth Leader Scheme Committee. On 28 May Mr Hughes received a letter from the Legal Branch of the Ministry of Education suggesting the possibility of the PCC obtaining a lease of the Welfare Institute, and that provided the lease did not exceed twenty-two years the consent of the Minister would not be required. Mr Hughes forwarded this letter to the Revd Baker and W M Jones with the suggestion that this might be a satisfactory solution and offering to assist in furthering the negotiations by arranging a meeting of the various interested parties. But W M Jones was unhappy about the concept of a lease, "with the ultimate uncertainty of tenure". He continued in his reply to Mr Hughes dated 30 May, "We have never had a direct reply from the Divisional Welfare Committee to the letter dated 8 February signed by the Vicar and Mr Button, a Trustee of the Hall and secretary of the Church Council. In it they asked 'the committee to consider the lowest figure they would accept. It will enable us to devote the Hall to its original purpose.' Could you ask for a reply to this point. They would treat you more seriously than anything I might say. I could then decide what to do."

What price the local community?

By July 1962 the situation had worsened in that the premises was once again in danger of being sold to the highest bidder with little or no consideration being shown for the needs of the local community. Things improved when a month later the Legal Branch of the Ministry of Education had agreed to the PCC applying to acquire the Welfare Institute "for a figure to be agreed between the PCC, the Coal Industry Social Welfare Organisation and the Trustees".

Now the diocese stepped in with a letter from the Diocesan Registrar on 4 September advising that if the PCC purchased the property, "it will have to be vested in the Diocesan Board of Finance in compliance with the provisions of the PCC (Powers) Measure 1956, but local administration remains solely in the hands of the [Parochial Church] Council". This was a formality and did not present any potential difficulty, unlike the letter received from E D Davies, the Regional Social Welfare Officer of the Coal Industry Social Welfare Organisation. His letter, dated 10 September and addressed to

Mr Hughes, was in reply to Mr Hughes' letter of 21 August, in which he had written, "You will be aware of the protracted correspondence relating to this building and the views expressed …" And he referred to "the interest of the local inhabitants in this building by reason of the manner in which contributions were raised towards the cost of the premises in the beginning …" (This is an indirect reference to Mrs Knatchbull's concert which raised £100, but there now seems to be an element of folklore creeping into the facts which interprets the concert as a larger scale fundraising effort by the local community to actually build the hall.)

A stinging rebuke …

Mr Davies replied to Mr Hughes in stinging terms: "The Parochial Church Council, as far as I am informed, have no funds to purchase the … property. The desire of the Church Council to buy the property was motivated by Mr W M Jones. I am not aware of any benefits that would accrue to the inhabitants of Coleford because the inhabitants of late years have not shown the slightest interest in the Hall. The Minister has only heard one side of the story, and it is proposed to let him have the South Western Divisional Welfare Committee's observations in due course. I am not aware of protracted correspondence relating to the building. This is the first time you have written to me on this matter. The cost of the building—many years ago—was paid from the Miners' Welfare Fund. It is true that a Mrs Knatchbull donated the area of land on which it stands to the Trustees. The Divisional Welfare Committee have rules that the Hall must be sold to the highest bidder, and this ruling was reiterated at a meeting of the Budget Committee … on the 29th August 1962 … Three tenders were received for the purchase of the building. We know that, in one case at least, Mr W M Jones 'persuaded' one of the bidders to withdraw, and we have reason to believe the same in the other case. That leaves the Parochial Church Council's offer of £1100 as the highest figure— an offer motivated … by Mr W M Jones. It appears now that after having the two other higher offers withdrawn, it is sought to purchase the Institute at a lesser figure. The Divisional Welfare Committee will not agree to this … The new Legion Hall at Coleford is quite capable of coping with the requirements of the Coleford district." Finally, he contradicted himself; having denied receiving or seeing any earlier letters, he summed up by saying, "If it is assured that the Parochial Church Council's offer of £1100, as given me in a letter dated 12th February 1962, is honoured, the South Western Divisional Welfare Committee will, I believe, approve of the sale of the Institute at that figure." Copies of the letter were sent to all the parties involved in the negotiations.

… And a gracious reply

The Revd Baker replied very graciously, almost naively, though one suspects he knew exactly what he was doing. "Our latest letter," he wrote on 14 September, "offering £500 for the Hall crossed your letter in the post. In view of the contents of the latter I would be grateful if you could … meet our Churchwardens and myself … What is disturbing to people here is the fact that for many years a levy of tuppence per ton on all coal mined by three pits in this neighbourhood was given by Coleford miners for supporting the costs connected with the Hall. Your generous assistance to schemes for the benefit of other mining villages in North Somerset is well known and if you could see your way to show Coleford similar consideration your help would be gratefully appreciated by all concerned …" A few days earlier, at a special PCC meeting, W M Jones had said he would be prepared to pay to the PCC the sum of £500 for the purchase of the Welfare Institute. It had been noted that the Diocesan Board of Finance would hold the Hall in Trust. Mr Jones also said that he was willing to make good any debt on the year's working of the Institute.

Mr Davies replied to the Revd Baker on 17 September in acid terms. "I am prepared to meet you and the Churchwardens if you will let me know that the offer … [of] £1100 will be honoured. The Divisional Welfare Committee has given definite instructions that the highest sum … should be accepted … As I have said … it is known for a fact that Mr W M Jones persuaded one of the tenderers to withdraw, presumably in favour of the Parochial Church Council tender. There is also reason to believe that he persuaded the other gentleman who offered a higher price than £1100 to withdraw. In view of his action the highest tender is £1100. I do not see any point in meeting you and the Churchwardens if there is no guarantee that the highest figure … will be honoured. Regarding your mention that the Coleford miners gave a levy of 2d per ton … We have no record of any contributions by miners to help to raise the building, or to cover maintenance. The whole of the money for erecting the building was paid for by the former Miners' Welfare Commission …"

The question of the levy of 2d per ton is possibly a case of confusion with the fact that the money for the establishment of the national Miners' Welfare Fund was originally raised by a levy of 1d per ton on all coal mined throughout the country. It is easy to understand how, with the passage of time, the reason for a levy was misinterpreted. Indeed it was stated in *Coleford as 'twere* that the local miners paid a levy to build the Welfare Institute, but as noted above this is not true. However, the local miners may have paid a levy of 2d per ton towards the *upkeep*, as opposed to the actual building, of the Coleford Institute, as the Revd Baker suggested in his letter of 14 September.

"Futile and unnecessary"

The Revd Baker replied to Mr Davies' letter on 20 September, taking it paragraph by paragraph. He pointed out that a meeting would be "futile and unnecessary" if Mr Davies would only meet the Vicar and Churchwardens if they agreed to the terms beforehand. He also noted that in his letter of 8 February, countersigned by Mr Button, he had stated that "with the help of members of our Church *we might eventually* [my italics] be able to offer a sum not exceeding £1,100 if that be considered necessary." Furthermore, the Revd Baker defended Mr Jones saying that the other two tenderers were personal friends of Mr Jones and that he had told them of the PCC's hopes and they voluntarily offered to withdraw their tenders. After querying Mr Davies' denial about the levy, his final point was that Mr J Carpenter, one of the two local Trustees, had been ignored throughout the negotiations and that he was opposed to the loss of the Hall by the local community.

The Revd Baker's letter to Mr Davies was met with a reply on 21 September in which Mr Davies continued to insist on nothing less than £1,100, and passing the buck for the decision to the South Western Divisional Welfare Committee. Mr Davies continued, "I certainly deny that the coal sold from the local colliery was subject to a contribution of 2d per ton for welfare purposes." This was followed by a vehement denial that Mr Carpenter had been ignored, followed by the final barb, "It was I who was ignored, and I could tell much of the means taken by Mr Jones without consulting me, to obtain possession of the Institute." This letter, with its aspersions on the integrity of William Marchant Jones, was passed to him by the Revd Baker. W M Jones duly replied on 27 September, denying the accusation of ignoring Mr Davies and reminding him of when they had met each other at Writhlington colliery and had discussed the matter. Mr Davies replied the next day denying this and going over the old ground yet again by insisting on £1,100 for the sale of the Hall. He continued, "I have written a letter to Mr Button saying that unless the Parochial Church Council are prepared to honour their offer, made through you, within four weeks, the question of the sale will be deemed to have lapsed, and the Institute will be re-advertised for sale." W M Jones replied, saying, "My own personal offer is for £500, without any conditions. It is very disappointing to find my action has failed to get the support I had hoped for it."

Many local needs

By this time Mr Hyrons, the headmaster of the neighbouring Church School, had expressed an interest in hiring the Hall from the PCC if their bid was successful. On 8 October 1962 he wrote to Mr Hughes, Clerk to the Frome Rural District Council, proposing the hire of the Welfare Institute from the church for PE, Music and Movement, drama and religious assemblies, amounting to a total of five hours a week. Accordingly, on 22 October Mr Hughes wrote a letter to the Secretary of the Legal Branch of the Ministry of Education in support of the PCC's bid. Summarising the local need for the Institute, he was able to make a considerable list: the need for a Church Hall; the needs of the Church School; the needs of the Frome RDC for a Youth Centre; and the occasional needs of the wider parish. He continued by summarising the situation regarding the NCB's insistence on £1,100: "Due to the deadlock which has arisen, perhaps it can be arranged for the Ministry [of Education] to act as an intermediary … I would suggest that if a Meeting were to be convened of all the interested Parties, an amicable solution might be found which would be of benefit locally … The correspondence has become protracted and little progress is likely to be made unless some definite line of action is pursued."

"Get rid of it"

Mr J Carpenter, one of the surviving Trustees, now entered the fray by writing to Mr Davies, registering his opposition to the Institute being lost to the people of Coleford.

Mr Davies replied very rudely and dismissively, claiming that the two Trustees (Mr Leonard Button and Mr Carpenter) had signed a form in March 1961 to say that the Institute was not needed for Welfare purposes and that it was best to get rid of it. No copy of that form exists in the parish file, but it may well be that such a form was signed because clearly the Institute had ceased to serve the mining community in the way it was originally intended, hence the decision by the NCB to sell it. But that is not to suggest that either of the Trustees would have wished for the Institute to pass out of parish and village use if it could be saved for the purpose. A further missive was sent by Mr Davies to the Revd Baker, criticising W M Jones: "I do not think it is either an honourable or honest thing to make an offer, get rid of all competitors, and then try to obtain the commodity at a much lower figure." He also defended Mr Button, who was in an increasingly difficult position being both PCC secretary and a Trustee.

Hopes dashed

Mr Hughes of Frome RDC had his hopes of a meeting facilitated by the Ministry of Education dashed when he received a letter from the Legal Department upholding the action of the Trustees in selling the property to the highest bidder. Thus if the PCC wished to purchase the Institute, they had to offer a sum not less than £1,100. Copies of the letter were sent to Mr Davies and to William Marchant Jones.

The paper trail stops

Frustratingly, the file of correspondence in the PCC records stops at this point, so although we know that the PCC acquired the former Miners' Welfare Institute, thanks

---

The Parochial Church Council (Powers) Measure 1956 states:

(1)   After the commencement of this Measure, a council shall not acquire any interest in land (other than a short lease as hereinafter defined) or in any personal property to be held on permanent trusts, without the consent of the diocesan authority.

(2)   Where, at or after the commencement of this Measure, a council holds or acquires an interest in land (other than a short lease as hereinafter defined) or any interest in personal property to be held on permanent trusts, such interest shall be vested in the diocesan authority subject to all trusts, debts and liabilities affecting the same, and all persons concerned shall make or concur in making such transfers (if any) as are requisite for giving effect to the provisions of this subsection.

(3)   Where any property is vested in the diocesan authority pursuant to subsection (2) of this section, the council shall not sell, lease, let, exchange, charge or take any legal proceedings with respect to the property without the consent of the authority; but save as aforesaid, nothing in this section shall affect the powers of the council in relation to the management, administration or disposition of any such property.

---

to the generosity of William Marchant Jones, there are still some unanswered questions. It took a good two more years before the business was concluded, and the PCC did not acquire the Hall until 1964. The Conveyance is dated 21 April 1964, and the sum of £900 was specifically stated. The document was signed, sealed and delivered in the presence of W M Jones. In accordance with the terms of the Parochial Church Councils (Powers) Measure 1956, the Bath and Wells Diocesan Board of Finance became the custodian trustees.

"You impugn my honour"

Whatever the sum paid, the Hall was a boon to the church. No longer would it be necessary to pay a fee for the use of the premises for Church events. William Marchant Jones was an old man by this time and was failing in health, and the lengthy and increasingly angry correspondence had taken its toll. He was deeply hurt by the attitude of the Coal Board and had concluded his letter of 9 October 1962 to Mr Davies, "In your letter you impugn my honour. I am content to leave the record to present and future generations of Colefordians." The continued use of the Church Hall, almost half a century after he began negotiations for its purchase, restores his name to an honourable place in the history of the church and village.

A strong letter of protest

The PCC Minutes throughout the 1960s are strewn with references to damage done to the Church Hall by the Youth Club and other users. For instance, the following Minute recorded in February 1967 is typical of many others: "Mrs Habershon reported on the amount of damage done in the Hall by the Youth Club. A strong letter of protest had been sent to the youth leader with a copy to Mr Hughes, warning them that unless matters were improved, they would be refused access to the Hall. In the meantime, the Youth Club would be refused permission to use the upstairs room." By May the damage was so great that the decision was made to give them only one more chance, and if it continued they would be unable to use the hall. Excessive use of electricity was another issue and meters were installed.

An unsolved mystery

Because the parish file of correspondence is incomplete, we do not know the exact terms under which W M Jones made the funding available. (The Bath and Wells Diocesan Board of Finance holds correspondence as the "custodian Trustees" but would not make it available for the purpose of this book, although other documents were made available.) It is possible that W M Jones paid part of the cost (£500 is likely) and made a loan to the PCC of the balance. The Church Accounts for 1965–67 (D/P/Coleford 4/1/3) show repayments on loans to Reconstructed Bath Stone Ltd (W M Jones' company at Newbury). While these loans could relate to other church work, it is also likely that they relate, at least in part, to the purchase of the hall or to its refurbishment:

27 August 1965 Repayment of loan (RBS Ltd) 1st instalment £350.0.0
5 December 1966 Repayment of loan (RBS) 2nd payment £175.0.0
26 April 1967 Repayment of loan (RBS) £175.0.0
26 October 1967 Repayment of loan (RBS) £125.0.0

The last Will and Testament of William Marchant Jones

The PCC Minutes of 3 May 1967 reported a conversation between PCC member Mr Townsend and Richard Jones (W M Jones' son), regarding the recovery of Income Tax on his father's "covenanted subscription". At the meeting it was agreed that Miss Ackroyd, the PCC Secretary, should ask the Diocesan Board of Finance for advice. Meanwhile, William Marchant Jones died on 7 June, the very day that Miss Ackroyd saw the DBF Secretary. The PCC had a long discussion on 7 June and decided that Jack Coles and Miss Ackroyd should seek an immediate meeting with Mr Barrett, Secretary of the DBF. At this meeting Mr Barrett advised that no action should be taken until further information had been sought from the solicitor on the terms of Mr Jones' Will. The PCC members were told on 5 July that "the contents of Mr Jones' Will showed a legacy of £100 to the choir fund, details about the cancellation of any remaining debt, and the provision of a brass tablet in the church". An extraordinary meeting of the PCC was called on 27 September to discuss the hall situation. Mr Barrett had written to say that the PCC was under no legal obligation to pay any money towards the purchase of the hall but that the PCC might wish to make an ex gratia payment. Due to the vicar's absence through illness, Jack Coles was chairing the meeting, and he proposed that the PCC should make an ex gratia payment equal to the amount of tax reclaimed on one year's payment of W M Jones' covenant. This was agreed. On 1 May 1968 the Treasurer (Jack Coles) reported that he had received the cheque from W M Jones' legacy, and that this had been paid to the Solicitors of Reconstructed Bath Stone Ltd., discharging any debt.

"In accordance with his wish …"

At the parish Annual General Meeting in 1970, "Mr Withers gave a brief resume of the wishes of the late Mr W M Jones when giving the Church Hall to the Church. In accordance with his wish, the Committee had now been able to create a reserve fund of £200 and in the current account they had £74. Now it was felt that the officers of the Hall Committee wished to resign and to hand over the responsibility to the PCC at the same time making a recommendation that the reserve fund be kept intact for emergencies. The officers were thanked for their work and it was agreed that the PCC would discuss the matter at their next meeting." In May the Hall Committee was dissolved and a new sub-Committee of the PCC elected in its place.

By September 1970 the Church School was on the move, with the new Bishop Henderson Church of England Primary School opening in Farley Dell. This eventually opened up the possibility of the old school buildings being used for Youth Club purposes instead of the Church Hall.

The Miners' Welfare Institute, now the Church Hall

Restoration

Over the next few years a tremendous amount of work was done on the restoration of the Church Hall. This also involved repairs following continued vandalism and occasional break-ins. In the 1970s a caretaker was first employed to be responsible for cleaning and general maintenance. In September 1974 a long list of requirements was presented to the PCC. These included attention to the fire escape; lavatories needing to be renewed; electrical work; repairs to floorboards, wall heaters, and redecoration in all rooms. A year later most of this work had been done. Much of this work was done by local builders, including Dennis Hodges, who was a member of Holy Trinity. Fundraising such as whist drives, coffee mornings and concerts were held to raise the money for restoration and maintenance work. As a result, bookings were increasing and these would bring in more funds for further work.

The future in question

On 1 February 1984 the PCC agreed that a complete review of the Church Hall was needed, and John Kestin agreed to ask advice from Mr D Olive of the architects Beech Tyldesley. Of particular concern was the roof, extensive and costly work being required. By September 1984 the suggestion had been made to make the hall into a "Church and Community Hall" but this idea was soon dropped. A Committee of Management was formed consisting of the Rector in the Chair, four members of the PCC, and two members from organisations using the hall. A loan of £5,000 would be sought from the diocese; in fact a loan of £4,000 was offered and accepted, to be repaid over four years at 5% interest rate. It had also been discovered that the hall was grossly underinsured and the premium was increased. The work of re-roofing the hall was carried out during May and June of 1985 at a cost of £5,364.

The future of the Church Hall again came under review in the period 1998–2000. The cost of maintenance was weighing heavily on the PCC, especially as major work needed to be carried out on the Church. Also new Health and Safety legislation was about to be passed, which would affect public buildings, and the PCC feared that its implementation would involve further high costs, and that the lack of these provisions would lead to the closure of the hall. Mr Paul Sander Jackson, who worked for a rural body at Shepton Mallet, had inspected all meeting places in the village and was going to make recommendations to the Millennium Committee. He had asked to attend a PCC meeting and did so on 6 May 1998, when he suggested the idea of using the Church Hall as a Community Centre. The idea was attractive because it would ease the burden of maintenance costs. The PCC members favoured further exploration without committing themselves to a final decision at that stage. On 9 November a feasibility study was carried out, and this was followed on 20 January 1999 by a meeting in the hall to be addressed by a member of Somerset Community Council to which PCC members were invited. Meanwhile, advice was sought from the diocese regarding the PCC's ownership and legal position regarding disposal of the Hall.

More concern about the future

On 3 March 1999 the PCC heard a report on the meeting with the Somerset Community Council, though details were not recorded in the Minutes. It was also revealed that a number of parishioners were seriously concerned about the future of the hall, and so it was decided to openly discuss the matter at the parish Annual General Meeting. The April 1999 issue of *On the Map* set out three possibilities for the hall. Firstly, for the PCC to retain ownership and face the prospect of closure when the Disability Discrimination Act came into force. Secondly, to hand the hall over to a charitable body such as the Millennium Group, who would be able to obtain a grant to make the necessary alterations. And thirdly, to sell the hall and use the proceeds to make improvements in the church. Finally, after a long period of delay, it was decided to retain ownership of the hall and to restore it using local help wherever possible.

A stroke of luck Clearly the file of letters referred to above, together with the original Trust Deed, had been lost sight of. They were found, quite by accident, amongst copies of music in a cupboard in the choir vestry, by Dave Baker and the Revd Valerie Bonham, in 2008, while looking in vain for the Revd Sidney Wood's history of the church—a classic case of looking for one thing and finding something else!

A new lease of life

This work on the refurbishment of the hall was begun in 2001 and completed by the autumn of 2004. Rex Parfitt, Richard Usher and Geoffrey Plummer had been working hard to completely overhaul the facilities so that the hall would be viable for a wider range of bookings. New kitchen facilities were installed in the Committee Room and the Mendip Room, a new toilet for use by the disabled was created from a storeroom, extra storage space was made, and the team completely redecorated the rooms downstairs. The large room upstairs was restored and the redecoration was carried out by Community Service workers under the supervision of the Somerset Probation Services, using materials supplied by the PCC.

Church Hall maintenance by Rex Parfitt and Richard Usher

Work on the Church Hall continues to be carried out, but despite fewer bookings from the village community, the PCC acknowledge what a tremendous resource the hall is for the church. It provides a venue for coffee after the Sunday Eucharist as well as being the regular venue for the Wednesday Eucharist. The hall began to be used for the Wednesday Eucharist in about 1993, and in recent years the congregation has grown in numbers from four or five to over a dozen, and anything from fifteen to twenty when followed by a Coffee Morning. Fundraising events such as the Coffee Mornings are held on a regular basis, and the hall is often used for refreshments following funerals. The Lent lunches in collaboration with the Methodist Chapel are held in the hall, as well as the Easter and Harvest lunches. Also, from time to time the hall is let for fundraising lunches in aid of CLIC-Sargent (Children with Cancer and Leukaemia) and the Macmillan Nurses. The hall is used for serving refreshments after special services such as the Christmas Carol Service and following concerts held in the church. Also, it is used for PCC meetings and provides CF5 with a convenient meeting place for rehearsals for their productions as well as a large space to prepare the scenery and "props". During the 2007 redecoration of the church and the installation of the heating and carpets in 2009, the Church Hall was once again used for Sunday worship, following a long tradition at Holy Trinity.

- 13 -

HOLY TRINITY AND EDUCATION

This chapter gives some highlights of Holy Trinity's involvement with religious education, beginning firstly with the Sunday School and some of the later work that has followed it in more recent years. Then there is a glimpse of the Church School beginning in the 1830s and progressing into the 21st century. In both cases, this can be no more than a broad canvas. To do real justice to both aspects of children's work would require a much fuller study.

The Sunday School

The Revd George Newnham recorded the foundation and early days of the Sunday School: "A Sunday School was commenced a few weeks after the Church consecration and held in the Church—this plan being of course attended with both indecencies and inconvenience. The Teachers are gratuitous barring a gratuity twice a year and a sovereign at Xmas to the Leader ... In the spring of 1835 the School was moved to the new room then open and both scholars and teachers largely increased, until in 1839 they exceeded the number on the Wesleyan list. The encouragement to the children has been the giving of 2 tickets for 'Decent Appearance' and 'Good Behaviour' when deserved by 'neatness' and 'punctual attendance' and 'diligence and obedience': both of which were forfeited by either rudeness in going to church, or unruly behaviour during the service." (D/P/Coleford 8/3/1 p109–10)

The Revd G W Newnham's original Sunday School met at 9.00 am and continued to 1.30 pm or even 1.45 pm. Usually opening with a hymn, by the late 1830s a short litany had also been included. "By way of keeping them together as a body, the teachers have been wont to meet every two months on a moonlight evening to take tea in the Parsonage kitchen, which has been followed by a converse on school regulations and prospects, stating difficulties, giving counsels, and reading extracts from some book bearing on the subject, with sermon reading, a hymn and a prayer. Sometimes one or two of the elder scholars, who occasionally acted as monitor, were invited to attend the party." (D/P/Coleford 8/3/1)

As already noted in chapter 3, the annual sermon collection was used to aid the work of the Sunday School. The Revd Newnham experienced a difficulty early in his ministry regarding the timing of the Sunday service, which seems to indicate some rivalry with the Wesleyans just down the hill. He wrote thus: "The services were originally at 11.00 am and half past two but it being found that the late morning service induced many children to prefer the Wesleyan School—the parents foolishly giving them the option—it was resolved to start fair with the dissidents at half past ten. The afternoon service to lengthen the school time was deferred until 3.00 pm except during December and January." (D/P Coleford 8/3/1 p87)

The Millennium book *Coleford as 'twere* is full of the memories of Colefordians (many of whom have died since the book was published in 2000), and it is clear that in the first half of the 20th century both Church and Chapels had flourishing Sunday Schools. Lottie Taylor and her sister Florence James, both staunch Methodists, recalled that in their youth every child in the village went to Sunday School and that both Church and Chapel had large numbers.

Sunday School outings were memorable because it was practically the only time that children and their mothers travelled from the village. Lack of transport and money meant that very few had family holidays, so the annual outing was a real treat. It is not surprising, therefore, that these outings provided lifelong memories.

During Fr Sutters' time, the emphasis was on "Children's Church"; and in the *Coleford Parish Paper* of September 1955, he explained the difference between Children's Church and Sunday School: "It is difficult for boys and girls who never come to anything but children's services to settle down and feel at home when the time comes to change over to grown-up worship; so often they drop away. Those who never worship with their parents ... naturally come to think that religion is just for children, and that you leave Church when you leave school. So I say firmly to parents, '*Bring* your children to Church on Sunday mornings; and then send them to learn their Faith in the afternoon ...' We shall be delighted to see you."

> By the 1930s, there were regular annual outings of the Sunday School scholars, usually to Weston-super-Mare or Burnham. **Joyce Button** recalls that she started Sunday School when she was about seven years old, and they had a large open-top charabanc for the outings. "On one occasion they were going down Cheddar when Granny Steeds stopped the coach because she did not want to drive down, so she walked and they waited for her at the bottom."

Membership of the Children's Church required attendance at the 9.30 am Parish Eucharist as well as at the Children's Church at 2.30 pm. Those who regularly attended both over a period of six months qualified for the Canon Moore Memorial Prize.

In November 1956 the decision was made to rearrange the Children's Church by ages. Those up to 11 years were to attend at 2.15 pm for the Children's Church service and instruction. Those over 11 were to attend a Class at 3.00 pm during which there would be a chance for discussion. On 13 November the Junior Children's Church elected new officers:

Ron Brewer also remembers his early experiences at Sunday School:

My first recollection of Coleford Church is Sunday School which was then held in the Church School, which is now the Scout Hall.

Young Ron Brewer

John Turner was the Superintendent. Our teacher was Mrs Baynton. She was a dear old lady who got her clothes from jumble sales. She often had a new hat from a jumble sale. One particular hat was in the shape of a bowl of fruit. The cherries were stuck on wires, and we used to get behind her and snick the cherries and the fruit would wobble around like a trifle. If Mrs Baynton was ill, I would play the organ. I must have been about thirteen and played from time to time until I was thirty. Sunday School moved to the Church and then the Church Hall.

The Sunday School trip to the seaside was a great day. It seemed half of Coleford went. It was the only time most children saw the sea. On the way home we had singing in the coach. Then we would stop for fish and chips to end the day.

Mrs Baynton's brother, George Edgell, sold the *Christian Herald*. He delivered them on an old bike all round Coleford, Holcombe and Leigh-on-Mendip. They were 4d in old money. As he delivered he whistled hymns as he went; mostly it was "What a friend we have in Jesus".

Readers, Malcolm Plummer and Ronald Coles;
Wardens, Philip Kelly and John Moore;
Sidesmen, Jacqueline Trimby, Hilary Coles, Margaret Coles, Elizabeth Jones;
Registrar, Glyn Edgell (Hazel Price to remain Senior Registrar);
Ringers, Alan Seviour and David Price (junior).

From the end of 1956 the finances of the Sunday School and the Children's Church were to be joined together as the Sunday School no longer worked separately. John Turner had agreed to take charge of the joint fund.

A few months later a Children's Eucharist had been started at 10.45 am on the 3rd Sunday of each month for those who had found 9.30 too early. This had been well attended for the first two months, but attendance had dropped off and Fr Sutters decided to abandon it. He was also appealing at this time for more boys to join the choir.

In 1966 Mr Donald became Superintendent. Though at the time there were only a few regulars, numbers gradually increased.

The Revd Sidney Wood became Vicar in 1969, and he informed the PCC at its meeting in September 1970 that as from the Sunday following the Harvest Festival, the Parish Communion would be at 10.00 am and that the afternoon Sunday School would be replaced by a morning session with the children coming into the Parish Communion after the sermon. This reflected a growing trend in the wider church, hinted at in Fr Sutters' time and brought about by the number of children who "grew out" of afternoon Sunday School and did not transfer to Sunday morning worship. Evidently not everyone was convinced of the wisdom of the new arrangements because it was reported towards the end of the year that the morning "Sunday Club" was in existence and that an afternoon meeting was also being held.

By 1979 the Revd Alan Coleman was reporting in the November issue of *On the Map* that the Sunday School had not been functioning satisfactorily for some time. So, beginning on Advent Sunday (2 December), there would be Children's Church each Sunday at 2.30 pm, lasting half an hour, to be followed by Church Club until 4.00 pm at the Church Hall. It was hoped that it would be possible to extend the Club to one night a week from 6.00 pm until 7.30 pm. Children would still be welcome at the Sunday Eucharist.

Over the years, numbers in the Sunday School in its various guises dropped from fifty in 1976 to twenty in 1980. By the time of the Annual Parochial Church Meeting of 1982, it was reported that there was no formal Sunday School but some children attended the Parish Eucharist, and there were sixteen young people and one adult preparing for confirmation. By 1986 the Sunday School had been re-formed under the leadership of Sylvia Kestin and there were ten members. This number fluctuated and was difficult to maintain. A plea was made for a children's corner in church, but it took until 1999 before this was provided.

In the year 2000 Children's Services were begun on the second Sunday of each month. The Children's Services were led by Clarissa Cridland, and each one had a special theme and service booklet. Personal invitations were sent to the children, and the services were well supported. Later, around 2005, the services were themed according to the church year with the inclusion of some Family Eucharists. At the time of writing, work with families and children is again under review.

The Church School

The Church school has been in existence almost as long as Holy Trinity itself. Founded in 1834, its first building soon proved inadequate, and in 1846 the Revd Robert Whiteway provided land for the building of a new school. The Revd Whiteway formally transferred the deeds for the school and its land, including the original church school, the new school adjoining it, the master's house and the yard, to the church in 1874.

Just across the road from the church, it remained the home of the village school until 1970. In 1878, the original school building was restored, creating "a lighter, brighter and airier

> **Joyce Button** remembers that she started at the Church School at the age of four. She remembers that she was taught to knit at school and that the children would be given Horlicks mid-morning for a small fee.

room" to house the infants, and a public tea was given in an effort to encourage parents to enrol their children. This was not always easy when there was a 2d fee per child.

In 1879, the Revd Thomas Yewens came into conflict with some parishioners after allowing the schoolroom to be used for the entertainment of seventy elderly people, because provisions included beer and tobacco.

The Church School was not the only school in Coleford, the Wesleyans having their own school adjoining the Chapel. There was some rivalry between the children of the two schools, complete with name-calling ("chapel rats and church mice"), and some lunchtime fisticuffs. After the First World War, some ex-Army huts were brought to Coleford and erected in Anchor Road (opposite the present day Post Office). This became the Council School and the Wesleyan School closed. Mr Hollick, the Wesleyan schoolmaster, transferred to the new Council School so there was some continuity for the pupils.

The Schoolmaster's house and school yard

In 1953 the school performed a play called *The Forgetful Ghost*, and in 1954 their production was called *The King's Messenger*.

Throughout its history the clergy of Holy Trinity had kept close contact with the Church School, and by the 1950s church education had undergone many changes. In 1959 Mr Evans, the headmaster, announced his forthcoming retirement, and Fr John Sutters wrote a tribute in the February issue of the *Coleford Parish Paper*: "Mr Evans is to resign the Headmastership of Coleford School at Easter, and to retire from his life's work as a teacher. That means we shall lose Mrs Evans also … They have not only had a long time here—over fifteen years—but have seen the School through the

Above: *School staff in the early 1900s*

Below: *Pupils at the Church School, early 1900s*

Above: *School children celebrating the coronation, 1911*

Below: *The Church School football team in 1932*

Coleford Church of England School
football team, 1932 (left to right):
(Back row) Sid Perkins,
L. Sargent, K. Chivers;
(Middle row) Ron Button,
D. Moore, Phil Green,
Mr Webber; (Front row)
R. Gibbs, J. Trimby,
E. Coles, H. Perkins,
J. Harwood, E. Moore

Above: *School managers and top class* c. *1949; second from left: Jack Coles; fourth from left: headmaster Mr Evans*

Left: *Cast of the 1953 school play,* The Forgetful Ghost

Cast of the 1954 school play, The King's Messenger

greatest changes in all its history. They took over in the most difficult stage of the war years … They have seen the change-over from the School's being one of two 'all-age' schools in Coleford to its taking responsibility for all the under-11's in the village, and from being a purely Church School to 'controlled' status—that is, to accepting considerable restrictions on its Church character in return for substantial financial support from the County Education Authority. All this change and development has called for skill, wisdom, and devotion in those responsible for the administration … of the School … and it has not been achieved without a little difficulty at times. But the present happy state of things within the School … are due in no small measure to the hard work and wise administration of Mr and Mrs Evans during these years of change and development."

Fr Sutters then paid tribute to Mr and Mrs Evans' efficient teaching, readiness to help and work with children out of school hours, their hard work raising funds for extra amenities, the high standard of music, concerts and plays, and for the Christmas parties, which the children would long remember.

The priest's stall in Holy Trinity was given in memory of Mr Evans after his death in 1979. A brass plaque on the side reads:

> Wilfred John Lewis Evans 1897–1979. Headmaster of Coleford Church
> Junior School 1943–59.
> Given by Mrs Evans in loving memory of her husband.
> 'Life is everlasting and love is immortal'

More than 100 people applied for the Headship of the School, and the candidate appointed was Mr H C Hyrons, who would be moving from a church school at North Cheriton in Somerset. Mr Hyrons was also a Diocesan Lay Reader.

In 1970 the Church School was relocated to the top of the village, where new premises were dedicated by the Bishop of Bath and Wells, Bishop Edward Henderson, on 24 September. The building was named Bishop Henderson Church of England Voluntary Controlled Primary School.

Mr Hyrons retired from Bishop Henderson School on 30 March 1977, after a Headship lasting eighteen years. He was replaced by Mr Robin Clark, formerly Head of Farrington Gurney Primary School. He held office for seventeen years, retiring in July 1994. Writing in the July issue of *On the Map*, School Governor Ann Crawford paid tribute to Robin Clark's achievements, noting the new ideas he had introduced to the curriculum, such as swimming, sports, PE, computers and improving the academic standards. She noted that a number of former pupils had achieved academic success in higher education and the professions. And she also paid tribute to his pastoral care of several families who had lost children through terminal illness.

The new Head Teacher was David Hayward, who took up office in September 1994. During David Hayward's time as Head Teacher, the Rector, Fr Peter Down, forged close links with the School.

From the time of her appointment in 2002, the Revd Valerie Bonham has built up a good relationship with the school and both she and the Revd Clarissa Cridland visit regularly for Assembly. Revd Valerie is also an ex-officio Foundation Governor along with Ann Usher and Shirley Kite, both members of Holy Trinity. (Holy Trinity has provided a number of Foundation Governors over the years, including Ann Crawford, Dave Baker and Curtis Ilott.) The school children and their parents come to Holy Trinity for end of term Assembly, and individual classes make visits to the church to learn about Baptism and to make drawings of the building.

The school was extended in 2001 and blessed by the Revd Stephen Tudgey, and further building work, involving the demolition of two temporary classrooms and the building of new ones and additional teaching space, took place in 2005. On the latter occasion Revd Valerie blessed the new buildings. After twelve years, David Hayward left Bishop Henderson School at the end of 2005 for a new appointment.

In February 2006 the Governors appointed Mrs Tonie Scott, formerly Deputy Head, as Head Teacher as from April 2006. Revds Valerie and Clarissa continue to visit the school and to build on the good relationship nurtured over the years.

- 14 -

HOLY TRINITY IN THE 21ST CENTURY

REVD VALERIE **writes:** Many aspects of parish life have continued in the 21st century in much the same way as in former years and with former priests—the observance of the seasons of the Church Year, fundraising events, Gift Day, Bible study groups and Christian Nurture Courses such as "Emmaus". And also the familiar pattern of baptisms, weddings and funerals. Modern lifestyles impinge on church life in that while we have many baptisms, we have very few weddings. This is not just because fewer people marry, but principally because fewer people *marry in church*, opting instead for hotel "packages" or exotic beach weddings far away from Coleford.

Writing in 2009, I have been here long enough to be deeply saddened by the number of funerals I have taken, either in church or at the crematorium, of people I have come to know (and some I have not known) since my arrival in 2002. These have included babies, young mothers, village "characters", former and present members of the congregation, pillars of the various village organisations, and those who have lived to a great age. Whoever they are, they are all my parishioners—people whose pastoral care was entrusted to me at my licensing—and it is a privilege to be alongside their families at such times. For the purposes of this chapter, I have only mentioned the funerals of members of the congregation, simply because there have been *so many others* that it would be easy to miss a name out. But I should also mention here some of our good friends from the Methodist Chapel who have died since my arrival: Stella and Albert Treasure, Florence James, Myrtle Willis, Alf Payne, John Perry, Dennis and Teena Button, Lottie Taylor and Pearl Bull, some of whom have faithfully supported our Evensong and other Sunday evening services and other fundraising events.

As well as fundraising for our own church needs, the congregation of Holy Trinity is also quick to respond to the needs of the wider world, such as the tsunami appeal, the "Jar of Grace" appeal for the United Nations Children's Fund (UNICEF), Christian Aid, Claire Fleming's work with HIV/AIDS orphans, "Send a Cow", and The Children's Society, to name just a few of the good causes that have been supported in recent years. And in June 2009, Holy Trinity sponsored a concert by the Mendip Male Voice Choir in aid of three-year-old Ben Halford, suffering from a brain tumour, and raised £925 towards his care.

It is impossible to mention everything that has taken place in the past seven years, but here are **some of the highlights in the life of Holy Trinity from 2002 until 2009**, and at the end of the book you will find a photographic record of parish life since 2002 …

2002

As final preparations were made for the licensing of the Revd Valerie Bonham as Priest in Charge of the Benefice, the Churchwardens thanked the clergy who had helped during the long period of vacancy. These were Canon Brian Boyce, Fr Brian Sutton, the Revd Geoffrey Thomas, the Revd Marianne Atkinson and Fr Robert Webb. Thanks were also expressed to Don Thompson, Reader Emeritus, for all his help at St Andrew's. The licensing by the Right Revd Andrew Radford, Bishop of Taunton, took place on Wednesday 16 January in a church packed to its fullest capacity. A coachload came from the Revd Valerie's former parish at Cookham, together with their vicar the Revd Michael Smith, who officially handed their former curate over to her new parish and people.

The nation was saddened by the death of Queen Elizabeth the Queen Mother on 30 March (the day before Easter Sunday). A thanksgiving Eucharist for her long life was celebrated on Tuesday 2 April and twenty-eight people attended, of whom twenty-six received Holy Communion.

2002 marked the Golden Jubilee of the accession of Queen Elizabeth II to the throne in 1952, and the Country was getting ready to celebrate in style. Coleford and Holcombe was no exception, with many events in both villages during the Jubilee weekend of Saturday to Monday 1–3 June. At Holy Trinity there was a Flower Festival throughout the weekend, masterminded by Ann Mackie-Hunter. Floral arrangements were contributed by church members and also by the village organisations. Letters of invitation had been sent out to the organisations inviting them to contribute a flower arrangement and also to attend the special Jubilee service at 9.30 am on the Sunday. There was an enthusiastic response and sixty-one adults and five children attended the service. On the Monday, the new vicar opened the fete organised by the Luckington Carnival Club and then spent a good deal of time going from one event to the other in both villages—and back again!

There were some special anniversaries nearer home too. Ann Crawford, having

Left: *Ann Crawford celebrating 26 years on the PCC*
Centre: *Harold Crossley*
Right: *Rupert Shepherd celebrating his 100th birthday*

served twenty-six years on Holy Trinity PCC, decided at the Annual Parochial Church Meeting to stand down, and she was given a card of thanks the following Sunday.

Harold Crossley celebrated his 90th birthday on Sunday 4 May and was rather overwhelmed to be given a card and birthday cake at the start of the service.

Two people from the benefice celebrated their 100th birthdays—Lilian Conn from Brickhouse Farm in Holcombe on 17 May, and Rupert Shepherd from Coleford at the end of June. It was good to be able to join their celebrations.

Memorial Services for the departed had been held in former years by Fr David Watson and Fr Peter Down. On Sunday 3 November a Memorial Service was held, during the course of which the names of the departed were read out. This service was well attended, letters of invitation having been sent to those who had been bereaved during the course of 2002.

Remembrance Sunday saw special services in Holy Trinity and St Andrew's, and in addition Revd Valerie led the annual Remembrance Service at the Royal British Legion for the first time.

2003

The beginning of 2003 was marked by funerals. Early in January, the death occurred of Dorothy Brooks, a member of Holy Trinity who had recently celebrated her 90th birthday. Her funeral was held in church on 13 January. On 10 February the funeral of Clare Tresidder took place in church. Clare had been a very active church member in years past, and had latterly received Holy Communion at home.

Clare Tresidder

12 February marked the death in Oxford of Fr John Sutters, Vicar of Coleford from 1954–61. He had kept in touch with the parish ever since he left it, and his widow, Muriel Sutters, later sent a donation to the Restoration Fund.

As the world sank deeper into conflict in Iraq, vigils of Prayer for Peace were held in the benefice—at St Andrew's on Thursday 6 March from the end of the 10.00 am Eucharist until 1.00 pm, and at Holy Trinity on Sunday 9 March from the end of the 9.30 Eucharist until 3.00 pm.

Soon after Revd Valerie's arrival in the benefice, Clarissa Cridland began the Selection Process for ordination, having made the initial enquiries during the vacancy. Selection for ordination is a lot more difficult than it was in the early days of Holy Trinity, involving a series of interviews within the diocese culminating in an interview with the Diocesan Bishop, who subsequently makes the decision whether the candidate shall proceed to a Bishops' Selection Conference. Having overcome all these obstacles, Clarissa attended the three-day Selection Conference in June 2003. After a very anxious ten-day wait, the result came through that Clarissa had been recommended for training

Training for ordination can be either residential at a theological college, or on a non-residential ministry course, in both cases usually for two or three years. Clarissa opted for the non-residential Southern Theological Educational Training Scheme (STETS), which operates from Sarum College in Salisbury. (Revd Valerie had trained on a similar course in Oxford.) The STETS course is rigorous, with weekly meetings with a tutor, and residential weekends twice a term. The students study two modules each term and produce essays or other written assignments at the end of each module. In addition, there is an annual residential "Easter" school in Holy Week; and during the second year, each student undertakes a three-month placement in a different parish or in a different mode of ministry. The third aspect of the course is parish based, with the ordinand working alongside the training minister in order to gain insights into pastoral work as well as the church services. At the end of the course, assuming all the assignments have obtained the pass mark, the successful candidate is awarded a Diploma in Theological and Biblical Studies. During the course, there are further interviews with the Bishop, and if all goes well the student is finally recommended for ordination.

for the priesthood. Revd Valerie was designated her "training minister" for the duration of the three-year ordination course and, after ordination, her "training incumbent" for the duration of her first four years as a curate.

The harvest festival season began in earnest in September, and Revd Valerie and Clarissa led not only the Harvest Thanksgiving services in church but also at the Royal British Legion, and joined other village organisations for their services too. This has become a regular part of their September diary.

Another member of the congregation died in 2003. Peter Russell died on 22 October and his funeral took place on 29 October. Peter and his wife, Doris, had been confirmed at Holy Trinity in May 1997 and had been active members of the church ever since; in particular Peter helped with the preparation of the service booklets.

On the Map won an award from the Association for Church Editors as the best parish magazine, having "knocked for six" 500 other competitors. But no one in the benefice was really surprised at such a distinction! This triumph was repeated in 2004.

Peter and Doris Russell

2004

Early in the year Robyn Dexter, a young member of the congregation (the daughter of Julie and Mike Dexter), asked if she could work in the benefice with Revd Valerie and Clarissa for her week-long work experience from Somervale School. This was arranged for the end of June/early July and Robyn took part in a number of activities in both churches. As it was Gala Week at Holcombe, she was able to come to the Gala Service, which was also a pets' service. She also took part in baptism preparation, a visit to Scott's Close in Holcombe, and worked with Clarissa on her "home parish" module from STETS.

Julie, Robyn and Mike Dexter

As Holy Trinity prepared to celebrate its 175th anniversary of dedication, the thought began to formulate in Revd Valerie's mind about getting the church restored.

Revd Valerie recalls: When Clarissa, who was Churchwarden, showed me round Holy Trinity before my interview, my first impression was of an attractive open-planned building which was sorely in need of paint! The walls were discoloured by damp, there was a smell of dampness and the paint was peeling. I decided there and then that if I were appointed, I would get the church decorated within five years (though I didn't say so at the time!). Well, I was appointed, and the more I looked at those walls, the more I wanted to see the church restored—and the sheer impossibility seemed to increase. The walls were so high that it would need scaffolding; and then there was that plastered ceiling. The very thought was madness because I knew we hadn't got the funds for a major restoration. Even so, the challenge was there and it wouldn't go away!

On Sat 21 August 2004 Shirley Kite organised a "Coffin Path walk". Revd Valerie had been intrigued by the idea of the Coffin Path, and so Shirley Kite agreed to lead a group to Kilmersdon, following the route of the path if possible. Despite ankle deep mud and a group of steers who were very surprised to see so many muddy humans and followed them for some way, Kilmersdon was reached in safety.

As noted in chapter 12, work on the refurbishment of the Church Hall, begun in 2001 by Rex Parfitt, Richard Usher and Geoffrey Plummer, was completed by 2004.

A Pet Service was introduced in September 2004 and was attended by ten dogs, thirty-three adults and thirteen children.

On 10 November there was a confirmation by Bishop Peter Price at St Peter's

The Coffin Path walkers after safely arriving at Kilmersdon, 21 August 2004

Confirmation group with Bishop Peter Price

Westfield and four candidates from Holy Trinity were presented. Kevin and Pauline Smith and John Woodley were confirmed, and Maggie Woodley was received into the Church of England by Bishop Peter. A large number of people from Holy Trinity attended the confirmation in order to support the candidates.

In response to a request from a member of the congregation, a Memorial Service for Babies and Children was held on 21 November. While this filled a pastoral need at the time, only a few people attended, despite extensive publicity, and it has not been repeated.

During 2004, the Coleford Theatre Group reinvented itself under the title C5, soon to become CF5 (Coleford 5), the "5" being David and Sandra Hull, Jeffrey and Jean Power, and Graham Edgell. Early in 2004, they approached Revd Valerie, Clarissa and the PCC about the possibility of staging a production in Holy Trinity just before Christmas. It was to be called *A Christmas Journey* and was a combination of the Nativity story and *The Snowman*. A call was put out for members of the church and village to take part, and rehearsals began in earnest. The production took place on 17, 18, and 19 December, each performance being to a capacity audience. It did of course follow a long tradition of religious drama at Holy Trinity and gave many people food for thought about the true meaning of Christmas. In addition it raised £1,400 for Holy Trinity's Restoration Fund.

2005

The March/April 2005 issue of *On the Map* reported the completion of a major project at Holy Trinity, namely the resurfacing of the church drive. This work had been done by Dave Baker and his team, and the PCC was very grateful to Mrs Yeoman for subsidising the cost of the surfacing materials. The completion of this project did much to raise the morale of the congregation and to enable them to think positively about the restoration of the church interior.

Cast in order of appearance

Narrator (present day)	David Baker
Jonathan	George Kite
Jonathan's Mother	Kate Arthur
Jonathan's Father	Mike Turner
The Snowman	Megan Williams
Santa Claus	Richard Usher
Narrator (yesteryear)	Jean Power
Mary	Fleur Turner
Gabriel	Shirley Kite
Joseph	Simon Turner
Innkeeper	Jeff Power
Shepherd 1	Heather Allen
Shepherd 2	Jean Coles
Shepherd 3	Jean Lee
Angel	Sarah Ilott
Wise Man 1	Shirley Newton
Wise Man 2	Maggie Woodley
Wise Man 3	Pauline Smith
King Herod	Graham Edgell
Palace Guard 1	Colin Turner
Palace Guard 2	Jeff Power
Priest 1	Maryann Baker
Priest 2	Diane Pratt
Parish Priest	Valerie Bonham
Ordinand	Clarissa Cridland

Chorus
Jo Doggrell, Esme Harrison, Sandra Hull, Moira Mallinson, Liz Thompson, Julie Warwick

Cast list of A Christmas Journey

At the Annual Parochial Church Meeting on 20 April 2005, Clarissa Cridland relinquished her role as Churchwarden after ten years in order to concentrate on her theological studies. Her place as Churchwarden was taken by Curtis Illot. Clarissa paid tribute to her fellow Warden, Dave Baker, and thanked him for all his support. On 17 April Clarissa began a three-month-long placement at Radstock and Kilmersdon as part of her ordination course. The essence of a placement was to be in a different type of parish or ministry, and therefore being close geographically was not necessarily a drawback. While Kilmersdon is the mother parish of Coleford and is a similar type of parish, Radstock is quite different, both in the pattern of worship and in the way in which the parish is organised and administered. The Revd Colin Turner as Rector was to be responsible for Clarissa's placement. At the end of the three months, she was required by STETS to produce a 4,000-word report and a 1,000-word critical reflection.

In the Spring of 2005 Mary Plummer gave up the leadership of the Support Group but continued as a member and as a hard working fundraiser, particularly with regard to the Coffee Mornings held roughly every two months in the Church Hall after the Wednesday Eucharist. These help boost the church General Fund, which pays the running costs of the church, as well as providing good social events. In addition, Mary Plummer organises the Women's World Day of Prayer service and also the Lent lunches to support Christian Aid, in collaboration with Eve Tucker from the Methodist Chapel.

Looking ahead to the 175th anniversary of the Church's dedication in 2006, Revd Valerie began, in June 2005, to think about the possibility of producing a history of Holy Trinity.

Revd Valerie recalls: I had written several books on church history, and had contributed to the *Oxford Dictionary of National Biography*, some years previously, but I knew I wouldn't have the time to start from scratch on a new project. And yet, there were a sizeable number of people in the church and village who have, or have had in the past, connections with Holy Trinity, and who might contribute their memories. And also we are fortunate to have historian Julie Dexter in our congregation. Julie had already done extensive research into Coleford's history and, as well as writing one of the Millennium books with Les Kite, had appeared on a local history TV programme. So I asked Julie if she would co-ordinate the project. A number of open meetings were held in the Church Hall at which people came along and brought photographs and other mementoes, as well as their wealth of memories. Julie spent a lot of time visiting people and gathering their information. We both visited the Somerset Record Office to examine parish records deposited there, and then we began writing. Julie handed over what she had written at about the end of 2006. Then it was over to me. Much more information had come to light, including material from Lambeth Palace Library, the Census returns, the PCC Minutes and Parish Magazines, the Church Hall correspondence, further material from the Somerset Record Office, and other sources. It is a much bigger book than I originally envisaged, but a short booklet would not have done justice to Holy Trinity. There have been many delays due to health problems, and also due to the sheer amount of parish duties which must take precedence. But here is the result and I hope it is worthy of Holy Trinity and its people.

May 2005 marked the 60th anniversary of VE Day, which heralded the end of World War II in Europe. The actual day (7 May) was marked by an Entertainment at the Royal British Legion Hall. In addition, 10 July was designated National Commemoration Day, and invitations were sent to the village organisations to attend the special Sung Eucharists at Holy Trinity and at St Andrew's. There were good numbers at both services, which included thanksgiving prayers for those who served in the War, prayers for peace and an act of commitment to peace and freedom.

2006

As 2006, the 175th anniversary year, dawned, Revd Valerie issued a plea in the March issue of *On the Map*: "Holy Trinity desperately needs extra heating, better lighting and complete redecoration, but I fail to see how this can be achieved … Perhaps someone from the wider village community would like to go on *Who wants to be a Millionaire?* for us, or get sponsors and run in a marathon! I am quite serious because the church congregation is stretched to the limit, and Holy Trinity is here for everyone in the village … The building is in a sad state and will not last another 175 years if something isn't done urgently."

The response to this plea was overwhelmingly positive, as if it had lit a touchpaper! Alan Townsend had planned to take part in the Brussels 20km sponsored run at the end of May, and he offered to run for Holy Trinity. Sponsor forms were distributed far and wide, and by the day of the run (28 May), it looked as though he would raise around £500. By the time of the final count-up Alan had raised £622, and this not only gave a tremendous boost to the restoration fund, but also to the morale of the congregation. Meanwhile, in June Keith Marshall, assisted by Robin Thompson, carried out urgent repairs to the stone window mullions, which were badly cracked.

Fundraising began in earnest: a number of people designated donations to Holy Trinity from the funerals of loved ones; there were special collections at the Golden Wedding anniversaries of Alf and Jean Lee, Ernie and Pat Hedges, and the Diamond Wedding anniversary of Ken and Eve Tucker; Ron Brewer and Colin Turner both had significant birthdays and asked for donations in lieu of presents; Rosemary Spedding did a sponsored walk; Tony and Sue Marshall held a garden sale; Ann Mackie-Hunter organised a raffle for hand-made toys made by Mike Harrison; "Santa's sleigh" (courtesy of Ted Phillips) made two donations; Craig and Helen at the Kings Head, Coleford, held a collection and raised £276.50; Jean Lee held a Coffee Morning and open garden;

Craig presenting Revd Valerie with a cheque on behalf of the customers at the Kings Head

Alan Townsend on marathon day

Shirley Kite held a Coffee Morning; we received a grant of £100 from Coleford Parish Council; various people sold items and donated the proceeds; and there were many individual donations ranging from £5 to £500.

Although Holy Trinity needed new heating, lighting, and redecoration, it had seemed sensible to begin with the lighting and redecoration because these had the most visual impact. The peeling walls and dim lighting seemed to make this the priority, but while the quotations from various contractors seemed quite reasonable, it still left a huge challenge. All in all, a sum in the region of £16,000 would be needed for this first phase of the work. By November 2006 we had raised almost £11,000. The target was reached when the Ralph and Irma Sperring Charity gave a grant of £5,000. A date was pencilled in the diary for the work to begin after Easter 2007.

July was a very important month, beginning

Clarissa on her ordination day as deacon

with Clarissa's ordination as deacon on Sunday the 2nd, and this was closely followed by the 175th anniversary of the church's dedication. Clarissa's ordination came after many years' discernment and study, and the amount of love and support given by both churches, and the wider communities in both villages, was really overwhelming.

Revd Valerie recalls: As Clarissa's Training Incumbent, I had to ring the Cathedral Office to let them know how many seats would be required at the Ordination Service for Clarissa's guests. I think each candidate was allocated something like thirty tickets. There was a stunned silence when I said we would need *at least* seventy-five seats, if not more. There were, in fact, only six candidates, and even if they had all asked for seventy-five seats, surely that vast cathedral had enough for all. Be that as it may, Clarissa and I continued to tell everyone to come, and indeed they did! At least 130 people from the two villages came to the Cathedral, and most of them came to the lunch on the Rectory lawn afterwards. It was a glorious day, and just as all the empty plates were being cleared and people were deciding to go home, the heavens opened and there was a mighty downpour. But the sun was shining again by 6.30 pm when Clarissa presided at Evensong at Holcombe Old Church, her first service as a deacon.

Clarissa writes about her ordination … I was on retreat with all those who were being ordained Deacon, along with those who had been ordained Deacon last year and were now being ordained Priest. There were six Deacons, and twelve Priests. We Deacons began with interviews with the Bishop in Wells, and then had lunch with him, the Archdeacons, and a few others in the Bishop's Palace. After lunch, we went to the Cathedral for our rehearsal. Each of us had a sponsor to "give us away" and our vicar "to welcome us to our parish". I was very proud to be the only person who had both sponsor [Dave Baker] and vicar at the rehearsal.

We then went off to Abbey House, Glastonbury, for the ordination retreat, which was led by the Archdeacon of Taunton, the Venerable John Reed. For the first couple of days, we were silent during much of the time. We had four talks in total, and shared worship several times a day. We were very blessed with the weather, and were able to wander round the gardens and Abbey ruins, or sit outside and read or reflect.

On Friday evening, Bishop Peter came to wash our feet, following Jesus' example in John 13, when he washed his disciples' feet the night before he died. It was an incredibly moving experience. Those being ordained Priest went to their ordination on Saturday, and we attended one of the services, in Shepton Mallet (in Bath and Wells, priests' ordinations take place in parish churches, not the Cathedral). During the evening, as well as Night Prayer in the Abbey grounds, there was much ironing of outfits, and checking that we had all we needed.

The morning of my ordination began when I went into the Abbey ruins. I had gone in there a few days earlier in the early morning, and on the evening before the ordination we had all said Night Prayer standing in a circle in the ruins of the Abbey church. It had been an incredibly peaceful and moving occasion, and I wanted to pay a final visit. This time, I did not pray, but wandered around, absorbing the feel of the Abbey.

After I came in from the Abbey on Sunday morning, we had Morning Prayer. I had been worrying that I would cry during my ordination, but instead it all came out during Morning Prayer, and I cried my way through it! Afterwards, I was consoled by remarks such as "we'll need a bucket for Clarissa" and "we'd better wear gumboots". After breakfast it was off to the Bishop's Palace. The temperature was already hot, and it was to reach well over 30 degrees later. We robed in cassock and surplice (a cassock is the black ankle length garment, and a surplice is the white one over the top). Then began the solemnity, and we swore our oaths before the Diocesan Registrar, had an official photograph taken, and went back into the chapel for some quiet. And then we were collected by a verger and led in procession, with the Bishop and several other diocesan clergy and the Registrar, to the Cathedral. The bells were pealing, and suddenly all desire to cry left me.

As we entered the Cathedral by the great west door, there was a movement as the congregation rose, and I could hear the wonderful strains of the organ and the first hymn. From the moment I entered, all through the Cathedral I could see friends who were there for me. I felt really supported, and overwhelmed that so many had come. The whole service lasted about an hour and a half. It would be impossible to describe it in detail, but the highlights for me were: the Bishop laying his hands on my head and actually ordaining me: "*Therefore, Father, through Christ our Lord we pray: Send down the Holy Spirit upon your servant Clarissa for the office and work of a deacon in your church*"; having my stole put on me by Valerie; and turning round to face the whole congregation and hearing the applause, which seemed to go on forever. Others have told me how wonderful the organ was, how much they appreciated John Reed's sermon, and how moving it was to receive Communion in the cathedral. Many people also said how radiant I looked, and I did—and still do—feel completely radiant.

Processing out at the end was also completely wonderful, and then we stood outside the Cathedral afterwards greeting everyone, while cameras clicked, and cards and presents were pushed into my hands. Around 130 people from Coleford and Holcombe (as well as some other friends and family) came to the service, and there were over 100 in the Rectory garden for lunch afterwards. During lunch, it was lovely to be able to go round and to talk to as many people as possible. The temperature became hotter and hotter, and I did eventually take off my jacket and put a sun hat on. I was presented with a wonderful cake, made by Heather Allen, which had photographs of me on the top from the past few years (sitting on Father Christmas' lap, wearing a "pearly hat" at a RBL party, dancing at a Bishop Henderson School disco, and outside the church, robed, one Easter day). The cake was served, puddings were eaten, and … the heavens opened. Within seconds people were drenched—"you clearly know how to get rid of us"—and that was when most people left! (A couple of miles away, there was no rain at all!) How do I feel now? I felt different when the Bishop laid his hands on me, and I still *do* feel different. It is difficult to say *how*, but I do.

A stole is the scarf-like garment worn by those ordained. Deacons wear theirs over the left shoulder, and priests wear theirs hanging down round their necks. Stoles represent putting on the yoke of Christ, and are worn by most clergy when robed during services, often together with other vestments (some clergy prefer to wear a black preaching scarf rather than a stole). They come in the various liturgical colours (there is no limit to the number of stoles one can have), and can be very decorative. My "white" ordination stole, given to me by Valerie, is very decorative indeed—"very exotic" was the Bishop's comment!

Even though Clarissa had lived in the benefice since 1982 and had opted for non-stipendiary ministry within her home parish, the diocese insisted on Clarissa going through the same process for the placing of curates that would be applied to a curate coming new to a parish. It proved to be an exasperating process.

Revd Valerie recalls: Shortly before completing her ordination course with STETS, I was informed by the diocese that I would need to prepare a Parish Profile so that Clarissa would know in what sort of parish she would be serving. I explained that she had lived in Coleford since 1982 and had been one of the Churchwardens who had appointed me, and had been largely responsible for preparing the Parish Profile at the time of the vacancy: surely they were not suggesting that Clarissa would need to be sent a Parish Profile? "Oh yes," came the reply—and furthermore, as her prospective Training Incumbent, I would be required to attend an interview as all Incumbents who had asked for a curate were required to do. Meanwhile, I brought up to date the Parish Profile that Clarissa had prepared for my interview, so that she would know what the parish she had lived in for the past 24 years was like! Then I was called to an interview (which meant an early return from my post-Easter break), and I was told that "of course, just because you have asked for a curate does not mean you will be allocated one". I explained once more that the Diocese had already agreed that Clarissa would be ministering in Coleford with Holcombe, and in due course a letter arrived informing me that after her ordination Clarissa Cridland would be serving as curate in Coleford with Holcombe!

The 175th anniversary of the Dedication of Holy Trinity took place over the weekend of 15–16 July. The Summer Fair was held at the Royal British Legion on the Saturday and this raised about £1,050 for the General Fund. On the Sunday morning there was a special Sung Eucharist attended by representatives from the village organisations, and a Festal Evensong in the evening. Throughout the weekend, there had been a Flower Festival, masterminded by Ann Mackie-Hunter. There were sixty-four arrangements contributed or sponsored by church members, members of the village organisations, or individuals. Further help was contributed by members of Frome Women's Institute, and Malcolm and Margaret Champion and Lucy, their florist. Many of the arrangements were dedicated to past clergy and members of Holy Trinity, and to particular aspects of the 175 years of the church in Coleford. The church was open on the Sunday afternoon for people to look round it and to admire the flowers.

Holy Trinity lost a dear friend on 30 August in the death of Fr Brian Sutton. Writing in the August *On the Map*, Revd Clarissa paid tribute to him. "Father Brian ministered in both parishes during the two years before Revd Valerie came, and has taken services and helped out since on a number of occasions. He was due to come during Valerie's summer holiday … Then I had a call from his wife, Bridget, to say that he was not well. His death was sudden—he was rushed into the Royal United Hospital that morning. Valerie had telephoned to ask how he was, and, visiting the RUH in the afternoon, was able to be with him at the end, together with Bridget and other members of the family. He was a help and encouragement to all who met him, and he not only looked after parishes during vacancies but had a special ministry with the bereaved, taking many funeral services at Bath Crematorium. He was a particular mentor to me in my journey towards ordination, and taught me an enormous amount. He and Bridget attended my ordination service. He gave me a very beautiful white stole. I shall miss him more than I can say."

Left: *175th Anniversary of Dedication, Flower Festival, 2006*
Right: *Revds Valerie and Clarissa at the 175th Anniversary Flower Festival, 2006*

Bridget Sutton, Fr Brian Sutton, and Clarissa's uncle Roger Boissier
at her ordination

The final major event of 2006 was the Confirmation Service held at Holy Trinity on Wednesday 4 October. Two members of the congregation, Tony and Sue Marshall, were confirmed, along with candidates from St Mary's, Frome, and St John's, Midsomer Norton. Bishop Paul Barber, an assistant bishop in the diocese, officiated at the service and met the candidates in the Church Hall afterwards. As part of her preparation, Sue Marshall had been baptised at the 9.30 am Sung Eucharist on Sunday 28 May.

2007

Two major events defined the year 2007: the church restoration and the Revd Clarissa's ordination to the priesthood.

It seemed logical to begin with the renewal of the lighting because inevitably the removal of the old fittings would leave marks on the walls. The contractor for the work was Brian Hussey of Shepton Mallet, and the work was done towards the end of April with very little disruption to the church routine. (A spotlight to illuminate the altar Cross was added later in memory of Wyn Howell, who died in November 2007.) The decorating was a far more complicated project, involving the removal of the old emulsion paint and the application of three coats of oil-based distemper. The contractor was Andrew Kynaston and his team, though due to Andrew's declining health he was unable to be on site for much of the time. (Sadly, Andrew died in September 2007.) Work began on Monday 30 April, and the estimated time scale was four weeks. During this time, all services were held in the Church Hall; no bookings for baptisms were taken; and provision was made for funerals either at St Andrew's or at the Methodist Chapel. In fact there was only one funeral during this time, that of Dick Crawford, who had asked for Revd Clarissa to conduct his funeral. This took place at the Methodist Chapel on 3 May.

Meanwhile in church, the contractors were struggling against time because the removal of the old paint was proving far more difficult and hazardous than anyone could have guessed. The whole interior was covered in a platform of scaffolding with a moveable tower scaffold on top. The sanding process to remove the paint was producing a fine dust which, despite the covering of furnishings and fixtures, seeped in everywhere and took a good deal of cleaning before it was finally eradicated. And time was ticking away, and as the end of May approached it became clear that the work would over-run. The Mendip Male Voice Choir had been booked for over a year to give a concert on Saturday 16 June, and the church had to be ready. This began to seem increasingly unlikely, but after an all-out effort by the contractors they were able to vacate the building by Thursday 14 June. Next day a team from the congregation moved everything back into the church, as well as cleaning, polishing and preparing for the concert. The concert itself was a sell-out and raised £853 for the Restoration

Sue and Tony Marshall's confirmation, 4 October 2006, with Bob and Shirley Swallow

Revd Clarissa's first Mass, 3 July 2007

Fund. The redecorating had been confined to the walls and ceiling, and so, in order to complete the work, Revd Valerie undertook the painting of the organ gallery and all the doors.

As soon as the congregation returned to the church, it became obvious that the carpets in the sanctuary and aisles needed to be replaced. It was also obvious that these should be fitted after the heating had been installed, but for the time being there was no funding for either project. Meanwhile, people from the congregation and the village began to make donations towards the cost of the carpets, and this accumulated over the following two years. In addition, Ann Mackie-Hunter organised a wine raffle which raised £302, and the Ralph and Irma Sperring Charity gave a grant of £750. The 2007 phase of the restoration was concluded by essential work to the roof and to the drains to ensure there would be no further water ingress.

The other major event of 2007 was Revd Clarissa's ordination to the priesthood. Her year as a deacon had been somewhat curtailed by the onset of ME, the debilitating illness that sometimes follows a viral infection such as influenza. While she had been able to exercise her deacon's ministry to a large extent, she had found it necessary to take several weeks' sick leave, and this proved immensely frustrating for her. However, by the careful pacing of what she was able to undertake, she was able to go forward for her priestly ordination on Saturday 2 July at St John's, Midsomer Norton. A large number of supporters from both parishes descended on St John's on a rather damp and cold day. Priests had come from far and wide, and about fourteen stepped forward to lay their hands on Clarissa's head, along with the Bishop of Taunton (Peter Maurice), at the moment of ordination.

The next day, Sunday 3 July, Revd Clarissa presided at the Eucharist for the first time. It was a joyful occasion attended by members of her family, by the congregation of both churches, plus friends from the Chapel and the two villages. Unlike the previous year when lunch was provided in the Rectory garden, the inclement weather forced the use of the Church Hall. Even so, a wonderful meal, catered by Heather Allen, was enjoyed by a large number of people.

Clarissa writes: I have to confess that I had not expected my ordination to the Priesthood to be as special as when I was ordained Deacon, because it was not in the Cathedral. In a sense I was right, in that the setting was not so grand, but in another sense I was wrong—the occasion was very special indeed. And it was good to be ordained locally … I had spent the previous couple of days on retreat in Abbey House, Glastonbury, with all those being ordained … and as I did last year, I had gone into the Abbey grounds early each morning—but this year in my gumboots in the pouring rain! Notwithstanding that, it was a very special place to be …

There were four of us from the Bath Archdeaconry being ordained Priest in Midsomer Norton … and we were ordained by the Bishop of Taunton, Peter Maurice, who was consecrated earlier this year … I was actually the first person he ordained. I was a little anxious about numbers because we were supposed to limit numbers and I had asked everyone, but the Churchwardens managed to squeeze everyone in, and it was very good to be supported by so many people from Coleford and Holcombe. At the Ordination of Priests, it isn't only the Bishop who lays hands on the candidate, but also other priests. We were supposed to have just a few priests doing this, but I had about fourteen, some of whom came from as far as Ely and Weymouth. So I was incredibly fortunate.

My first Eucharist was an incredibly moving experience, in which all the particular elements of Priesthood—Absolving, Blessing and Consecrating—came together at once. It was really good to have so many people from both villages and to have so many people assisting in one way or another.

Most people came to lunch afterwards, in the hall due to the weather, and we had a delicious meal. I had a surprise cake made by Heather Allen, with a picture of me taken on the day I was ordained Deacon.

2008–9

In May 2008 Revd Valerie became ill from a relapse of ME, having had it nine years previously following chickenpox. Although she was only on sick leave for two weeks, her ministry was much curtailed during 2008. Even so, there were some aspects of ministry, such as funerals, with which she was able to assist. Meanwhile, Revd Clarissa was also still ministering within the limitations imposed by ME, but between them the two priests were able to look after the spiritual and pastoral needs of the parish. And Revd Valerie was able to finish *A Good Foundation*.

Revd Valerie writes: The first time I had ME was when I had only recently been ordained (a similar situation to Clarissa's own experience). I found this very challenging after all the training and build-up to ordination—it felt like "the Lord has given, and the Lord has taken away". But through the experience, I came to a position where I knew it could be a resource for ministry. Many people suffer from chronic illness, the sort that imposes limitations while having very little outward manifestation. I found the experience of ME gave me a deeper understanding of that type of illness, so that it did indeed become a resource for ministry. Nine years later it returned, and I must admit it has been more difficult to come to terms with this time. I think this is because as Priest in Charge I am aware of greater expectations being placed on me, and also greater expectations which I place on myself. And of course it is immensely frustrating to be unable to do many things I had previously been doing, such as hospital visiting and visiting the village organisations. But even so, writing in 2009, I can say that I am coming to a point where I can do much more than I could a year ago. Living within limitations is never easy—it is not something taught on ministry courses! However, as this book has progressed towards publication, I have become increasingly aware that had I been in full health, I would not have had the same amount of time available for the project. So the completion of the book has turned the negative experience of ME into a positive form of ministry.

Revd Clarissa here reflects on what it means to be a Priest:
What does a priest do? If I had written this just after I was ordained Deacon, my answers probably would have been very different, partly because I had not anticipated having ME and partly because my priestly ministry is something which has developed, and not something which was just there when I was ordained Priest. At the heart of everything I do is to try to follow Jesus and to do as He would want me to, and to try to show others how to follow Jesus, and to bring them to Him.

Prayer Praying the Daily Office is something which I did before I was ordained, but since then it has become more focussed. The Daily Office consists of Morning and Evening Prayer, and I also usually say Night Prayer (Compline) and sometimes Prayer during the Day. Some clergy pray in church, but Valerie and I pray in our homes, and so my day begins with Morning Prayer, before I do anything else. We have a new Common Worship service, and I follow this, but add in a different Old Testament reading. And I pray for each of the congregations by name, pausing particularly over those who are ill, and those who might have especial problems, and I know Valerie does, too. When I know them, I add in other people from the villages who need praying for in particular, and the village organisations. I also offer my day to God, going over things which I definitely plan to do, and saying a general prayer for things about which I don't yet know. Sometimes I add in prayers for the world, but I am not very good at this. Evening Prayer for me is a shorter service of about half an hour, and Night Prayer is just handing the day back to God—usually this is very quick, but it can be longer. I really only pray Prayer during the Day with other members of our Local Clergy Group, and so this is said in a corporate, rather than private, way.

Services Normally, Valerie and I attend all services together, sharing as to who will lead. We are very flexible about this, because it may be one of us takes over at the last moment if the other is not feeling so well. I had led many non-Communion services before I was ordained Priest, but celebrating Communion has been absolutely wonderful for me (and still is), and it isn't possible to write about just how wonderful it is. If you come to the Communion Service, I hope you will realise that it is not just another task, but something completely special and sacramental.

Preaching I had preached before I was ordained, but one thing I have been able to do since having ME is a lot of study of the Bible, particularly the Old Testament, and I think this has made my post-ordination sermons different to those before. Some sermons are quite quick to prepare, but often it can take up to six hours, because I find that I need to have the text in my heart as well as my head. I am sure the congregations know when this isn't the case!

Reading Theologically I also read before I was ordained, but I have continued to do this, and have probably read more because of the ME. I find it absolutely fascinating to choose books and usually I enjoy what I choose, but just occasionally I don't. Valerie and I both read a lot, and so we often swap books, and indeed lend them to others.

Occasional Offices This is the collective description for funerals, baptisms and weddings, and I have listed them in this order since this is the frequency with which they seem to occur. Obviously, funerals are much more solemn than baptisms or weddings, but really they all require a similar amount of preparation, and especially a funeral. I have found it the most enormous privilege to be able to lead funerals, and something which oddly enough I would describe as joyful, even though funerals are not joyful occasions. But I do feel joy when I know I have done the best that I can do.

Visiting I visit individual people, but not nearly as often as I would like. I am able to take Communion to members of the congregation who are either temporarily unwell, or who are simply no longer able to come to church. We have had several members from Holy Trinity who have been in Care Homes, and visiting them is an enormous privilege, just as visiting at home is. But since the onset of ME, it has been difficult to do hospital visiting because driving any distance takes so much energy. But when we hear of anyone in hospital, we always inform the hospital chaplain and ask him to visit.

Bishop Henderson School I always enjoy leading Assembly at BHS, although at the moment this doesn't happen as much as it used to, because of changes at BHS in the way in which things are done. But I go in at other times, too, and always try to attend BHS events. The children are hugely supportive, and very often have a real understanding of the Christian faith.

Being about in the village This is probably one of the most important parts of being a priest. We cannot pretend that Holy Trinity is full every week, so it is very important to go to events where we can meet people from the village. I try to always attend jumble sales, coffee mornings and other special events in the village, although because of my ME, in the evening I only attend important church events (and only till about 8.00). But most Saturdays will find me at something, and often during the week as well. Sometimes it is just saying hello to people, but very often someone wants to talk about a problem or wants to know how they have a baby christened. And always, as a Priest, I am there for people to talk to about their problems.

I have highlighted the main things I do as a priest, but not all. Within all of this, I have to earn a living, since I am what is known as an ONSM (ordained non-stipendiary minister). Once my four years post-ordination training is complete (at the end of June 2010), my official designation will be Associate Priest. I am lucky enough to be able to work around what I do as a priest, and indeed part of my job is to come to the Post Office most days, so I see people there.

 If I had to sum up what a priest does in just a few words, it would be "sacramental service"—serving members of both villages within the sacramental ministry of the priesthood as I try to follow Jesus.

 Despite the parlous health of the clergy, parish life proceeded as usual. On 21 May the Archdeacon of Bath came to Holy Trinity for his Visitation of the Midsomer Norton Deanery. During the service, the Churchwardens for the parishes within the deanery were sworn in, the Archdeacon delivered his Charge (a form of sermon), and refreshments were served in the Church Hall.

 In February 2008 Revd Valerie had begun the process for obtaining a Faculty for a new heating system for Holy Trinity. The contractor was to be K H Harris, who had

Ruth Nelson

installed a similar heating system at St Andrew's. The seeming impossibility of such a project, so soon after the redecoration, had become possible thanks to a bequest. The late Ruth Nelson had remembered Holy Trinity in her Will, and the prospect of completing our restoration seemed more like becoming a reality. The Will, however, was a complicated one and became a lengthy process, but by the end of the year it was possible to engage the contractor and set a date for the work to begin.

Towards the end of 2008, Rex Parfitt completed a major project. As noted in chapter 11, the west wall of the churchyard (i.e. the boundary wall furthest from the road) had been in a derelict state for many years and was getting worse. Something had to be done, but clearly it would cost thousands of pounds to rebuild the wall. Rex Parfitt had already done much manual work for Holy Trinity, and in 2005 he offered to repair the churchyard wall. The PCC gladly accepted and Rex set to work on what would become a complete rebuilding. It took him three years, and the only cost to the church was that of the materials.

Two former members of Holy Trinity's choir died in 2008: Hilda Hamblin and Rose Plummer. Hilda Hamblin, who is on the 1981 choir photograph, had been unable to attend Holy Trinity for many years but had received Holy Communion at home every few weeks. She followed church activities through reading *On the Map* and was enthusiastic about all the work being done to restore the building. She died peacefully at home on 25 February 2008.

Although Rose Plummer had sung for many years in the choir at Holy Trinity, she had lived in Scott's Close, Holcombe, since

Rose Plummer with Hilary, Sally and Barnaby

the early 1980s. In her introductory chapter to this book, Phyl Coles has paid tribute to Rose and her husband, Fred (Phyl's brother), both of whom were deeply committed to life at Holy Trinity. After moving to Holcombe, Fred was knocked down by a car near the Holcombe Inn and spent the next three years in the Royal United Hospital in Bath. Rose visited him almost every day until his death in 1990. Just as she had been a faithful member of Holy Trinity, so Rose became a faithful member of St Andrew's, Holcombe. Her support for the cake stalls at Gift Day and Coffee Mornings was greatly valued (everyone clamoured for her raspberry buns!), and she also supported the summer fete at Scott's Close, ably assisted by Phyl Coles. Even on the coldest Sunday mornings, Rose would often attend the 8.00 am Holy Communion, accompanied by Rita House. Revd Valerie once made the mistake of commenting that Rose was up early, and was told very firmly that 7.50 am was not early to someone who had been a miner's wife and had seen him off to work every day with a cooked breakfast inside him! Even so, St Andrew's on a Sunday morning in the days before the heating system was installed was a bitingly cold experience. If she was not at the "8 o'clock" Rose would often come to the 11.15 Service, and she also attended the monthly Communion at Scott's Close. As her health began to fail, she received Holy Communion at home or in hospital. Rose had a phenomenal number of friends, as the great display of cards on her birthday testified. She died peacefully in Frome Community Hospital on 28 October 2008, and St Andrew's was full for her funeral on 6 November. She was laid to rest in Holcombe churchyard with her husband, Fred.

John Woodley, a member of Holy Trinity's congregation, collapsed and died outside his house on 29 November. This was a tremendous shock to his family and friends, including all at Holy Trinity. John had been confirmed on 10 November 2004 at

Ted Ilott, Alf Lee, Genevieve Payne,
Stan and Ron Brewer

Ron Brewer cutting the ribbon at the
opening of Coleford Co-op

Holy Trinity after the completion of the restoration work 2007–9

Westfield, strongly supported by members of Holy Trinity. Like his friend David Poole, who died six weeks before him, John had been a staunch helper at Holy Trinity's sales. He always had a stall selling CDs, DVDs and videos, and had built up quite a clientele, who called him "the music man". In fact John had helped at Holy Trinity's Christmas Fair on 14 November, just two weeks before his death. His funeral took place in Holy Trinity on 10 December. His widow, Maggie, gave a ciborium in memory of John, for use at the Wednesday Eucharists.

Meanwhile, there were changes in the village. More new houses at the eastern end of the village had added to the population, and at the end of 2008 two village "institutions" came to an end. In September the Crawford family gave up the ownership and running of the village Post Office, which subsequently became Jones' Convenience Stores and Post Office. Revd Clarissa blessed the new shop and Post Office on Saturday 4 October. And Brewer's, an emporium where anything from a pin to (almost) an elephant could be purchased, became Coleford Co-op in December. The newly revamped shop had an official opening and blessing ceremony on Monday 8 December at which Ron Brewer cut the red ribbon with a large pair of scissors, the children of Bishop Henderson School sang carols, and Revds Valerie and Clarissa said a prayer.

It marked a return to the village by the Co-op after twenty-five years. Ron, Christine and Sylvia now retired, but sadly their father, Stan, who had owned the business, died early on 23 January 2009 after a short illness. Stan Brewer had been a firm supporter of Holy Trinity, contributing raffle prizes, the Christmas tree, and oranges for the Christingle Service for many years. His funeral took place on 2 February amidst a snowstorm, the like of which Coleford had not seen for over twenty years. The church was full for the funeral, though not overflowing as had been expected, due no doubt to the weather. But as the words of the committal were said at the graveside, it seemed as though Coleford would never be quite the same again.

The installation of the heating system had been scheduled to begin on the day following Stan Brewer's funeral, but the onset of deep snow and ice held things up by almost two weeks. Also, the provision of the utilities was subject to a long delay. Meanwhile, Sunday worship was held in the Church Hall. Keith and Sandra Brewer were due to lay the new carpets as soon as the heating system was completed, but there was a further delay because wet rot was discovered in the floor around the font and children's area. The affected timbers were removed and new flooring put in by Curtis Ilott, who also did some work to level the floor in preparation for the carpets, which were laid soon after Easter. The only part of the church that had shown any sign of dampness following the redecoration in 2007 was the porch. Following advice from

Robin Thompson

Above: *Phyllis Coles celebrating 80 years in the church choir*
Right: *Phyllis Coles cutting her commemorative cake*

the architect, George Chedburn, work was carried out to re-point the exterior and redecorate the interior of the porch. The contractor was Dominic Kynaston, who had carried out the work in 2007.

The church was reopened for worship on Sunday, 3 May 2009. David Baker and a team of helpers from the congregation were responsible for putting the church back in order ready for worship. The work had involved extensive removal of furnishings, and once these were back in place, other members of the congregation cleaned and polished everything. In addition, Keith Marshall plastered a large expanse of the choir vestry wall following the removal of wood panelling for the gas and water pipes.

Before moving back into church, Robin Thompson and his helpers did some work on the flagpole so that once again Holy Trinity could fly St George's flag. Robin has been responsible for a great deal of work in the tower over the past few years, endeavouring to overhaul the clock and keeping the church supplied with flags.

Holy Trinity has received many gifts in recent years, and these include a cruet tray to commemorate Clarissa's ordination, a new set of *Complete Anglican Hymns Old and New*, and a set of rose pink vestments. (Also, the green vestments given some years ago by Shirley Newton in memory of her husband, Jim, are still used at Holy Trinity.)

Following Stan Brewer's funeral, the family very generously designated part of the collection to Holy Trinity and this will be used for some major work to clean the organ, which Ron Brewer regularly plays for funerals and Evensong.

Even though the days have gone when a vicar could be in office for over fifty years, there is no such time limit on choir members! On 9 May 2009 Phyllis Coles celebrated her 89th birthday, thus marking eighty years membership of Holy Trinity's choir.

On 10 May she came to church and occupied her seat in the choir stalls, where she was presented with a special commemorative card. After the service she was presented with a birthday cake, which the congregation helped her to eat! So we come full circle. The story of Holy Trinity, Coleford, continues to unfold, but as that great priest Joseph Wade said, it is *A Good Foundation*.

Revd Valerie writes: In January 2009 I completed seven years in Coleford with Holcombe. My first instinct on reading the *Church Times* advertisement had proved correct, and I have been very happy here. There have, of course, been disappointments; for instance, it would be very good if the regular congregation were more numerous, and if we could count more families and children amongst them. But we live in an age where there is so much else for people to do at weekends and so we lose out. If you have read this far, you will see that this is something that began in the 1950s. But the important thing is that at Holy Trinity (and at St Andrew's) Revd Clarissa and I are here for everybody, and I think people know it.

I see myself as a country priest who tries to be alongside all aspects of village and church life. St Paul writes, "Rejoice with those who rejoice and weep with those who weep." Of all the past clergy of Holy Trinity, the one with whom I most closely identify is the Revd Joseph Wade—he restored the church, wrote books, and loved his parish and the people in it. That is a very good model for ministry.

Julie Dexter sums up: 178 years after opening its doors to the people of Coleford, Holy Trinity remains at the heart of Anglican worship. Its present vicar, the Revd Valerie Bonham, was the first female vicar in the church's history. (But not the first female priest to preside at the Eucharist, the Revd Marianne Atkinson having done so during the previous interregnum.) Valerie served on the General Synod of the Church of England from 1990 to 1995 as a lay person, and again from 1998 to 2001 after ordination, and was a member of General Synod when it voted to ordain women as priests. And now we also have the ministry of the Revd Clarissa Cridland, who has fulfilled many roles since moving here, and latterly has become our curate.

Baptisms, marriages and funerals, and regular services, make up the most easily recognised face of life at Holy Trinity; but like their predecessors, members of the congregation are involved in many other activities—quizzes, jumble sales, anniversary celebrations, Bible study and Lenten courses, sick visiting. Through now living in a residential home at Frome, Joyce Button and others like her may not be able to get to Holy Trinity, but as she herself has noted, "Where I cannot go, they come to me." Esme Harrison has fond memories of the Nativity and Passion plays performed at Holy Trinity in her younger days, and equally fond memories of more recent productions, including the children's Nativity plays helped by singing from the choir, and the *Christmas Journey* production of mime and song in 2004.

Strong links have been forged in recent years between the church and the wider community as a result of the Revds Valerie and Clarissa visiting the village clubs, groups and school. Close links with the Methodist community also continue, with shared Lenten lunches and Sunday evening worship alternating between church and chapel.

Responsibility for routine cleaning and maintenance of the church, Church Hall and churchyard, and for numerous social activities and fundraising events, is shared among many dedicated volunteers who, like their predecessors, devote countless hours of service to Holy Trinity as an expression of their faith. Without them Holy Trinity would not have survived its first 178 years. As today's members look back at the history of their church, and forward to its future, they can reflect on some of the previous events, whose highs and lows reflect the ebb and flow of community life … and pray for good weather!

A PANORAMA IN PICTURES OF PARISH LIFE …

Sybil Hodges in 2002

Sheila Perry

Colin and Marlene Turner

Revd Valerie with Ruth Nelson

Hilary Plummer and Margaret Flower

Shirley Newton, Pauline Smith and Santa

Doris Russell, Diane Pratt and Maryanne Baker

Joyce Button at her Coffee Morning in 2004

Tracey Button and Ann Turner at the Christmas Fair, 2006

Fred Bonham, Jean Lee and Shirley Kite at the tombola stall

Eva Heatley and Sophie Ilott with Esme Harrison and Anne Woolley

Curtis and Sarah Ilott, July 2007

Rona Bruniges at the Christmas Fair, 2006

Richard and Ann Usher, Christmas Fair 2007

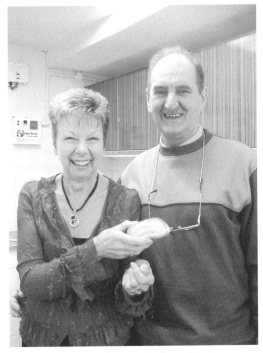

Maryanne and Dave Baker, Christmas Fair 2007

Tony and Diane Pratt celebrating their Silver Wedding Anniversary

Mary Plummer, Ann Usher and Doris Russell, Summer Fair

Ida Allen and Revd Valerie, Summer Fair 2007

Oliver Tasker, Eva Heatley, Lucy Tasker, Zoe and Sophie Ilott, and Jasmin Quennell

Jean and Alf Lee

Heather Allen and Jean Coles with Lukas and Eva Heatley and Ruby Jean and Chloe Coles

Myra Perry and Phyl Coles, Summer Fair 2007

*Nancy Parfitt at Holy Trinity Coffee
Morning*

*Geoffrey Plummer and Rex Parfitt
cleaning the church path*

*Revds Valerie and Clarissa with Lucy
Tasker, Zoe Ilott, Eva Heatley and
Sophie Ilott*

Tony Pratt and Ron Brewer

*Rosemary Spedding, Myra Perry, Ann
Mackie-Hunter and Dawn Townsend*

Mike and Esme Harrison

Liz Thompson

Doreen Pooley

Clive Smith

Eileen Pertt

Sue Marshall, Laura Nicholls, Shirley Swallow, Hilary Plummer, Cherry Moore and Bob Swallow

Jean and Gerald Coles

Carol Morse

Priscilla Thomas

Fred Bonham and Mary Plummer

Eileen Smith and Doris Russell

SOURCES CONSULTED

Somerset Record Office

D/P/Coleford 2/1/1 Baptism Register 1831–1862 (contains the seating plan inside the front cover)

D/P/Coleford 4/1/1 Churchwardens' Accounts 1869–1932

D/P/Coleford 4/1/2 Church Accounts 1935–1963

D/P/Coleford 4/1/3 Church Accounts 1964–1975

D/P/Coleford 8/3/1 Minutes of the Church Building Committee 1829–1833 (with notes by various incumbents on the life of the church)

D/P/Coleford 8/3/2 1830 Contract and specification for building Coleford church

D/P/Coleford 9/1/1 Vestry Minutes 1846–1921

D/P/Coleford 9/1/2 Vestry (1920–1975) and annual church meeting Minutes (latter from 1964)

D/P/Coleford 9/3/2 1939–1948 PCC Minutes and annual church meetings

D/P/Coleford 9/3/5 1960–1963 PCC Minutes and annual church meetings

D/P/Coleford 17/1/1 1925 Copy of deed of the Village Institute with plan of site

D/P/Coleford 18/1/1 1874 Deed of school with plan of site

D/D/Va 5/8 1851 Bishop's Visitation Articles of Enquiry

D/D/Va 7/9 1855 Bishop's Visitation Articles of Enquiry

D/D/Va 8/8 1858 Bishop's Visitation Articles of Enquiry

D/D/Va 9/8 1861 Bishop's Visitation Articles of Enquiry

D/D/Va 10/8 1864 Bishop's Visitation Articles of Enquiry

D/D/Va 11/8 1867 Bishop's Visitation Articles of Enquiry

D/D/Va 12/8 1870 Bishop's Visitation Articles of Enquiry

D/D/Va 13/8 1873 Bishop's Visitation Articles of Enquiry

D/D/Va 14/8 1876 Bishop's Visitation Articles of Enquiry

D/D/Va 15/8 1879 Bishop's Visitation Articles of Enquiry

D/D/Va 17/8 1885 Bishop's Visitation Articles of Enquiry

D/D/Va 19/8 1891 Bishop's Visitation Articles of Enquiry

D/D/Va 21/8 1898 Bishop's Visitation Articles of Enquiry

D/D/Coleford/1931/71 Petition for Faculty 28 April 1931 (and accompanying correspondence)

Somerset Local Studies Library, Taunton

Various issues of:

Somerset Standard

East Somerset Telegraph

Frome Library
Various issues of:
Somerset Guardian and Standard

Lambeth Palace Library
Archives of the Incorporated Church Building Society (ICBS) File 1109

Bath and Wells Diocesan Board of Finance
Conveyances, Trust Deeds and other documents relating to the sale of the Miners'
Welfare Institute, Coleford, to the PCC of Holy Trinity Church

Records at Holy Trinity, Coleford
Coleford Parish Magazine January 1901–May 1914
Coleford Parish Paper July 1955–December 1961
On the Map January 1976–present date
Registers of Services, 1896–present date
PCC Minutes September 1965–present date
Correspondence relating to window by Keith New
Faculty papers for various works
File of correspondence relating to the sale of the Miners' Welfare Institute.
Trust Deed for Miners' Welfare Institute dated 2 November 1927
Conveyance dated 21 April 1964 of Miners' Welfare Institute to Coleford PCC

Printed sources
Cleverdon, The Revd F W *A History of Mells* 2nd edition 1974
Clifford, Colin *The Asquiths* John Murray 2002
Coleford Oral History Group *Coleford as 'twere* 2000
Coventry Cathedral guidebooks
Crockford's Clerical Directories 1860–1990
Dexter, J and Kite, L *Coleford and Highbury: A Short History* 2000
Forsyth, Michael *Bath* (*Pevsner's Architectural Guides*) 2003
Hansard House of Lords debates, 21 June 1922 Miners' Welfare Fund
Hansard House of Lords debates, 2 August 1922 Somerset Miners' Welfare Fund
Heath, Frank R *The Little Guides, Wiltshire* 7th edition 1949
Hylton, Lord *Some notes on the history of Kilmersdon* 1912
Lambert, Angela *Unquiet Souls* Macmillan 1984
Macmorran, Kenneth M and Briden, Timothy *A Handbook for Churchwardens and
Parochial Church Councillors* Mowbray, 2001 (reprint)
Medlycott, Sir Mervyn *Monumental Inscriptions of Coleford, Somerset* 2006
(unpublished MS)
Ollard, S L and Crosse, G (Eds) *A Dictionary of English Church History* 1912
Port, Michael *600 New Churches* Spire Books 2006

Ralph-Bowman, Peter *Ah-Yes: An Introspective Retrospect* Gracewing, Leominster 1999

St Margaret's Magazine vol 1, p211 quoted in *The Planting of the Lord. The History of the Society of Saint Margaret in England, Scotland and the USA 1855–1995* by Sister Catherine Louise, SSM.

Internet Sources

1841 England Census
1851 England Census
1861 England Census
1871 England Census
1881 England Census
1891 England Census
1901 England Census

Miscellaneous

Correspondence by William Marchant Jones relating to the Belgian refugees